Vulnerability and Violence

Vulnerability and Violence

The Impact of Globalisation

Peadar Kirby

Pluto Press

LONDON • ANN ARBOR, MI

First published 2006 by Pluto Press
345 Archway Road, London N6 5AA
and 839 Greene Street, Ann Arbor, MI 48106

www.plutobooks.com

British Library Cataloguing in Publication Data
A catalogue record for this book is available from the British Library

ISBN   0 7453 2288 3 hardback
ISBN   0 7453 2287 5 paperback

Library of Congress Cataloging in Publication Data applied for

10   9   8   7   6   5   4   3   2   1

Designed and produced for Pluto Press by
Chase Publishing Services Ltd, Fortescue, Sidmouth, EX10 9QG, England
Typeset from disk by Stanford DTP Services, Northampton, England
Printed and bound in the European Union by
Antony Rowe Ltd, Chippenham and Eastbourne, England

Contents

List of Boxes   vi
Preface   vii

1 Globalisation, Vulnerability and Violence   1

Part I   Description

2 Risk's New Riskiness   31
3 Coping with Risk   54

Part II   Diagnosis

4 The Political Economy of Globalisation   77
5 Globalisation's Cultural Worlds   101

Part III   Interrogation

6 Society and Market   129
7 The Individual and Society   151

Part IV   Remedies

8 'So What Should We Do?'   173
9 Contesting Globalisation   196

Bibliography   223
Index   236

List of Boxes

1.1 Keohane and Nye: vulnerability and interdependence 5
1.2 A more violent world 12
1.3 Voices of the Poor 18
1.4 Adding vulnerability to IPE's conceptual toolkit 24
2.1 'Basic questions about global finance' 34
2.2 Getting bigger, smarter, faster to survive 36
2.3 Women at risk 42
2.4 Globalised terrorism 47
2.5 Mass extinction threatens 49
2.6 Childhood at risk 51
3.1 Stiglitz on 'making risk a way of life' 58
3.2 Globalisation's health threats: HIV/AIDS and SARS 63
3.3 Eroding social capital: 'More people watch *Friends* than have friends' 67
3.4 Facing a 'global water crisis' 70
4.1 Does globalisation make famines more likely? 83
4.2 Bridging the digital divide or e-imperialism? 86
4.3 The vulnerabilities of Ireland's success 93
4.4 Cox's integrated, precarious and excluded workers 98
5.1 Languages under threat 107
5.2 Monopolising the media 112
5.3 Chile's 'credit-card citizenship' 118
5.4 Masculinity in crisis or identity politics? 124
6.1 The power of the market 133
6.2 Waxing and waning of 'embedded liberalism' 141
6.3 Poverty: do we know what it means? 143
7.1 *Homo economicus* makes a comeback 155
7.2 Trauma: society has become emotionally numb 161
7.3 Human security: Rambo warrior or Mother and Child? 164
7.4 Vulnerability: between life and death 168
8.1 The new physics: Western physicists meet Eastern mystics 177
8.2 Ushering in 'the age of the fund manager' 184
8.3 Putting poverty on the global agenda 188
9.1 Are alternatives now the mainstream? 201
9.2 A new global movement is born 209
9.3 Are South American states creating an alternative? 214

Preface

The book was conceived in Latin America but born in Ireland, two regions that I have been studying and holding in a somewhat uneasy but very fruitful embrace for over a quarter of a century. These two areas have taught me much of what I know about the dynamics of social change and this learning continues as intensively as ever under the impact of the manifold forces we label 'globalisation'. As will become clear to the reader of this book, vulnerability has become an issue of concern to authoritative analysts of both Latin America and Ireland as they try to make sense of how our lives as individuals, as families and communities, and as countries are being reshaped at a time of breathtaking and rather scary change. Having written books on globalisation's impact on Ireland and Latin America over recent years, it was perhaps not as strange as it may seem at first sight that my attention would turn to the topic of vulnerability.

It was, however, a number of invitations by groups of Catholic missionaries during my sabbatical year in Chile in 2001–02 that convinced me that this topic, which I was encountering more and more in my reading, was worthy of further investigation. When I was invited to give a talk on globalisation to a continental meeting in Chile of Maryknoll missionaries – Catholic lay people, sisters and priests, almost all from the United States – who work in countries throughout Latin America, it struck me that the themes of vulnerability and violence might help connect the rather technical details of the state–market shifts we associate with globalisation with the real changes they experience in their everyday lives among the poor of the region. My hunch proved correct, as my argument that vulnerability constitutes the distinctive way in which globalisation is reshaping all our lives, resulting in an extension of violence, found a very strong echo and sparked much discussion among those present. This led to a further invitation to talk to a meeting of lay Maryknoll missionaries from all over the world, this time in Venezuela, where again my analysis of globalisation gave them much food for thought and led to animated discussion. Of course, Venezuela proved a conducive environment for consideration of vulnerability and globalisation since this topic forms a central theme in the discourse of President Hugo Chávez. I remember in particular one Sunday evening at the meeting where a large group of us sat transfixed watching the President's weekly TV show. Indeed, unlike much of the Catholic Church in Venezuela, the Maryknoll group gave their critical and at times public support to the President because they witnessed what his government was doing for and with the poor. My third talk was to a group of Catholic missionaries in Santiago, members of the Society of St Columban, made up largely of Irish priests and sisters but with some others present from Australia, New Zealand, the Philippines, Fiji and Papua New Guinea. Again, the term vulnerability caught their attention and articulated for them the reality within which they live and work.

What began as a vague hunch, therefore, became a firmer conviction that the term 'vulnerability' (in which I include violence as both a cause and an expression) does capture in a valuable way an important dimension of today's world. As I have worked on the book between November 2003 and May 2005, and given academic papers drawing on this work, my conviction has grown that vulnerability is an essential characteristic of globalisation and that without giving it central attention we fail to understand key aspects and events of the world around us – from the French *non* to the EU Constitution in their May 2005 referendum to the remarkable mobilising capacity of the alter-globalisation movement, or from the growing strength of the political right in the United States and many Western European countries to the implosion of countries through civil strife in former Yugoslavia or parts of Africa. For, if the globalisation label means anything, it is an attempt to find some term that can express fundamental shifts in power, in social structures and even in cultural sensibilities that are impacting on all our lives. Such shifts challenge those of us who are professional social scientists to look more critically at inherited frameworks of understanding and theoretical maps as they seem increasingly inadequate to interpret with any depth or genuine insight what we see happening around us – and thereby fail to give us any firm idea of what we need to do. My hope is that the category of vulnerability as it is defined, described, discussed and interrogated in these pages will find some echo among social scientists and others interested in progressive social change and will come to find a place in their toolkit.

As always, 18 months' work leaves many debts. The first that requires mention, and without which this work would not have begun life, is to Roger van Zwanenberg, publisher of Pluto Press. From the first offer he made to me in August 2001 to write a book on some aspect of international affairs (I think he had imperialism in mind), I was considering what I might like to write about and so my encounters with vulnerability found a ready outlet. Roger passed me over to Julie Stoll, who very ably saw the project through proposal stage and into the first few chapters before she left Pluto Press to travel the world. Since then I have been guided through the final stages by Sejal Chad. To all of them I owe a lot of thanks, for their enthusiasm for the project after I outlined it to them, their friendly support through the months of writing, and their trust in aspects of what I was proposing that must have seemed somewhat opaque to them. It has been a pleasure to work with them. Finding a supportive publisher was, however, just the beginning. Having set myself a deadline I then needed to get down to work. In this I was greatly assisted by a research grant from the Irish Research Council for the Humanities and Social Sciences (IRCHSS), for which I would like to express my gratitude here. This grant allowed me buy out some teaching over two semesters but, far more importantly, allowed me employ the invaluable research assistance of David Doyle. From day one, Dave has shown a very lively interest that went far beyond what professional duty warranted. His understanding of what I was doing allowed him to search out sources for me, discovering gems that I could never have come across, and always doing so efficiently and reliably. Without Dave's assistance I am doubtful that I could have covered the range of issues required to do justice to the book's subject. His imprint marks many parts of the book and I thank him for his many contributions.

Beyond those immediately involved in the project, I of course owe a great debt of gratitude to my colleagues in the School of Law and Government, Dublin City University and especially my head of School, Professor Robert Elgie. In the very best academic traditions, the School under Robert's leadership offers both practical support and an excellent collegial environment in which to develop and debate ideas. The success of our MA and BA programmes in international governance means that we attract fine students from around the world whose thoughtful engagement with the great issues of our time contributes to a stimulating and at times challenging learning environment. To all of them, colleagues and students, I offer my thanks; it is a very privileged place to work. I want to make a special mention of Dr Seán Phelan, a former PhD student of mine and now a lecturer at Massey University, New Zealand, whose comments on draft chapters were incisive and drew my attention to some serious weaknesses. I appreciate very much the trouble he took to engage with my work.

As always, of course, the greatest debt is owed to my family. Toni, Bríd and Caoimhe are by now very used to my long sojourns before the computer and to the ever more untidy state of my study. On this occasion, Toni agreed from the beginning to co-author a chapter with me, thereby becoming more intimately involved with this book than she had been with any of my previous books. I appreciate that it has not been an easy involvement, yet I believe she has brought an immense richness to the book, deepening inestimably its analysis of vulnerability. For this, I thank her in a very special way and know what it has cost her. To all three, for the innumerable ways in which they provide me with intellectual stimulation, affirmation and relaxation, *gabhaim mo bhuíochas ó chroí leo.*

Peadar Kirby
Dublin
May 2005

To Capacitar International and its founder, Dr Patricia Cane, I dedicate this book. If the book analyses vulnerability and violence then Pat and her Capacitar co-workers who work with those experiencing violence, poverty and HIV/AIDS in 25 countries of North, Central and South America, Africa, Asia and Europe, offer practical and effective means to empower people amid the vulnerabilities and violence of today's world. Capacitar's work is a rare example of helping people rediscover the fullness and strength of their vulnerable humanity.

1
Globalisation, Vulnerability and Violence

While vulnerability, uncertainty and insecurity in the life of people are not new, what is new is that their causes and manifestations have multiplied and changed profoundly over the last decade. Examples include civil strife and the proliferation of conflicts, growing inequalities within and among countries further accentuated by globalization, mixed outcomes of poverty reduction efforts, increased mobility of populations and changes in family structures. (UN, 2003: 2)

Unusually for an academic term, 'globalisation' has become a field not just of intellectual debate but of political battle. As the twenty-first century opened, it became commonplace for most international meetings of political or economic leaders to attract groups of often very colourful protesters, labelled by the media as being 'anti-globalisation'. Indeed, these protesters can take credit for catapulting to the attention of the general public such organisations as the G-8, the World Economic Forum at Davos, the International Monetary Fund, the World Bank and the World Trade Organisation – up to then rather secretive elite organisations to which few people paid much attention, even though their decisions often had major consequences on the lives of all our societies. Suddenly these organisations were mounting rearguard PR campaigns to try to counteract the negative prime-time media focus on them, and they took to meeting in obscure places (a resort in the Canadian Rockies, the Gulf state of Qatar) to be able to carry on their business. The mobilising power of this relatively new social scientific concept of globalisation is all the more surprising in that some academics still dispute whether it actually exists, claiming it to be a 'myth' (Hirst and Thompson, 1999).

In using the word 'myth' to describe globalisation these 'sceptics', as they are called, may unwittingly be on to something. While they use the team to mean an untruth, it may be more positively understood as meaning the foundational story of a culture or civilisation which explains fundamental natural or social phenomena and is usually invested with a deeper religious or transcendent significance.

Increasingly the term 'globalisation' and its story of deeper flows of investment, trade and information uniting the fates of distant peoples around the world is functioning as the myth of today's economic and political elites. Just as religious leaders down the ages used myths to persuade people that they had no choice but to accept what the leaders were telling them and insisted that it would bring them happiness, so too our leaders promote globalisation as something that offers us all the prospect of a better life, warning us that to resist or oppose it invites disaster. Yet, as is clear from the size, persistence and worldwide resonance of the 'anti-globalisation' protesters, this particular myth is being increasingly challenged even if no alternative way of organising the world's economy is yet clearly evident.

The emergence of globalisation as a field of battle has therefore served to expose an increasingly interested and concerned public to what Held and McGrew have called 'some of the most fundamental issues of our time', relating to 'the organization of human affairs and the trajectory of global social change' (Held and McGrew, 2002: 118). Among these, perhaps the most fundamental issue of all concerns the impact of globalisation on our individual and social well-being. Is globalisation really making us all better off or are some reaping most of the benefits while most of us are worse off, either absolutely or relatively? Put simply, is globalisation increasing poverty and inequality or is it reducing them? These are the sorts of concerns that enrage enough people to fuel a wave of global activism that has surprised politicians and commentators alike, forcing reconsideration of the accepted wisdom that politics interests people less and less, especially the younger generation. Finding answers to these questions is therefore very important, either to confirm the argument of pro-globalisers that what we need to help eliminate poverty is a deepening of globalisation, or to lend support to the demands by 'anti-globalisers' for more public regulation of global markets to help ensure most of the world's people reap more of the benefits. Yet, surprisingly, answers are not easily come by; fierce debates rage among academics about how globalisation is impacting on the poor, with diametrically different conclusions being reached. World Bank researcher Martin Ravallion reports different surveys concluding that poverty fell sharply in the 1990s, that it fell modestly, or that it rose, and ones that find inequality has risen while others find it has fallen. As he puts it: 'Both sides in the debate have sought support from "hard" data on what is happening to poverty and inequality in the world. A "numbers debate" has developed, underlying the more high-profile protests and debates on globalization' (Ravallion, 2003: 739). What we have are two opposing camps talking past one another, due often to differences in how key concepts are defined or in methods of data collection and analysis, with no resolution or consensus in sight.

The purpose of this book is to help break this logjam. Its writing is motivated by the conviction that both sides of the argument are, to some extent, correct in the claims they are making about globalisation – where it results in economic growth it does help reduce some kinds of poverty though the evidence shows that globalisation does not necessarily result in sustainable growth – but that they are failing to identify the central distinctive feature that characterises the impact of globalisation on our lives and our societies. It could be said that they are locked into a conceptual vocabulary that obscures rather than elucidates the core issues at stake. In other words, they are failing to probe deeply enough, or to fashion categories that adequately capture what is happening in this period of intense economic, social, cultural and political change. As expressed in the epigraph to this chapter, the term 'vulnerability' may be a much more appropriate category to capture the distinctive ways in which the economic, social, political, cultural and environmental changes associated with the term 'globalisation' are impacting on all of us, especially the poor, while the term 'violence' constitutes both a cause of vulnerability and also an expression of it. This book argues that 'vulnerability' expresses much more adequately the novel and multifaceted features of the impact of globalisation on our personal and social lives than do concepts like 'poverty', 'inequality', 'risk' or 'insecurity', concepts that up to now have dominated academic discussion of that impact. While analyses of globalisation (especially by intergovernmental organisations like the World Bank and various UN bodies) widely refer to many ways in which globalisation is making more vulnerable such features of our social world as national economies, social groups, fragile ecosystems, political systems or cultures, this book is the first to focus attention on the concept of vulnerability itself, a concept that is so widely used but rarely interrogated. As the UN Department of Economic and Social Affairs recognised in its *Report on the World Social Situation* in 2003, since the mid 1990s reference has increasingly been made to the notion of vulnerability in the context of social policy. However, it adds that 'use of the words "vulnerability" and "vulnerable" has been quite loose in policy contexts and has entailed neither the theoretical rigour nor the degree of elaboration that one finds in analytical works' (UN, 2003: 14). Through examining the ways in which the concept is used to describe the impact of globalisation and through situating the concept in social theory, this book hopes to offer such theoretical rigour and to illustrate its practical usefulness. It will identify the central features that make it such a rich concept and one uniquely able to express how today's dominant form of globalisation is changing all our lives. In analysing and describing vulnerability, the book again and again shows how it is linked to violence and to social and environmental destruction.

Following this introduction, the present chapter undertakes three tasks. The first is to assemble evidence to support the claim that the term vulnerability is being widely used in the literature on globalisation. The various uses identified will be analysed to flesh out what is being meant by the term and to offer a definition. This discussion will introduce the theme of violence as an essential feature of vulnerability in today's world. Having identified the book's core concepts, the second task of this chapter is to distinguish them from other concepts widely used to analyse the social impact of globalisation, especially those mentioned above – poverty/inequality, risk and insecurity. This discussion will help clarify why vulnerability is a more adequate concept to capture the complex and multifaceted impact of globalisation. Finally, the chapter outlines the rest of the book, using the metaphor of mapping globalisation to express how this work is seeking to describe the contours and delineate the boundaries of the sort of world being fashioned by the forces we label globalisation.

VULNERABILITY: MEANINGS AND USES

Use of the concept of vulnerability in international relations discourse can be traced to the 1970s (see Box 1.1) but, since the early 1990s, it has come to be widely used by some leading intergovernmental organisations to characterise, define and measure aspects of globalisation's impact on a range of areas relating to the well-being of society. These include economic vulnerability, social vulnerability, financial vulnerability and environmental vulnerability. The United Nations Department of Economic and Social Affairs offers the following definition:

> In essence, vulnerability can be seen as a state of high exposure to certain risks and uncertainties, in combination with a reduced ability to protect or

defend oneself against those risks and uncertainties and cope with their negative consequences. It exists at all levels and dimensions of society and forms an integral part of the human condition, affecting both individuals and society as a whole. (UN, 2003: 14)

It goes on in its 2003 report to identify groups that are especially vulnerable such as the young, the elderly, people with disabilities, migrants and indigenous peoples, and specifies that vulnerability is not limited to the poor but can affect any group in society as 'all groups face vulnerabilities that are largely the outcome of economic, social and cultural barriers that restrict opportunities for, and impede the social integration/participation of the groups' (2003: 15). Furthermore,

---

BOX 1.1   KEOHANE AND NYE: VULNERABILITY AND INTERDEPENDENCE

When Keohane and Nye proposed in their classic work *Power and Interdependence* (1977/2001) the concept of 'complex interdependence' to challenge the dominance of the state in realist accounts of international relations, they distinguished interdependence from interconnectedness on the grounds that the former involves potential costs and requires action in order to avoid incurring those costs whereas the latter does not. In analysing the costs involved in interdependence, they introduced two dimensions – sensitivity and vulnerability (2001: 10–12). The first refers to the threats (either economic or political) faced by a country whereas vulnerability refers to whether a country has the ability to implement policies that minimise the costs arising from such threats. Taking oil price rises, for example, two countries may have similar levels of sensitivity but if country A can reduce consumption or discovers domestic sources of oil, it is less vulnerable than country B which maintains its previous consumption and has no alternative supplies available to it. 'The vulnerability dimension of interdependence rests on the relative availability and costliness of the alternatives that various actors face', they write (2001: 11).

While Keohane and Nye recognise the multifaceted nature of vulnerability – economic, political, cultural, social and environmental – and see today's globalisation as intensifying interdependence and therefore vulnerability, they devote cursory attention to its impact and manifestations. Thus, for example, though their dimensions of sensitivity and vulnerability bear a loose relationship to the dimensions of increased risks and reduced coping mechanisms that in this book are seen to constitute vulnerability, they capture far less adequately the manifold expressions of vulnerability as described in Chapters 2 and 3 of this book. Furthermore, their treatment rests on assumptions about state capacity and the availability of alternatives (indeed, it largely limits itself to the action of states or intergovernmental bodies) that fail to examine more fully the implications of the shifts in economic, political, social and cultural power analysed in Part II of this book, or the social impacts of these shifts as discussed in Part III.

the UN Department of Economic and Social Affairs echoes the views of the UN Development Programme (UNDP) in identifying globalisation as an important source of growing vulnerability. In its 1999 *Human Development Report* on the subject of globalisation, the UNDP states that 'people everywhere are more vulnerable':

> Changing labour markets are making people insecure in their jobs and livelihoods. The erosion of the welfare state removes safety nets. And the financial crisis is now a social crisis. All this is happening as globalization erodes the fiscal base of countries, particularly developing countries, shrinking the public resources and institutions to protect people. (UNDP, 1999: 90)

The World Bank, on the other hand, discusses vulnerability in relation to the poor only. In its keynote study of poverty, the 2000–01 *World Development Report* entitled 'Attacking Poverty', the World Bank sees vulnerability as a dimension of poverty, alongside other dimensions such as income poverty, health and education, voicelessness and powerlessness. 'In the dimensions of income and health, vulnerability is the risk that a household or individual will experience an episode of income or health poverty over time. But vulnerability also means the probability of being exposed to a number of other risks (violence, crime, natural disasters, being pulled out of school)' (World Bank, 2000: 19). The report sees vulnerability as a dynamic concept, capturing the ways in which people move into and out of poverty over time, though it acknowledges that measuring it is especially difficult as it would require a continuous monitoring of the same households over a period, necessitating a range of data not currently available through the household surveys of income or expenditure that provide the basis for measuring poverty today. However, the Bank has included a table entitled 'Assessing vulnerability' in its annual World Development Indicators publication. This is made up of indicators such as the percentage of employment that is in the informal sector, the percentage of children aged 10–14 in the labour force, female-headed households as a percentage of total households, percentages of the labour force and of the population who make pension contributions, and private health expenditure as a percentage of total health expenditure. These measure risks faced by households of falling into poverty (World Bank, 2005: Table 2.8). This illustrates, therefore, that vulnerability is primarily seen by the World Bank as the risk some sectors of the population face of falling into income poverty.

Economic vulnerability has been developed as a concept to help identify those states most vulnerable in a globalised economy. The idea of measuring the extent and dimensions of economic vulnerability first arose in the early 1990s when UNCTAD carried out a study on the feasibility of constructing an index of vulnerability. The idea was afterwards taken up by the UN Economic and Social Council and in 2000 the first Economic Vulnerability Index (EVI) was drawn up with a composite indicator based on five components, reflecting three dimensions of countries' economic vulnerability: firstly, the magnitude of external shocks beyond domestic control measured through indicators of the instability of agricultural production and the instability of exports of goods and services; secondly, the exposure of the economy to these shocks measured through the share of manufacturing and modern services in GDP, and merchandise export concentration; and finally, the structural handicaps explaining the country's high exposure measured through population size. Tuvalu was top of the 2003 EVI followed by Kiribati, Brunei Darussalam, Afghanistan, Mongolia and Cambodia (ESCAP, 2003). A similar index is the Commonwealth Vulnerability Index which uses a sample of 111 developing countries to measure two aspects of vulnerability: firstly, the impact of external shocks over which the country affected has little or no control and, secondly, the resilience of a country to withstand and recover from such shocks. The index is compiled from the three most significant indicators of countries' income volatility, namely: lack of economic diversification, export dependence and the impact of natural disasters. Of the 28 most vulnerable countries on this index, 26 are small states, 18 of them islands. Lesotho and Mauritania are the only exceptions.

For the International Monetary Fund (IMF), the currency crises in Mexico, East Asia, Russia and Brazil in the 1990s have led them to develop vulnerability indicators identifying which countries are vulnerable to such financial crises and to what extent. The Fund states that 'timely and detailed data on international reserves, external debt, and capital flows strengthen the ability to detect vulnerabilities, giving policy makers enough time to put remedial measures in place' (IMF, 2003). Four groups of indicators are monitored by the IMF to identify vulnerability. First are indicators of external and domestic debt, with special attention to countries' ability to pay back their debts, such as the ratios of external debt to exports and to GDP and, where public sector borrowing is significant, the ratio of tax revenues to debt. The second set of indicators relates to reserves and is particularly important for those countries with significant but uncertain access to capital markets. Thirdly, there are what the IMF calls 'financial soundness indicators', used to assess the strengths and weaknesses of countries' financial sectors, including the profitability and liquidity of financial institutions and the pace and quality of credit growth. These are used to assess sensitivity to market risk such as changes in interest and exchange rates. Finally, the Fund has a set of corporate sector indicators that trace the exposure of companies to foreign exchange and interest rate exposure. These vulnerability assessments are now incorporated into the IMF's consultations with its member countries and, based on these data, the IMF produces Early Warning System (EWS) models to estimate the likelihood of currency crises.

The UN Environmental Programme (UNEP) sees environmental vulnerability as an essential element of human vulnerability. 'Since everyone is vulnerable to environmental threats, in some way, the issue cuts across rich and poor, urban and rural, North and South, and may undermine the entire sustainable development process in developing countries', writes the UNEP. It adds that 'coping capacity that was adequate in the past has not kept pace with environmental change' and urges two types of policy response: firstly, to reduce the threat through prevention and preparedness initiatives; and secondly, to improve the coping capacity of vulnerable groups (UNEP, 2003: 302–3). The UN Development Programme (UNDP) recognises that over the past 40 years there has been a significant increase in natural disasters and in the losses they cause to society: 'Vulnerability of populations and ecosystems has increased, often as a result of inadequate development practices, leading to environmental degradation and human poverty' (UNDP, 2003b). While many regions of the world are at risk from exceptional natural events (earthquakes, volcanoes, hurricanes) and from freak weather patterns caused by the impact of human activity on the environment (drought, torrential rainfall, flooding), the concept of vulnerability relates not to these risks but to the underlying exposure of human communities to them. To identify this exposure and to seek to avoid the worst impact of these events, specialists draw up vulnerability assessment maps of vulnerable regions based on such indicators as environmental factors (forests, rivers, slopes, soil permeability and vegetation), population, social factors (levels of poverty) and infrastructure (its condition and exposure). An example of the results of such vulnerability assessments is that, in the Central American region, Honduras has been identified as a high-risk country and detailed maps have been able to identify the top 60 high-risk municipalities in that country, listing them in three groups beginning with the ten most at risk.

The UN Economic Commission for Latin America and the Caribbean (ECLAC) writes that 'the opening up of markets and the downgrading of the state's role in the economy and society have exacerbated the insecurity and defencelessness affecting large groups of individuals and families, who are now exposed to increased risk'. It argues that this problem affects not only the poor but far wider sections of the population 'to such an extent that vulnerability may be regarded as a distinctive feature of the social situation in the 1990s' (ECLAC, 2000: 52). In developing a concept of social vulnerability, it focuses upon both the 'perception of risk, insecurity and defencelessness' and also 'the quantity and quality of the resources or assets controlled by individuals and families' and the opportunities they have to use them in the new economic, social, political and cultural circumstances. These resources and assets include work, human capital, productive resources, social relationships and family relationships. For much of the population, ECLAC argues, these assets and resources are under pressure and are being eroded by the conditions of the liberalised economy. In the Caribbean region, ECLAC is helping develop a Social Vulnerability Index (SVI) compiled from the following components: poverty, crime, natural disasters, migration, health status and social marginalisation (Briguglio, 2003).

Apart from these general uses, the concept of vulnerability has also been used to analyse the situation of specific population groups. Identifying the ever-increasing threat of HIV/AIDS to the population of Southeast Asia, the Asian Development Bank (ADB) argues that 'increasing linkages within and between countries further hasten the epidemics, as more and more people move and interact' (ADB, 2003). While mobility does not in itself place people at risk of HIV infection, the Bank argues that such mobility may increase people's vulnerability to the disease in a number of ways: migrants may be marginalised, subject to discrimination and have little social or legal protection in their host community; they may be forced to trade unprotected sex for goods, services or cash in order to survive; they may have little access to health services or means of HIV prevention; finally, separation from regular partners may encourage them to take risks that make them vulnerable to infection. Another application of the concept is in the Aging Vulnerability Index, sponsored by the European Union (EU). This assesses the capacity of twelve developed countries to meet the challenge of a fast-aging population. It is developed from four indicators: the public spending burden; room for fiscal growth; dependence of the elderly on public benefits; and the relative affluence of the old versus the young (Jackson and Howe, 2003). France, Italy and Spain were found to have the highest vulnerability in the 2003 index.

An aspect of vulnerability not explicitly mentioned in these treatments is violence. It deserves explicit mention here as the threat or use of physical force causing damage or injury to people is one major way in which vulnerability is being manifested in the lives of states, communities and individuals in the globalised world. Indeed, violence inflicted on innocent people – whether through neighbour turning against neighbour in Rwanda, some countries of former Yugoslavia and East Timor; through state collapse as in Somalia, Sierra Leone and Liberia; or through the suicide bombings carried out by conspiratorial groups in Istanbul, Bali, Baghdad, Casablanca, Madrid, Mombasa, Riyadh and, most dramatically, in New York and Washington on 9/11 – has become emblematic of a more globalised world. Kaldor calls these 'new wars' and sees them as 'one aspect of the current globalized era' with its global interconnectedness and the growing privatisation of organised violence (Kaldor, 2001: 1). Though some of these forms of violence developed before the end of the Cold War, especially in Africa, and evolved out of guerrilla and counter-insurgency wars of an earlier period, Kaldor writes that 'it is also the case that these wars greatly increased in number during this [globalised] period, and, moreover, there was also a big increase in civilian suffering, as measured by the ratio of military to civilian casualties and by the explosion of refugees and internally displaced persons' (Kaldor, 2003: 119–20). Furthermore, argues Rogers, Western strategies to address a growing sense of insecurity in an ever more violent and unequal world may increase vulnerability: 'Attempting to keep the lid on insecurity – "liddism" – without addressing the core reasons for dissent, will not work. It is more likely to make western elite societies more vulnerable, a trend already beginning to be recognised by some military analysts' (Rogers, 2000: 10).

But the 'new wars' of a globalised world are only one way in which people's lives are becoming more vulnerable to violence. Box 1.2 details evidence of growing levels of interpersonal violence (homicides, domestic violence, sexual violence) that characterise societies in all regions of the world. Scholte posits that one possible cause of this derives from higher levels of stress:

The stresses induced by unceasing pressures for greater productivity and worries about job security can heighten tensions in the household and on the street. It would be difficult to demonstrate precisely that flexibilization has fuelled domestic strife, uncivil driving, hooliganism and other violence; and no doubt other factors have also played their part. However, it seems reasonable to posit that insecurity at work has fed insecurity elsewhere. (Scholte, 2000: 223)

He concludes that 'faster and fuller time in a highly globalized life can present substantial coping challenges' and sees it as no accident that stress has grown concurrently with globalisation (2000: 196–7). While our lives are ever more vulnerable to the risk of violence, therefore, more and more people are also reacting more violently as coping mechanisms and supports are eroded. Violence is both a source of vulnerability (increasing threats) and also a reaction to vulnerability (a response to threats); examples of both occur throughout this book. Indeed, beyond such examples of violence, one major conclusion of the examination of the changing nature of the relation of the market to society and of the individual to society (in Chapters 6 and 7) is the increasingly destructive impact on individual, social and environmental well-being. This constitutes a further form of violence, not dissimilar to Pierre Bourdieu's notion of 'symbolic violence': 'that properly symbolic force which allows force to be fully exercised while disguising its true nature as force and gaining recognition, approval and acceptance by dint of the fact that it can present itself under the appearances of universality – that of reason or morality' (Bourdieu, 1990: 85).

A number of conclusions are warranted from the foregoing discussion. Firstly, it demonstrates how, over the course of the 1990s, the concept of vulnerability has come to occupy a central place in the attempts of some leading intergovernmental organisations (IGOs) to analyse the impacts on social groups of changes associated with globalisation. Secondly, the concept has been applied at different levels, from the nation state to local livelihoods. Thirdly, it has been found useful in a range of areas, including poverty alleviation, financial monitoring, environmental analyses and economic and social risk assessment. It can be concluded that, while there is disagreement on the range of groups suffering vulnerability and on its sources, there is a general agreement that vulnerability is an important concept capturing the dynamic way that people's well-

BOX 1.2   A MORE VIOLENT WORLD

In response to the globalisation of crime and the threat it poses to societies worldwide, the UN Secretary General, Kofi Annan, established an Office for Drug Control and Crime Prevention which in 1999 published a *Global Report on Crime and Justice* (UN, 1999). For the first time, this attempts to provide comparable data on the state of crime around the world. It reports the percentages of those living in cities with a population of 100,000 or more who reported being victims of various crimes over the period 1989 to 1996. These data are divided according to six regions and are compiled from national surveys. Under 'contact crimes', which covers sexual harassment and/or violence, assaults/threats and robbery, it reports the following percentages of urban populations in different regions which have been victims of such crimes over this period: Africa: 32 per cent; Asia: 13 per cent; Central and Eastern Europe: 17 per cent; Latin America: 36 per cent; New World (US, Canada, Australia and New Zealand): 20 per cent; Western Europe: 16 per cent. The figure for the world was 20 per cent.

By and large, the report offers a snapshot of the recent situation rather than trends over time. However, the percentages of those reporting being victims of assaults or threats increased between 1988 and 1995 from 4.7 per cent to 4.85 per cent in the United States but from 2.7 per cent to 4.66 per cent in Western Europe. The average number of homicides per 100,000 of the population fluctuated between 3.5 and 4.1 from 1974 to 1988 but had jumped to 6.1 in 1993, the latest data presented. Examining overall trends in the numbers of homicides and rapes reported to the UN between 1986 and 1994, the report shows how, out of 39 countries, the number of homicides fell in nine countries, was stable in four countries and rose in 26 countries, increasing by over 100 per cent in 13 of these. In the case of rape, data from 41 countries is reported. Rapes fell in seven of these, were stable in five and rose in 29. Examining various forms of violence against women, the report states that these are 'increasingly recognized as important public health and human rights issues' (UN, 1999: 155). It offers a sample of national survey results on the percentage of women in the population who suffered violence by their spouse, though it emphasises that differences in methodology, in the understanding of what constituted violence in each case, and in the time period covered mean that these data are not comparable. The following is the percentage of women in certain countries who reported sexual or physical violence by their spouse:

Papua New Guinea, 1996: 62 per cent	Canada, 1993: 29 per cent
Nicaragua, 1996: 52 per cent	Chile, 1993: 26 per cent
Malaysia, 1989: 39 per cent	Australia, 1996: 23 per cent
Korea, 1992: 37 per cent	United States, 1996: 21 per cent
Mexico, 1992: 33 per cent	Cambodia, 1995: 16 per cent
Colombia, 1990: 30 per cent	England and Wales, 1996: 1 per cent

(UN, 1999: 155)

being in today's world is affected by wider changes in the economic, financial, social, institutional, cultural and environmental spheres. Furthermore, a common meaning can be identified in the many uses of the term. This is a combination of two factors: firstly, the frequency and nature of risks that impact on people's lives and, secondly, the ability of people to cope with these risks. The World Bank identifies three different types of assets that help people to cope with risks: physical assets (like savings, land or property), human assets (like education and good health) and social assets (networks of social support like the family, and social groups such as community associations, trade unions or peasant organisations) while the Voices of the Poor survey (see Box 1.3) adds environmental assets (land, water sources). These two factors – risks and coping mechanisms – will guide the examination of vulnerability in Chapters 2 and 3. Finally, it has been argued that evidence of growing violence at levels from the interpersonal to the intercommunal can be understood both as a dimension of vulnerability but also as a reaction to it.

WHY VULNERABILITY?

Establishing that vulnerability is being employed as a concept to analyse the impacts of globalisation is not, of course, on its own a sufficient reason to use it. It could be argued that resorting to yet another concept will only confuse the task of reaching a deeper understanding of the nature and causes of such impacts and thereby even impede a wider consensus on how to address them. In other words, we have to ask why vulnerability is a useful concept in undertaking this task. This section offers an answer through clarifying the differences between vulnerability and three other sets of concepts that have been more widely used in discussing globalisation's impacts – poverty/inequality, risk and insecurity. It will be argued that the concept of vulnerability goes further than any of them in being able to capture more fully what is distinctive about the way globalisation is impacting on society. This is not to say that concepts such as poverty/inequality, risk and insecurity are not applicable to discussing globalisation; indeed, all of them express aspects of growing vulnerability in the increasingly globalised world. The argument here is that vulnerability is a more adequate concept because it focuses attention in an analytically precise way on the complex and multifaceted social impacts of the changes being wrought by globalisation, their dynamics and their interconnections.

i) Poverty/Inequality

By far the most common way of trying to assess the impact of globalisation on society is through examining data on trends in poverty and inequality. Though poverty and inequality are distinct concepts, they are treated together here since both relate to distibutional issues and since, as stated earlier in this chapter, they are intimately related in debates on globalisation. The pro-globalisation view can be summed up in the words of a major World Bank report on globalisation and poverty:

> [S]ince 1980 the overall number of poor people has at last stopped increasing, and has indeed fallen by an estimated 200 million. It is falling rapidly in the new globalizers and rising in the rest of the developing world. ... This third wave of globalization [since 1980] may mark the turning point at which participation has widened sufficiently for it to reduce both poverty and inequality. (World Bank, 2002: 7)

Central to this argument is the claim that countries which have strongly increased their participation in global flows of trade and investment (two important indicators of how globalised they are) have seen their per capita incomes increase and poverty fall to the point where they are beginning to catch up with the world's richer countries (examples are China, India, Brazil, Hungary and Mexico), whereas the 2 billion people in countries that are not participating strongly in such global flows (such as those in Africa and those of the former Soviet Union) are growing poorer and are falling further behind. This argument is widely propagated through the media (for example, it is explicitly promoted in the *Financial Times* and *The Economist*) to argue for more and faster economic liberalisation. However, there are three main difficulties with it which help identify the limitations of over-reliance on poverty and inequality as a way of assessing the impact of globalisation on livelihoods and well-being.

The first relates to measurement. In his analysis of World Bank data (and he emphasises that the Bank 'is effectively the sole producer of the world poverty headcount'), Wade casts serious doubt on the accuracy of world poverty measures (Wade, 2003a: 19). He writes that counting the number of people in extreme poverty inevitably involves 'a large margin of error' but 'we can be reasonably confident that it is higher than the World Bank says' for a number of reasons. Firstly, the Bank's comparison of poverty in 1980 and 1998 (on which the argument of the pro-globalisers rests) is not legitimate since the Bank changed its methodology in the late 1990s involving a substantial change even for estimates of the same country in the same year once the change was made (for details, see Wade, 2003a: 19–20). Secondly, the Bank's new poverty line (of $1.08 a day rather than $1 a day) had the effect of actually lowering the poverty line in most countries, thereby automatically reducing the numbers in poverty. Thirdly, the poverty count is based on household surveys at national level. The limitations of such surveys, however, 'add up to a large margin of error in national poverty numbers' (Wade 2003a: 22). Finally, Wade draws attention to the Bank's inconsistency, showing how its 2000–01 World Development Report on poverty showed an increase in world poverty of 20 million between 1987 and 1998 whereas its major report on globalisation and poverty two years later showed a decrease of 200 million between 1980 and 1998. He points out that, at the time of the first Report, Joseph Stiglitz was the Bank's chief economist and Ravi Kanbur was the Report's director, both of them critical of neoliberalism. However, both had left the Bank by the time of the second Report, and the institution was under pressure from the US Congress for its failure to reduce poverty. Wade speculates that 'the comparison between the two reports suggests that the data and the choice of methodologies may change with the people and the organization's tactical objectives' (Wade, 2003b: 141). On inequality, he writes that there is even less agreement on how to measure it so that estimates depend greatly on what one chooses to measure (for example, inequality within countries or between countries) (see Wade, 2003a: 23–30). On the World Bank's claim that the globalising countries are reducing poverty and inequality while those globalising less decisively are not, Wade points out that the Bank's category of 'pro-globalisers' is based on those whose ratio of trade to GDP increased most between 1977 and 1997. Prominent among these are China, India, Bangladesh and Brazil. This is therefore a category of countries which are liberalising fastest; it does not mean that they are the most globalised as many poor countries which have been exporters of primary raw materials for over a century have had a high ratio of trade to GDP for a far longer period and therefore don't make in into the World Bank's list. However, they are in many cases far more globalised than are the so-called pro-globalisers (that is, they have higher ratios of trade to GDP than have the fast-liberalising countries), yet they are not performing spectacularly nor are they reducing poverty and inequality. Indeed, *Foreign Policy*'s

2004 globalisation index lists China, India, Bangladesh and Brazil as among 'the world's bottom ten' on the index (*Foreign Policy*, 2004: 67). Furthermore, Wade makes the case that China and India began to perform well *before* they began to liberalise their trade and that they still remain highly protected economies. He therefore concludes: 'The Bank's argument about the benign effects of globalization on growth, poverty and income distribution does not survive scrutiny' (Wade, 2003a: 32).

However, even if we were to reach the point where we had reliable measures of poverty and inequality over a long enough time period to allow credible trends be discerned, other more substantive difficulties would remain. The second main difficulty with relying on poverty/ inequality data is that it is far from clear what they tell us about people's lives. Though widely accepted as measures of poverty, the World Bank's poverty line of $1 a day (now updated to $1.08 a day) adjusted to take account of its purchasing power parity or PPP (making the value of what this can purchase comparable across countries) bears no relationship to whether this amount of income or expenditure might meet basic needs or not. In other words, even if the measure were accurate, it may well be true that hundreds of millions of people with incomes higher than this are unable to satisfy their minimal needs for nutrition, clothing or shelter. Other measures of poverty are based on estimates of how much income or expenditure is required to satisfy such basic needs, with the result that poverty lines can be drawn related to such requirements. One example is the *canasta basica* or 'basic basket of goods' method used throughout Latin America. This derives two poverty lines from the expenditure needed to buy a basket of goods required for survival in that region: households whose average expenditure is lower than this amount are labelled the indigent while households whose expenditure is less than double the value of such a basket of basic goods are classed as poor. Interestingly, poverty estimates by the UN Economic Commission for Latin America and the Caribbean (ECLAC) using the *canasta basica* method are much higher in most cases than those of the World Bank (ECLAC, 2001: 51). This casts further doubt on the value of World Bank poverty counts.

The third main difficulty follows from this since over recent decades the definition of poverty has moved further and further away from one based on income poverty alone to a much more multifaceted understanding of what constitutes it. Early definitions of poverty, going back to the nineteenth century, concentrated on levels of income sufficient for survival. Over time, this focus was complemented by attention to social indicators such as life expectancy, school enrolment and infant mortality, also seen as indicators of alleviating poverty. These have found their most authoritative expression in the Human Development Index of the UNDP. However, in an extensive survey of the views of the poor carried out for the 2000–01 World Development Report on poverty (see Box 1.3), the World Bank identifies two key aspects of poverty not captured in conventional surveys. These were highlighted by Kanbur and Squire:

> One is a concern with risk and volatility of incomes, and is often expressed as a feeling of vulnerability. In talking about their situation, the poor detailed the ways in which fluctuations, seasons, and crises affected their well-being. From these descriptions, we come to understand the particular importance of poverty not just as a state of having little, but also of being vulnerable to losing the little one has. The poor also described their interactions with government employees and institutions, revealing another important aspect of life in poverty: lack of political power. (Kanbur and Squire, 1999: 21)

So important were these for the poor, that at times they took precedence over increases in income. As Kanbur and Squire said: 'Frequently the idea of a secure livelihood is perceived as more important than maximizing income, and thus the local understandings of people about their livelihoods have more to do with vulnerability than poverty' (1999: 21). This echoes concerns that have been raised elsewhere about the inability of poverty data to capture the threat to livelihoods that results from high levels of vulnerability. For example, Briguglio has highlighted the fact that small island states like Singapore, Cyprus and Malta have managed to generate high income per capita but 'are very economically vulnerable' due to their high level of dependence on trade and on inward investment, as well as their vulnerability to environmental disasters (Briguglio, 2003: 42). Focusing on poverty and inequality, therefore, raises complex problems of definition and measurement; even if there were consensus on these (which there is not), it is clear that these concepts fail to capture in a comprehensive way threats to livelihoods and well-being.

The three difficulties outlined here highlight the limitations of using measures of poverty and/or inequality as a way of examining the impact globalisation is having on the well-being of people and

BOX 1.3   VOICES OF THE POOR

To inform its 2000–01 *World Development Report* on the subject of poverty, the World Bank commissioned the most extensive qualitative survey ever of poor people, to find out what, in their view, constitutes poverty. This was published in three volumes under the general title 'Voices of the Poor' (see Narayan, 2000). Not only did this gather the views of over 60,000 poor men and women in 60 countries in Africa, Asia, Latin America and Eastern Europe, but its use of the Participatory Poverty Assessment (PPA) method allowed the poor to define their agenda rather than agree or disagree with an agenda set by outside surveyors. As a result, it constitutes a rare 'view of the world from the perspective of the poor' (Narayan, 2000: 3). In some important ways, the evidence gathered serves to turn on its head our conventional view of poverty since the poor rarely spoke about lack of income but emphasised instead the importance of cultural identity and social belonging, identifying powerlessness, voicelessness, dependency, shame and humiliation as important aspects of what it means to be poor.

Much more than income, what matters to the poor are assets. The survey identifies four kinds of assets mentioned by the poor. The first are physical assets, including land and material belongings. The second are human assets such as education and training, health and ability to work. Third come social assets, referring to the extent and nature of the social networks to which they belong, including family networks, neighbours and associations. Finally they mention environmental assets, such as grass, trees, water and non-timber products. The poor see a link between the lack of these assets and their vulnerability to risks. This draws attention to factors other than the lack of possessions as contributing to poverty, such as the failure of the state or NGOs to provide accessible educational and health services, and the erosion of social networks through the breakdown of the family or the decline in social cohesion as a result of economic opportunities, migration, lawlessness or crime and violence. Finally, environmental degradation is putting pressure on natural assets that enabled coping strategies for the poor such as gathering wood, harvesting wild herbs, fruits or nuts, and fishing or hunting. Furthermore, as assets decline women are often the first to suffer: it is their goods which are sold first, it is they who have to nurse sick children or relatives, it is they who have to hold the family together when men are absent.

The Voices of the Poor survey therefore reveals that poor people's fears derive from a lack of assets and from anxiety about their ability to survive in increasingly unpredictable and insecure environments. The survey states: 'Families that lack certain key assets may not necessarily be poor, but nonetheless may be extremely vulnerable in times of need or crisis' (Narayan, 2000: 65). This draws our attention to the fact that conventional measures of poverty may fail to include many of those whose well-being is at risk. It highlights two issues of supreme importance to the poor which are neglected by conventional approaches towards poverty alleviation. The first relates to power relations (from the household to the national institutional level), since this often determines who gets access to resources, while the second draws attention to the importance of such assets as family and social networks, health and education, land and labour, since these are

▶

> the resources that make self-provisioning possible. As the then British Minister for International Development, Clare Short, and the then World Bank President, James D. Wolfensohn, write in their Foreword to *Can Anyone Hear Us?*, this survey provides telling evidence of how the poor view their future, no matter what World Bank or other headcounts of the poor may show: 'What poor people share with us is sobering. A majority of them feel they are worse off and more insecure than in the past' (Narayan, 2000: ix).

societies. If these limitations are not acknowledged, claims made about globalisation's impact can be misleading and can neglect forms of impact (such as growing vulnerability) that really do matter to the poor.

ii) Risk

The concept of 'risk' was applied to society by the German sociologist, Ulrich Beck, who developed the notion of the 'risk society' (Beck, 1992). It has been used to understand the distinctive impact of globalisation on people's lives. Giddens argues that 'this apparently simple notion unlocks some of the most basic characteristics of the world in which we now live' (Giddens, 1999: 21). He argues that the notion of risk was unknown in the Middle Ages and is associated with modernity since it refers, not just to hazards or dangers, but to hazards that are assessed in relation to future possibilities. It is, in other words, a concept related to an uncertain future: this future-orientation gives it a positive connotation. What changes with globalisation, however, is that 'there is a new riskiness to risk' (Giddens, 1999: 28) which arises for two main reasons. In the past risks were more predictable but we now face incalculable risks associated with climate change, changes in the food we eat (remember the BSE scare), new diseases such as HIV/AIDS, and the volatility of economic activity. The second change is that the means we had developed of protecting ourselves against risk, through insurance policies or the welfare state, are now breaking down as they are proving unsustainable in the face of unpredictable risk. Giddens concludes:

> Our age is not more dangerous – not more risky – than those of earlier gen-
> erations, but the balance of risks and dangers has shifted. We live in a world
> where hazards created by ourselves are as, or more, threatening than those
> that come from the outside. Some of these are genuinely catastrophic, such
> as global ecological risk, nuclear proliferation or the meltdown of the world

economy. Others affect us as individuals much more directly, for instance those involved in diet, medicine or even marriage. (Giddens, 1999: 34)

While this discussion usefully clarifies the changing nature of risk in our globalised world, it is not as broad a concept as vulnerability as it focuses most attention on the nature of the threats we face. Vulnerability, on the other hand, also focuses attention on our ability to cope with these threats. Indeed, Beck seems to value the concept of risk since it functions as 'a magic political wand through which a smugly settled society learns to fear itself and, against its will, is compelled to become politically active in its core areas' (Beck, 2000b: 100). In responding to risk, Beck sees the contours of a 'utopian ecological democracy' beginning to emerge, which would for him be 'the essence of a responsible modernity' (2000b: 99). Yet, this is to create a notion of a future society out of very partial and fragmentary evidence. Employing instead the concept of vulnerability allows a treatment both of the changing nature of risk but also of the changing capability to cope with it. Whether this leads to a new utopian democracy and a new version of modernity, or whether it leads to growing social fragmentation and breakdown accompanied by the erosion of democracy, it is far too early to say.

iii) Insecurity

The concept of insecurity takes the focus off the nature of the risks we face and puts it back on their impacts; it is used by some analysts (Harriss-White, 2002; Scholte, 2000; Bakker and Gill, 2003) to undertake 'a normative evaluation of globalization' (Scholte, 2000: 207). The focus on security in relation to well-being derives from the emergence of the concept of 'human security' following the end of the Cold War. The UNDP Human Development Report 1994 was an early attempt to define this new security agenda. Its two-part definition bears some similarities to the definition of vulnerability offered in the previous section: 'It means, first, safety from such chronic threats as hunger, disease and repression. And second, it means protection from sudden and hurtful disruptions in the patterns of daily life – whether in homes, in jobs or in communities. Such threats can exist at all levels of national income and development' (UNDP, 1994: 23). The UNDP considers human security as deriving mainly from the following forms of security: economic, food, health, environmental, personal, community and political; the main threats to it come from unchecked population growth, disparities in economic opportunities, excessive international migration, environmental degradation, drug production and trafficking, and international terrorism (for a discussion, see UNDP, 1994: 24–37). Since then, the concept of human security has come into widespread use and in 2005 the first Human Security Report with its Human Security Index was published to complement the UNDP's Human Development Index.

Clearly, human security is a valuable concept that draws attention to ways in which human well-being is being undermined in today's world. However, uses of it illustrate its conceptual imprecision. In seeking to assess globalisation's impact on society, Scholte undertakes a broad assessment of the state of human well-being under a range of headings: peace, ecological integrity, subsistence, financial stability, employment, working conditions, identity and knowledge (Scholte, 2000: 208–31). While this describes and assesses its subjects well, it offers little precision in identifying what exactly is meant by security and how it relates to human well-being. The treatment of insecurity in Harriss-White's edited volume describes aspects of insecurity generated by processes associated with globalisation but leaves the concept itself loose and undeveloped. In her introductory chapter, Harriss-White identifies four dimensions of insecurity: physical insecurity, threats to state autonomy, instability and vulnerability which is described as 'a susceptibility to damage' (Harriss-White, 2002: 3). This is no more than a useful list of threats and lacks the focus on people's and collectivities' coping capacities contained in the definition of vulnerability given in the previous section. Bakker and Gill's treatment of the concept of security is more satisfactory, basing it on the UNDP's concept of human security and contrasting it with national security and the security of capital (Bakker and Gill, 2003: 9–12). However, they see no problem in using the same concept of security (with different adjectives) to mean very different things.

Employing the concept of vulnerability offers the potential for greater precision as is shown by its use across a range of fields by various intergovernmental organisations. Furthermore, since it derives from a broadening of the concept of state security, human security may run the risk of focusing too much analytical attention on the unit (whether that of the nation-state as in concepts of state security, or on the individual in achieving human security). This can be described as a danger of methodological individualism. An example is the way in which individuals and communities seek security through trying to put up secure barriers against the world around them (such as 'gated communities', security guards, etc.). Vulnerability, on the other hand, gives analytical attention to the erosion of bonds of secure belonging, as indicated in Box 1.3. Prescriptions deriving from the concept will require that this challenge is addressed, which may not always be the case when using the concept of security. For these reasons, the concept of vulnerability seems a better one to use, though it can draw usefully on analyses of human security. A fuller discussion of the distinction between vulnerability and security is pursued in Chapter 7.

This section has traced the uses of various terms to analyse the impact of globalisation on society, highlighting the limitations of each. In the light of this discussion, it can be concluded that the concept of vulnerability is more adequate for four principal reasons:

1) it has the advantage of analytical precision;
2) it is concerned not just with damage that is already done to people's and communities' well-being (as are the concepts of poverty and inequality) but also with the risks of such damage being done;
3) it focuses on mechanisms and capabilities for coping with risks, thereby giving analytical attention to issues of power at different levels (the individual, the local, the national);
4) it is based on an understanding of well-being that is not limited to the material and therefore reflects more fully the concerns of the poor themselves with vulnerability and powerlessness.

Clearly, employing the concept of vulnerability will require attending to evidence of trends in poverty and inequality but, recognising difficulties of methodology and definition, it will avoid treating these as sufficient and will also devote attention to dimensions of psychological or cultural poverty not captured by headcount measures as well as focusing attention on violence as a dimension of vulnerability. Vulnerability will obviously seek to identify risks associated with globalisation but will complement this by examining how globalisation is affecting coping mechanisms. Finally, while acknowledging its closeness to the concept of human security, vulnerability has the potential to achieve an analytical rigour, particularly in relationship to globalisation, that human security has not so far displayed and, as argued in Chapter 7, it points to quite distinct prescriptions about what needs to be done to lessen vulnerability and reinforce security. The ever more frequent employment of the concept of vulnerability by intergovernmental organisations indicates its practical usefulness and suggests that the time has come to employ it as a key conceptual tool in academic analyses of globalisation.

MAPPING GLOBALISATION

The metaphor of mapping helps express a lot of what the scholarly output on globalisation is doing since it is seeking to outline the nature and features of the 'new world' emerging under globalisation's impact. Just as the early European explorers of Africa or the Americas first drew maps containing fragments of coastlines, mountain ranges or river mouths and left many features of these territories blank because they remained unknown to them, so too books and articles on globalisation highlight features of a globalised world as they come into focus. Yet a full map of a new territory requires that the relationships between the different features be identified clearly so that their interconnections are known. Only then can a complete map be provided and the nature of the territory be fully understood. In a similar way, many features of globalisation's impact on people's personal and social lives, on their security and on their livelihoods, are known, yet the interconnections between them, their causes and effects, are still the subject of fierce debates, as outlined at the beginning of this chapter. Central to these debates is the question of whether globalisation is the cause of, or the solution to, the absence of well-being so amply documented around the world. In this regard, vulnerability offers a conceptual tool to help uncover how the shifts in political, economic and cultural power that we label globalisation are impacting in distinctive ways on society; this is why it is being employed more and more by intergovernmental organisations and this is the reason for introducing it into the academic debates through this book. In particular, as Box 1.4 outlines, vulnerability could be a valuable addition to the toolkit of International Political Economy, which might thereby make a contribution to our understanding of the social impact of globalisation as theoretically rich and distinctive as it has made to our understanding of issues of power, the state, regionalism and social forces as they are reconfigured by and respond to globalisation. In this way, yet more of the contours and boundaries of this emerging globalised world can be delineated.

The remainder of the book is divided into four parts, each with two chapters. Part I, entitled 'Description', contains chapters describing the nature of vulnerability as it manifests itself today. Chapter 2

BOX 1.4   ADDING VULNERABILITY TO IPE'S CONCEPTUAL TOOLKIT

The swift emergence of globalisation as a core interpretative category throughout the social sciences challenges not just our understanding of the world but also the tools we use to develop that understanding. Though the challenge is being felt in all the disciplinary areas into which the social sciences have progressively fragmented over the past century and a half, perhaps its greatest impact has been felt in the field of International Relations (IR). Dominated by a focus on inter-state relations, particularly in the diplomatic and military spheres, the tools offered by IR proved blunt instruments to make subtle sense of a world in which power had gravitated from the political to the economic, and from the level of the state to multiple levels such as multinational corporations, intergovernmental organisations, non-governmental organisations and social movements. With its ability to focus on economic power, on historical change and on power above and beyond the boundaries of the state, International Political Economy (IPE) quickly moved from being a sub-discipline of IR to becoming, in Philip Cerny's words, 'not merely a minor academic specialisation, a niche subdiscipline, but the expanding core of a new paradigmatic understanding of the world' (Cerny, 1999: 153).

For Robert W. Cox, the 'real achievement of IPE was not to bring in economics, but to open up a critical investigation into change in historical structures' (Cox, 2002: 79). Cox's own significant contribution to the field has been described as being the raising of critical questions about the system of international order and contemplating 'how one might get to a more egalitarian and sustainable system' (O'Brien and Williams, 2004: 32). Cox has made a number of important contributions to IPE's conceptual toolkit, providing it with categories to analyse more fully the nature of power in the emerging world order and the impacts of that power on society; among these is his focus on the role of social forces, on how men and women are differently incorporated into the global economy, and on people's relationship to the environment. Furthermore, his description of the 'covert world' and its relationship to the overt world of 'visible, legitimately recognized activities and institutions' focuses attention in a new and qualitative way on the structured worlds of inclusion and exclusion emerging under the impact of globalisation (Cox, 2002: 118). Cox's normative concerns and his imaginative expansion of the conceptual boundaries of IPE challenge scholars to address the task of theorising more adequately the links between the global and the local. While recognised as a key issue within IPE research, this is usually conceptualised in terms derived from sociology, such as inequality and marginalisation (see, for example, O'Brien and Williams's description of 'the problem of national and global inequality' as one of the four major themes of contemporary IPE research (2004: 32–5)).

Yet, while such research within all the main theoretical approaches of IPE (economic nationalism, liberal internationalism and critical theory) helps reveal dynamics of inclusion and exclusion, it largely fails to elucidate the principal theoretical question as to whether these dynamics result from too much or too little globalisation. It therefore fails largely to offer any original contribution to match that offered by IPE in theorising the nature of power in the world system, the reconstitution of the state or the ambiguities of regionalism. This is despite the

▶

fact that regular reference to the work of Karl Polanyi, especially among critical theorists, offers the potential to theorise in a far fuller, more robust and original way, the impact of market forces on society. One of Polanyi's contributions is his view of poverty as 'primarily a cultural not an economic phenomenon that can be measured by income figures or population statistics' (Polanyi, 2001: 164), his identification of 'the lethal injury to the institutions in which [a person's] social existence is embodied' as the essence of this 'social calamity' (2001: 164.), caused by 'the running of society as an adjunct to the market' (2001: 60), and that 'the essence of purely economic progress ... is to achieve improvement at the price of social dislocation' (2001: 36) (see Chapter 6 for a fuller treatment of Polanyi's contribution).

In adding vulnerability to the conceptual toolkit of IPE, therefore, this book intends to provide a new tool that has the potential to analyse in a way far more faithful to the insights of Polanyi the dislocating and marginalising impacts of global market forces on society. It will help broaden the focus on poverty and inequality to one that looks at risks and vulnerabilities; it will conceptualise these impacts not just as economic but also as cultural; and it will show how these insights apply not just to issues of poverty within nation states but to vulnerability at different levels, including the vulnerability of states themselves, and to different spheres such as the environment, politics, finance, the economy, as well as the social and the cultural. By showing its potential in these ways, vulnerability is offered as a tool to contribute rich and robust insights to the battles on globalisation's impact.

examines the types of risks that characterise our world, looking in turn at financial, economic, social, political, environmental and personal risks. Chapter 3 takes the other side of the concept of vulnerability, namely people's abilities to cope with risks, and analyses these under the headings of the assets identified by the World Bank – physical, human, social and environmental assets. It identifies how globalisation is impacting on each of these. Part II is entitled 'Diagnosis' as its purpose is to substantiate how and to what extent globalisation is causing the different forms of vulnerability identified in the previous part. Chapter 4 examines the political economy of globalisation, namely the shifts in power as the state, formerly central to processes of national development, has given way to the market, particularly to globalised or transnational market forces. Chapter 5 turns to cultural worlds, that is, to the changes in personal and social consciousness, in values and in social meanings, that are associated with globalisation. It surveys debates about the impact of globalisation on culture, identifying the role of the media and the culture of consumerism as distinctive cultural features of today's globalisation. The chapter ends by examining the influences these features of globalisation are having on links between power and identity. These two chapters identify ways in which changes in political economy and culture relate to the vulnerabilities identified in Part I.

The purpose of Part III is to examine the implications of vulnerability for social and individual well-being, and in this way to offer a theoretical depth and grounding to the concept and a deeper understanding of its destructive and violent impact. For this reason, Part III is entitled 'Interrogation', since it asks what vulnerability means for society and for individuals. Chapter 6 uses the work of Karl Polanyi to develop a deeper theoretical understanding of how market forces have a destructive impact on society through eroding people's sense of belonging in a secure way to a wider social community. The concept of vulnerability will be linked to Polanyi's concept of poverty as a cultural rather than an economic calamity. Chapter 7 turns to look at the roots of human well-being for the individual, highlighting how prominent pro-globalisation views rest on an understanding of individual self-sufficiency and rational endeavour that fails to take into account the findings of modern psychological theory. As a result, they place burdens on individuals that many are not capable of carrying or carry at great costs to themselves, their physical and mental health, and their families. Part III will also conclude that the concept of vulnerability draws attention to core elements of what is required for social and human well-being and how globalisation is eroding these. The final part, Part IV, looks at 'Remedies'. Chapter 8 examines *what* needs to be done to respond to growing vulnerability and violence. It identifies the principal 'ideologies' of globalisation and examines in turn the adequacy of the different agendas being advanced for reducing vulnerability and violence. Chapter 9 asks *who* is advancing remedies and *how* they are seeking to realise them. It devotes particular attention to the potential of an active, transnational civil society to fashion new forms of transnational political power for a globalised world as a means of reducing vulnerability and violence.

CONCLUSIONS

This chapter began by highlighting the main issue about globalisation that is being actively disputed (including on the streets) – is it really making us all better off or are its benefits limited to certain sectors of the human race? It was argued that the difficulties of reaching an answer to this important question, or at least an answer that might gain widespread acceptance, are compounded by the concepts being used to analyse the issues involved. The result is that contradictory claims are being made as if they were incontestable facts. The chapter has introduced the concept of vulnerability and linked it to violence, arguing that these have the potential to identify in a fuller and more adequate way the distinctive impact globalisation is having on our individual and social lives. It has offered a definition of vulnerability and has clarified how violence is both a dimension of vulnerability and a reaction against it. It has illustrated its widespread use since the early 1990s by intergovernmental organisations. It has distinguished it from such concepts as poverty/inequality, risk and insecurity, arguing that vulnerability is a more precise term, capturing dimensions of well-being that matter to the poor themselves, such as threats to their livelihood and their powerlessness. Finally, as well as outlining the book's contents, the chapter situated the concept in the theoretical field of International Political Economy (IPE) and outlined the potential it holds to contribute to the conceptual toolkit of IPE. The following chapter will describe the new risks associated with globalisation.

Part I

Description

2
Risk's New Riskiness

I want to argue that in the current period risk assumes a new and peculiar importance. Risk was supposed to be a way of regulating the future, of normalising it and bringing it under our domination. Things haven't turned out that way. Our very attempts to control the future tend to rebound upon us, forcing us to look for different ways of relating to uncertainty ...

External risk is risk experienced as coming from the outside, from the fixities of tradition or nature. I want to distinguish this from manufactured risk, by which I mean risk created by the very impact of our developing knowledge upon the world. Manufactured risk refers to risk situations which we have very little historical experience of confronting. Most environmental risks, such as those connected with global warming, fall into this category. They are directly influenced by ... intensifying globalisation ...

As manufactured risk expands, there is a new riskiness to risk. (Giddens, 1999: 25; 26; 28)

Life, by its very nature, is full of risk. Yet, as Anthony Giddens reminds us, risk has not always been with us. Though people in the Middle Ages faced ill-health, robbery, violence, environmental disasters or poverty as much or often a lot more than we do, they had no word for risk. This is because they put such things down to fate and so saw them as inevitable. Risk, by contrast, involves calculating future probabilities and is intimately linked to the opportunities opened up by modern industrial society. As Giddens puts it: 'Risk is the mobilising dynamic of a society bent on change, that wants to determine its own future rather than leaving it to religion, tradition, or the vagaries of nature. Modern capitalism differs from all previous forms of economic system in terms of its attitudes towards the future' (Giddens, 1999: 24). Central to such attitudes is the calculation of future risks (after all, making profits is an inherently risky business) so that forms of insurance and protection (including the welfare state) were developed to cushion the impact of such risks on people's livelihoods and well-being.

Surveying the use of the concept of risk, Tulloch finds that 'over the last decade, risk discourse has become an increasingly salient issue in social scientific research' with an increasing flow of books on the topic from a variety of disciplines (Tulloch, 2004: 452). Indeed, he observes that the concept of risk has become the defining mark of late or post-modernity. This focuses on the new forms of risk associated with the 'techno-hazards' such as chemical pollution, atomic radiation and genetically modified organisms that are such a defining feature of today's world (Adam and van Loon, 2000: 1–3). But, as Beck puts it, the pervasive nature of such risks has also 'set off a dynamic of cultural and political change that undermines state bureaucracies, challenges the dominance of science and redraws the boundaries and battle lines of contemporary politics' (Beck, 2000a: 225). These form the subject matter of debates on the 'risk society', focusing on the nature of such risks, their construction (particularly by media discourse), and their challenges to dominant epistemologies in the social sciences.

The focus of this book is less on the 'risk society' and more on well-being, both individual and social, and on how fundamental changes associated with globalisation are resulting in increased vulnerability and violence. It situates itself in the disciplinary field of International Political Economy since this concerns itself with shifts in the relationships of state, market and society. The focus of this book, however, is more on the *consequences* of these shifts for individual and social well-being. This is why it begins in this two-chapter part with a description of these consequences. This involves two dimensions, the first of which concerns the increased risks to which people are subjected and their impacts at various levels of society, from the nation state to the most intimate spheres of interpersonal relationships. This is the subject of the present chapter. But increased risk is only one dimension of the concept of vulnerability. The second derives from the erosion of the coping mechanisms that helped people survive such risks, mechanisms such as networks of social support, social welfare systems and even nature itself that enhanced people's power or capacity to survive. Chapter 3 examines how such coping mechanisms are faring under the impact of globalisation. Taken together, therefore, these two chapters describe key dimensions of how vulnerability and violence are increasing through the impact of processes associated with globalisation. Part II, entitled 'Diagnosis', will link these to shifts in structures, power and culture that are associated with globalisation.

FINANCIAL

The financial system may seem a strange place to begin a survey of some of the key risks associated with globalisation. Yet it needs to be borne in mind that, as Andrew Crockett, general manager of the Bank of International Settlements (BIS, often called the central bankers' central bank), puts it: 'the financial system is, in a sense, the central nervous system of the economy', directing real resources to end users (in Scholte and Schnabel, 2002: xv). It also 'has shown some of the most far-reaching globalization in recent history' as 24-hour financial markets around the globe trade an ever-burgeoning array of financial products whose value has soared over recent decades (Scholte, 2002a: 15–17). It was estimated that the average volume of foreign exchange transactions by the dawn of the new millennium had reached $2,000 billion *every day* (Ferguson, 2001: 281). What concerns us here, however, is not the size nor even primarily the structure of the financial system in itself but the fact that it 'has become increasingly volatile and unpredictable, with shocks originating in one part of the world spreading to other parts of the world at exceptional speed through the processes of "financial contagion"' (Dicken, 2003: 469). Indeed, FitzGerald writes that 'world leaders ... seem to regard currency instability as the critical threat to western civilization at the close of the twentieth century – in sharp contrast to the threat of socialist revolution with which it opened' (FitzGerald, 2002: 149).

Five main sources of risk can be identified in today's international financial system giving rise to its volatility and unpredictability. The first arises from the interconnected nature of the system as crises in one part reverberate almost instantaneously throughout the global system (see Box 2.1). As Held et al. write: 'In a "wired world" high levels of enmeshment between national markets mean that disturbances in one very rapidly spill over into others. Since the bulk of international financial transactions are carried out among a small number of banks, financial difficulties facing one or more have consequences for the rest' (Held, et al., 1999: 233). The second source of risk lies in the new financial instruments such as derivatives that have been developed to anticipate and seek to profit from price movements in currencies, commodities and equities; the most common types are futures, swaps and options. Yet, while the swift growth of such instruments indicates that they have the potential to make huge profits, Scholte reminds us that they have also produced 'a succession of spectacular

---

BOX 2.1   'BASIC QUESTIONS ABOUT GLOBAL FINANCE'

The forced devaluation of the Thai baht in 1997 triggered, domino-like, speculative attacks on the currencies of South Korea, Indonesia and Malaysia, causing interest rates to sky-rocket and then banking systems to collapse (the impact on Malaysia was checked through the imposition of controls on currency movements), and its effects reverberated around the world in the following years affecting first Russia and then Brazil. The devaluation of the Brazilian real, in turn, helped precipitate the severe Argentine crisis of 2001–02 as it made that country's goods much more expensive in its main market, Brazil. While these swift crises impoverished countless millions in these countries, as former US Federal Reserve chairman Paul A. Volcker recognised, they also raised 'basic questions about global finance and its implications for economic development' (Volcker, 2001: 76). Financial crises have always been part of capitalism, Volcker wrote, but 'somehow they seem to be coming more frequently and with greater force these days' (2001: 76). Unlike some US critics who blamed the weak regulatory systems of the countries involved, Volcker acknowledged that all these countries, with the exception of Russia, had high domestic savings, exceptionally good economic growth rates and were making progress towards more open markets for goods and capital. Indeed, the IMF and the World Bank had, virtually on the eve of the crisis, acknowledged the effectiveness of their macro-economic policies. For Volcker, therefore, the problem lay primarily not in the countries involved but instead in the nature of the international financial system itself.

---

losses' such as the collapse of Barings Bank in 1995 as a result of the $1.3 billion losses built up by one of the bank's traders, Nick Leeson (Scholte, 2000: 119). The third form of risk results from the lack of regulation of international financial flows. As FitzGerald puts it: 'At the international level, it is precisely at the interstices between regulatory authorities that the largest short-term profits are to be made and the greatest risks of systematic collapse are to be found' (FitzGerald, 2002: 153). Furthermore, in a world characterised by such vast and instantaneous capital flows, states find it more and more difficult to enact and enforce effective regulations. Volcker writes that 'countries with strong banks, honest and democratic governments, relatively transparent accounting systems, and experienced regulators have not been immune to banking crises' and gives the example of the collapse of the Texan banking system in the mid 1980s to illustrate his point (Volcker, 2001: 81).

A fourth aspect of the new riskiness is that, as Castells reminds us, its impact is by no means limited to those who consciously gamble on it. For, whether we like it or not, most of us are now players in this new 'casino capitalism' as institutional investors invest our savings through pension funds and mutual funds; between 1980 and 1995 such investments increased ten-fold in the United States, reaching $20 billion. In 1997, for the first time, a higher proportion of US household assets were in securities than in property (Castells, 2001: 54). In this way, the risk is generalised throughout society. Finally, the system as a whole is driven by a complex mixture of rational calculation and irrational activity that heightens its unpredictability. Castells describes it as follows: 'Movements in financial markets are induced by a mixture of market rules, business and political strategies, crowd psychology, rational expectations, irrational behaviour, speculative manoeuvres and information turbulences of all sorts. All these elements are recombined in increasingly unpredictable patterns' (2001: 56–7).

ECONOMIC

While much attention is today devoted to the emergence of a 'knowledge economy' and an 'information society', the characteristic feature of this new economy that concerns us here is its intensified competitiveness. The central role of competitiveness in economic success worldwide is illustrated by the annual publication of a Global Competitiveness Report by the World Economic Forum. The 2003–04 Report ranked according to their economic competitiveness 102 of the world's countries representing 98.7 per cent of global GDP. What this does not tell us, however, are the growing risks associated with these intensified competitive pressures (see Box 2.2). This is examined here through looking at the consequences for firms, for countries and for labour; the section ends by describing another result of the economic pressures in a globalised world, namely the emergence of a global criminal economy.

Under the pressure of intensified competitiveness, firms survive by growing bigger. This has resulted in the concentration of ownership and control in fewer and fewer hands. From 1990–98 the annual number of mergers and acquisitions worldwide more than doubled, from 11,300 to 26,200. This is creating global corporations with sales totalling more than the GDP of many countries and dominating key sectors of the world's economy. Illustrating how economic power has become consolidated among a few key players, the UNDP estimated the percentage of the global market controlled by the top ten corporations in a number of key industries in 1998 as follows:

- in commercial seeds, 32 per cent of a $23 billion industry;
- in pharmaceuticals, 35 per cent of a $297 billion industry;
- in veterinary medicine, 60 per cent of a $17 billion industry;
- in computers, almost 70 per cent of a $334 billion industry;
- in pesticides, 85 per cent of a $31 billion industry;
- in telecommunications, more than 86 per cent of a $262 billion industry (UNDP, 1999: 67).

Increasingly this growing concentration of ownership is driving the growth of transnational production chains, as companies from developed countries buy out those in developing countries. Yet most of this activity is concentrated in a small number of countries: 70 per cent of all foreign direct investment (FDI) to developing countries went to only ten countries in 2000, with 40 per cent going to China alone (including Hong Kong) (Dicken, 2003: 61). These recipients of FDI have become Newly Industrialising Countries or NICs, the most successful being the East Asian Tigers of South Korea, Taiwan and Singapore, and Latin American countries like Brazil, Mexico and Chile. However, to stay ahead, these face ever more intensifying competition from emerging countries able to compete in the lower-skill, labour-intensive activities that provided the original basis for the success of the NICs. Among these are Malaysia, Thailand,

---

BOX 2.2   GETTING BIGGER, SMARTER, FASTER TO SURVIVE

In his book on globalisation entitled *The Lexus and the Olive Tree*, journalist Thomas Friedman of the *New York Times* describes the competitive pressures on one small US company, Valley Lighting, Inc., of Baltimore, Maryland. Owned and run by Jerry Portnoy, the company employs 35 people supplying material to electrical contractors and developers for large commercial projects. In the early 1990s, Portnoy told Friedman that he noticed customers becoming far more demanding and his sales team reported a far more competitive environment. 'I started to feel that our company was at risk', said Portnoy. His response was to become faster and more efficient, providing the same business at lower costs and requiring harder work from his staff. By 1994, he was surviving but making less money. He then took a major risk, investing $350,000 in a new software programme that allowed his sales team to produce estimates for jobs far more quickly and efficiently. As a result, sales and profits rose by 33 per cent in 1998 while the number of employees remained the same. As Portnoy put it: '[I]n this winner-take-all environment, you have to get bigger, smarter, faster than your competition, or get out of the way. I don't know if it's sustainable, but I know that it has given me an opportunity for survival into the next phase – until somebody becomes more efficient' (Friedman, 2000: 91–5).

Indonesia and Vietnam or the Dominican Republic and Costa Rica. Indeed, intensified competitive pressure is what characterises the international environment for all these countries. Gwynne and Kay see the growing integration of Latin American economies into the global economy as making them 'more dependent on, and hence vulnerable to, global economic shifts' (2004: 255). As Hillebrand put it, the development of a unified system of world trade is 'leading to intensified competition between countries of the South' with Asian countries, led by China, capturing larger shares of export markets while Latin American countries have 'been increasingly faced with a situation marked by a diminishing presence in the world market and losses of shares of their own domestic markets' (2003: 1). Meanwhile, the 60 or so low-income countries, many in Sub-Saharan Africa, face even greater challenges as their continuing dependence on primary commodities mean they fall further and further behind, receiving virtually no foreign investment other than that put into resource extraction. These inequalities in the productive structure of the world's economy are illustrated by the fact that the top fifth of the world's people in the richest countries enjoy 82 per cent of the world's expanding trade in exports and 68 per cent of foreign direct investment whereas the bottom fifth of the population gain barely more than one per cent of these (UNDP, 1999: 31).

Turning to the nature of employment, the International Labour Office reports that there were 160 million unemployed people at the beginning of the twenty-first century, of whom 53 million were in Europe and North America. The late 1990s saw a considerable improvement in the employment situation in most developed countries; however, Dicken highlights the volatility of employment trends in these countries compared to earlier periods and the growing inequality in wages (what is called wage dispersion) as the wages of high-income groups increase far faster than do the wages of those on low incomes (this has been most marked in Britain and the United States) (Dicken, 2003: 528–31). Measuring the evolution of wage inequality in the global economy, Galbraith, Jiaqing and Darity also found that 'the predominant trend in inequality worldwide has been decisively upwards' in both developed and developing regions (1999: 8). Furthermore, the security that used to be associated with work in the formal sector has been severely undermined. As George and Wilding put it: 'The pattern is widespread – deregulation of labour markets, more use of temporary, short-term contracts, more use of part-time and shift work, the proliferation of low-paid jobs, the tightening of conditions for receipt of social benefits and reductions in their real value' (2002: 50). This pattern manifests itself in different ways in different places. Dicken points out that in New York the emphasis has been on informal work while in London most growth has been in part-time work (Dicken, 2003: 537). While this greatly increases the vulnerability of many workers and their families, it also results in 'a high degree of social and spatial polarization within these cities' (Dicken, 2003: 536), a characteristic of the occupational and social structure emerging in a more globalised world (see Chapter 4).

Outside the developed world, the ILO points out that in most countries people cannot survive without employment of some kind since unemployment benefits are not provided; it therefore highlights the fact that 530 million are classified as the 'working poor' because they are engaged in low-pay and low-productivity work. A further 330 million are underemployed, not having enough work. It concludes: 'Taken together, either because they are unemployed, underemployed, or with incomes inadequate to support their families despite their work, a full third of the world's labour force of 3 billion people cannot obtain the material rewards from work which they need and to which they aspire' (ILO, 2002: 2). Most new jobs created are in the small-enterprise sectors, reports the ILO, and many of these in the developing world are in the informal economy. For example, seven out of every ten new jobs created in Latin America between 1990 and 2002 were in this sector, characterised by low-pay, highly flexible employment conditions and lack of social security protection. Women are particularly vulnerable to this kind of employment: in Latin America 80 per cent of economically active women lacked any social security protection, according to the ILO's Latin America office. Despite the focus on modern industrial and service activities in much analysis of employment trends, it must not be forgotten that nearly 50 per cent of the world's labour force still works in agriculture, mostly in precarious subsistence agriculture throughout the developing world. Finally, the ILO predicts that some 500 million more people will be added to the world's labour force over the coming decade, many of them with better education than those older than them. Nearly all of this increase will take place in the developing world, with 65 per cent of it being in Asia.

In this situation, it is not surprising that transnational organised crime flourishes. The UNDP argues that crime syndicates have been quick to exploit the new opportunities opened by globalisation, such as money laundering through Eastern European banks following financial liberalisation there, Chinese triads moving into the restaurant trade in London, the Sicilian Mafia selling heroin in New York and the Japanese Yakuza financing pornography in the Netherlands (UNDP, 1999: 43). Globalisation is creating a burgeoning underclass on the margins of the legal economy ripe for exploitation by criminal gangs, such as the trafficking of women and girls to Western Europe for sexual purposes or the illegal trade in diamonds from African countries. In the mid 1990s, the illegal trade in drugs was estimated to be worth $400 billion, about 8 per cent of world trade and more than trade in iron and steel or in motor vehicles. Illegal migrant trafficking was estimated to move 4 million people a year – 500,000 into the sex industry in Western Europe alone – and was worth $9.5 billion a year (George and Wilding, 2002: 55). Overall, organised crime was estimated to be worth $1.5 trillion a year, 'a major economic power rivalling multinational corporations' (UNDP, 1999: 42). Increasing competitiveness and the pressures for survival it engenders are placing added strains on the world's economic system, on countries, on firms and, most particularly, on labour.

SOCIAL

Economic risks reinforce various forms of social risk evident in today's world. A central precondition for these is population growth which serves to exacerbate for certain groups and regions the risks associated with globalisation. While the world's total fertility rate dropped from 4.5 children per woman in 1970–75 to 2.7 in 2000–05, it still remains very high in the world's least developed regions. In Sub-Saharan Africa, it has only declined from 6.8 to 5.4 over this 30-year period so that the population of this region, which has increased from 305 million in 1975 to 626 million in 2001, is expected to increase to 843 million by 2015. Though the fertility rate in Arab states has declined from 6.7 to 3.8 over this period, the population has increased from 143 million in 1975 to 290 million in 2001, and is expected to be almost 400 million by 2015. Overall, the fertility rate in least developed countries has only declined from 6.1 to 5.5 in 30 years while the population has almost doubled from 353 million to 684 million over this period, and is expected to be approaching 950 million by 2015. This results in two very different trends, both of them associated with growing vulnerability for those involved. In those countries with the fastest population growth, the percentage of the population aged under 15 remains very high. In the least developed countries, as well as in Sub-Saharan Africa, over 40 per cent of the population will be under 15 years of age by the year 2015 while in Arab states 33 per cent will be. This places added social and economic pressures on those countries that are least able to bear them. Countries with low levels of population growth, however, will see a big growth in the percentage of those aged 65 and over; in the high-income OECD countries, this is expected to grow from 14.6 per cent to 18 per cent of the population between 2001 and 2015 while in the OECD as a whole it will grow from 13 to 16 per cent (UNDP, 2003a: Table 5, p. 253). This will put increased pressure on pension systems and on the economically active population.

Population growth therefore worsens problems of poverty and inequality worldwide. The most comprehensive estimate of world poverty levels is supplied by the World Bank which showed that, while the number of people living on $1 a day increased from 1,183 million in 1987 to 1,198 million in 1998, the percentage of the world's population in this situation decreased from 28.3 per cent to 24 per cent over the same period. The biggest increase in the numbers in poverty over this period was in Europe and Central Asia (from 1.1 million to 24 million, associated with the collapse of communism), in South Asia (from 474 million to 522 million) and in Sub-Saharan Africa (from 217 million to 291 million), though only in the first of these did the percentages of poor increase (from 0.2 to 5.5 per cent; in South Asia it decreased from 45 to 40 per cent, and in Sub-Saharan Africa from 46.6 to 46.3 per cent) (World Bank, 2000: Table 1.1, p. 23). However, as already discussed in Chapter 1, there are serious difficulties associated with these data (deriving both from the way they are drawn up and from what they actually tell us about the well-being of the world's people). The human development measure offers a more adequate way of identifying trends in well-being since it combines indicators of health and education with those for income. Surveying how far countries have got to meeting the 2015 Millennium Development Goals (MDGs), the UNDP concluded that 'stark differences are emerging between regions, with some pulling ahead and reaching new levels of development – while others are left behind' (UNDP, 2003a: 34). Significant progress was made in South Asia in the 1990s, though it remains one of the world's poorest regions, while East Asia and the Pacific performed well, with some exceptions. However, Latin America and the Caribbean showed stalled progress and the Arab states made some progress but gaps persisted between levels of income and levels of human development.

In two regions, the situation of poverty worsened – Sub-Saharan Africa, which 'is being left behind', and Eastern Europe and countries of the former Soviet Union which ended the 1990s less healthy and with poverty more than tripling to 100 million or 25 per cent of the population (UNDP, 2003a: 37). Overall, the UNDP concludes: 'What is most striking is the extent of the stagnation and reversals – not seen in previous decades', particularly in the latter two regions (2003: 40).

This points to a situation of growing inequality around the world. The level of income inequality in the world today is, as the UNDP puts it, 'grotesque', with the richest 5 per cent of the world's people receiving 114 times the income of the poorest 5 per cent while the richest 1 per cent receive as much as the poorest 57 per cent. The 25 richest Americans have as much income as almost 2 billion of the world's poorest people. However, as with data on poverty, there is little consensus on what the data tell us about trends in inequality due to broad differences in how it is defined. Surveying the range of studies about trends in world inequality, the UNDP identifies three broad categories. The first is inequality between countries; here it finds that the countries with the highest per capita incomes in 1800 are still the world's richest countries but that, when countries are weighted by population, inequality between the country averages has been constant or falling since 1980. (Wade argues that this is entirely due to fast average growth in India and China and that, if these two countries are excluded, even this measure shows widening inequality since 1980 (see Wade, 2003a: 27).) The second category is inequality across all the world's people; here it finds a widening gap between the world's richest and poorest people and a shrinkage of the middle-income group. The final category measures inequality across people within countries and here again it finds that inequality increased within most countries in the 1990s. Finally, while there may be debate on income inequality, the UNDP says that inequality in child mortality has got unambiguously worse. In the early 1990s children under five were 19 times more likely to die in Sub-Saharan African than in rich countries whereas by 2003 they were 26 times more likely. It concludes: 'If sharp increases in inequality persist, they may have dire effects on human development and social stability (including violence and crime rates)' (UNDP, 2003a: 39).

The impact of inequality on society can be identified by examining trends in migration and in urbanisation, trends that have their own specific impact on women (see Box 2.3). Many factors have been responsible for the large increase in migratory flows throughout the twentieth century, some of them associated with war and civil conflict driving people from their homes, but others associated with the growing disparities in opportunities available to people in their home countries as against those available in the countries to which they migrate. This latter case is illustrated by the growing number of Mexicans migrating, legally and illegally, to the United States. About 640,000 Mexicans migrated legally in the 1970s, 1.65 million in the 1980s and 2.25 million in the 1990s. A further 350,000 were estimated to have entered illegally each year during the 1990s. By 2000, 7.84 million Mexican-born people were living in the US, far higher than the 1.39 million Chinese-born and 1.22 million Filipino-born, the next two largest immigrant groups (Huntington, 2004: 33). Referring to refugee flows, the United Nations High Commissioner for Refugees (UNHCR) was providing assistance to

---

BOX 2.3   WOMEN AT RISK

In 2004, the human rights organisation Amnesty International launched a campaign to highlight the extent of violence against women. This showed that at least one in every three women has been beaten, coerced into sex or otherwise abused in their lifetime. Up to 70 per cent of female murder victims are killed by their male partners and one in five women is a victim of rape or attempted rape in her lifetime. More than 135 million girls and women have undergone female genital mutilation and an additional 2 million girls and women are at risk every year. Female genital mutilation is practised in more than 28 countries in Africa, has been reported in Asian countries such as India, Indonesia, Malaysia and Sri Lanka, and is performed among immigrant communities in Australia, Denmark, France, Italy, the Netherlands, Sweden, Switzerland and the United Kingdom.

Millions of women and children are caught up in 34 armed conflicts in different parts of the world. Trafficking of women and girls was reported in 85 per cent of conflict zones. In Rwanda, between 250,000 and 500,000 women, about 20 per cent of the country's female population, were raped during the 1994 genocide. In Bosnia, 20,000 to 50,000 women were raped during five months of the conflict there in 1992. In Kosovo, 30 to 50 per cent of women of child bearing age were raped by Serbian forces during the war there. Eighty per cent of the world's refugees are women and children.

Amnesty cautioned that these statistics do not show the true extent of the situation as there is a lack of systematic research and statistics on violence against women. This is because many do not report it, and there are some countries in which no information is provided on the subject. One study for the World Health Organisation found that between 20 and 70 per cent of the women interviewed had never told anyone else about being abused until they revealed it during the study (Amnesty International, 2004).

over 20 million people in 2003, of whom half were refugees and a quarter internally displaced people (IDPs). However, it quotes a UN estimate of between 20 and 25 million IDPs in that year. Most of the 10.4 million refugees were fleeing civil unrest in countries like Afghanistan, Burundi, Sudan, Angola, Somalia, Democratic Republic of Congo, Liberia, Côte d'Ivoire, Iraq and Bosnia; most of them ended up in neighbouring countries. These dwarfed the numbers claiming asylum in industrialised countries in 2002, of which the largest were 110,700 in Britain, 81,100 in the US, 71,100 in Germany and 50,800 in France (UNHCR, 2003).

Population movement results in growing urbanisation. In the second half of the twentieth century, the percentage of the world's population living in cities increased from 29 per cent to 47 per cent, or 2.8 billion people. Most of this growth has taken place in the developing world where the number of urban residents has increased from 17 per cent in 1950 to 40 per cent or 1.9 billion people in 2000, and is expected to double in the next three decades. Particularly noteworthy is the swift growth of megacities throughout the developing world such as Bangkok, Bombay, Cairo, Djakarta, Lagos, Manila, Mexico City, Nairobi and São Paulo. According to Kim and Gottdiener, this scale of urbanisation is unprecedented in human history and 'implies an immense social crisis for the developing countries' (2004: 175). It brings with it many pressing social problems with which developing-country governments are poorly equipped to cope, such as poverty, underemployment, ghettoisation, poor housing conditions, homelessness and crime. These are 'alarming and increasingly serious in recent years' (Kim and Gottdiener, 2004: 177).

POLITICAL

Economic and social risks result in a new riskiness in political life which became evident over the 1990s. This derives from two major shifts in the nature of organised political systems: on the one hand there is a growing disenchantment with the consensus-oriented moderate centre ground of established democratic systems while, on the other, support is shifting to more extremist parties within these systems or is ebbing away from such systems altogether. Most disturbingly, we are witnessing the emergence of a new and ruthless form of violent power politics that shows no interest in institutionalised systems. Through attacks such as those in New York and Washington DC on 11 September 2001 or in Madrid on 11 March 2004, this form of power struggle has greatly increased the sense of risk felt by citizens in large cities throughout the world. Each of these forms of political riskiness is briefly described in turn.

It is paradoxical that, at a time when democratic political systems are being established in more countries than ever before, 'people around the world seem to have lost confidence in the effectiveness of their governments – and often seem to be losing faith in democracy' (UNDP, 2002: 63). This is most clearly evident in the decline in electoral participation. Surveying elections around the world, the International Institute for Democracy and Electoral Assistance (IDEA) found a steady rise in the percentage of the electorate who turned out to vote between 1950 and 1990; however, over the 1990s there has been a steady decline both in the participation rate of all eligible voters and even more so in the participation rate of those actually registered to vote (IDEA, 2004). For example, only 51 per cent of US voters voted in the 2000 presidential election, down from 55 per cent in 1992, while the turnout in the British general election of 1997 was 69 per cent, down six points from 1992 and the lowest turnout since the Second World War. Even in countries which have recently reinstituted a competitive democratic system, abstention is growing. In the 1990 Czech election, 93 per cent of the electorate voted but this had fallen to 77 per cent by 1998; in Hungary, turnout fell from a high of 76 per cent in 1990 to 60 per cent in 1998 (Hertz, 2001: 107). In Latin America, a 2001 poll showed that only 48 per cent of the population supported democracy while only 25 per cent were satisfied with it (Kirby, 2003: 145). 'People are growing more distant from political parties, and more critical of political institutions', writes Hertz. 'Never since the development of the mass franchise has there been such disengagement from politics' (Hertz, 2001: 105).

Hertz also finds 'a striking correlation between economic status and voter turnout. The poor have disproportionately not been voting' (Hertz, 2003: 15). As support for established parties ebbs among those being marginalised by the socio-economic system, new extreme right-wing parties are emerging and targeting such sectors of the population. Indeed, Ignazi finds that 'the massive presence of working-class people in the extreme right electorate' is one of the distinguishing features of this emergence in the 1990s (Ignazi, 2003: 155), offering as it does an extreme anti-systemic discourse emphasising anti-liberalism, anti-pluralism, anti-egalitarianism and hostility to immigrants. These are now established features of the political systems of most Western European countries; by the early years of the new century extreme right-wing parties shared government for periods in Austria, the Netherlands, Switzerland and Italy, and provided support for the governing parties in Denmark. In France, the National Front leader, Jean-Marie Le Pen, won nearly 17 per cent of the vote in the 2002 presidential election to contest the second round against Jacques Chirac. In the Netherlands, following the murder of extreme right-wing leader Pim Fortuyn, his party, the Pim Fortuyn List (LPF), came second in the 2002 elections. In Denmark, the Danish People's Party of Pia Kjaersgaard won 18 per cent of the vote to establish itself as the country's third largest party. In Norway, the Progress Party of Carl Hagan has won 15 per cent of the vote. In Belgium, the Vlaams Blok of Filip Dewinter receives about 10 per cent of the vote nationally but 33 per cent in Antwerp. In Austria, Jorg Haider's Freedom Party has won up to 27 per cent of the vote nationally. In Germany, though the parties of the extreme right remain divided, a xenophobic and anti-Semitic sub-culture 'is now so deeply ingrained into the attitudes of the young that it bodes ill for the future', especially in the former East Germany (Merkl, 2003: 42). While quite distinct from earlier fascist parties, these new parties are no longer simply registering a protest against the dominant system but 'represent a specific constituency mobilized by feelings of alienation towards the political system and dissatisfaction towards the socioeconomic dynamics of postmodernization and globalization, which they do not control and feel excluded from' (Ignazi, 2003: 155). Their presence brings a destabilising risk to the political systems and social cohesion of some of the world's most prosperous societies.

But in the early years of the new century, a new political risk became dramatically apparent, eclipsing the risk from the extreme right. This has come to be referred to as the 'new terrorism', and is linked by experts to the new environment for terrorist activities that has emerged with the end of the Cold War. As Martin writes: 'Unlike the previous decades, the 1990s were distinguished by new and innovatively configured terrorist networks that were responsible for significant international incidents. These networks and incidents were different from those of previous years and were harbingers of a new era of terrorism', one that drew dramatic attention to itself with the attacks of 11 September 2001 (Martin, 2004: 357). During the Cold War, terrorist groups (meaning groups that use violence for political or ideological objectives often against civilian targets in ways calculated to sow terror among the general population), usually inserted themselves in some way into the wider geopolitical division between capitalism and communism, West and East, that defined the era. This was true even when their objectives were national independence (Basque, Irish or Tamil nationalism) or a change of regime in their own country (South African, Filipino or Salvadorean guerrillas). In some cases, local groups were mere proxies for US power, such as the Contras in Nicaragua. Groups were organised hierarchically, targets were selected for their symbolic value and casualties were relatively modest. Three features distinguish the 'new terrorism' of the globalised world: its organisation, its mode of operation and its motivation.

- Organisation: Groups are organised in networks; in the case of al-Qaeda these networks are fluid and increasingly global, being scattered in Europe, Africa, the Gulf and parts of Asia (see Box 2.4). For this reason, al-Qaeda is often referred to as a 'bank' or a 'franchise' as it offers funding or networking to groups that have emerged out of local grievances.
- Mode of operation: Groups are highly adaptable and flexible, showing meticulous planning and efficiency in the execution of operations. Their use of civilian planes as weapons to attack the World Trade Center and the Pentagon, of mobile phones to trigger bombs on crowded trains in Madrid or of anti-aircraft missiles against an Israeli civilian airliner in Kenya in late 2002, show them to be unpredictable and calculating. Muslim groups have been linked by police in France and Britain to attempts to manufacture the deadly poison ricin, while al-Qaeda operatives are said to be attempting to acquire biological, chemical and radiological agents.
- Motivation: The worldview of these new terrorists is religious, and they interpret their struggle as one between good and evil. Seeing themselves as the righteous ones and their enemies as the infidel, their objectives are primarily not to overthrow governments or change their policies but to inflict significant casualties and to terrorise or disrupt whole societies.

While most attention is now devoted to terrorist groups of Islamic inspiration, it must be remembered that there have been other examples of this new terrorism, such as the Aum Shinrikyo cult that gassed the Tokyo underground in 1995 with the nerve gas sarin, or

---

BOX 2.4   GLOBALISED TERRORISM

The new terrorism is globalised. After the US invasion of Afghanistan in 2002 and attacks on his bases there, Osama bin Laden is reported to have ordered his followers to move back to the Gulf, Africa and Europe. Long before that, however, the reach and organisation of this network was global. It has been linked to attacks in Saudi Arabia in 1996, in Tanzania and Kenya in 1998, in the Yemen in 2000, in the US in 2001, in Indonesia in 2002, in Turkey and Iraq in 2003, in Spain in 2004. Reports from Morocco following the Madrid bombs in 2004, indicated that for over a decade young disaffected Moroccans had been fighting in Afghanistan and participating in networks stretching across North Africa, into Spain and down to Senegal, Mali and Liberia. A report from the French city of Lyons showed how marginalised Algerian immigrants in France were involved in Muslim causes stretching from Chechnya to Bosnia to Afghanistan – what the French police call the 'international Jihad network' (Marlowe, 2004). With the coalition invasion of Iraq in 2003, the network found a new focus for its activity, and was linked to major bombing attacks such as that which killed 271 people in Baghdad and Karbala during the Ashura Shia religious festival on 2 March 2004. Iraq was also said to be providing the network with new recruits.

---

the Michigan Militia, linked to fundamentalist Christian sects, that planted a bomb in an Oklahoma federal building in 1995, killing 168 people. This new terrorism represents 'an extraordinary challenge for governments and societies during the twenty-first century' (Martin, 2004: 357), as these terrorists aim to kill large numbers of civilians and their adaptable and mobile activities are proving very difficult for governments to monitor.

ENVIRONMENTAL

After having been neglected for decades, risks resulting from environmental change emerged as a major cause of concern in the 1990s. Figures compiled by the insurance industry show a steady increase in the number of what it calls 'great natural catastrophes' over the decades since the 1950s, such as tornadoes and severe storms, earthquakes, heat waves, droughts and floods. These are classified as great 'if the ability of the region to help itself is distinctly overtaxed, making interregional or international assistance necessary' and it usually involves thousands of people being killed, hundreds of thousands being made homeless or substantial economic losses to the country or countries involved. The number of such catastrophes increased from 20 in the 1950s to 91 in the 1990s while the economic losses they inflicted increased from $42.7 billion in the 1950s to

$670.4 billion in the 1990s (calculated in 2003 values) (Munich Re Group, 2004). The UN Environmental Programme found that the number of geophysical disasters remained fairly steady but the number of hydrometeorological disasters, caused by weather and water, increased; in the 1990s more than 90 per cent of those killed by natural catastrophes died in events such as droughts, windstorms and floods. Furthermore, 90 per cent of such disasters, and 95 per cent of the deaths caused by them, occur in developing countries. Overall, the UN Office for the Coordination of Humanitarian Affairs (OCHA) estimates that over 3 million people have lost their lives in natural disasters over the past 20 years, that 1 billion others have suffered injury, homelessness, or disease as a result of such disasters, and that such disasters cost an average of $440 billion a year. For example, the economic costs of the European heat wave in the summer of 2003, an event statistically calculated to occur less than once every 450 years, was estimated at $13 billion. In its survey for the insurance industry, the Munich Re Group writes: 'It is to be feared that extreme events which can be traced to climate change will have increasingly grave consequences in the future. This means that we must reckon with new types of weather risks and greater loss potentials' (Munich Re Group, 2004: 3).

Evidence has grown that 'most of the global warming observed over the last 50 years is attributable to human activities' (UNEP, 2002: 3). The years 1998, 2002 and 2003 have been probably the warmest summers since records began. These climate changes are associated with greenhouse gases such as carbon dioxide emitted mostly by industrialised countries through fuel consumption, gas flaring and cement production. Their effects, however, spread throughout the world, affecting water and food security in Africa due to the impact of floods, drought and desertification; threatening the future of island states in the Caribbean and the Pacific by rising sea levels; decreasing crop yields and spreading diseases in Latin America; reducing food production in West Asia; and leading to an increased risk of tropical cyclones in many countries of arid, tropical and temperate Asia. In Europe, decreased agricultural productivity is expected in southern and eastern regions but positive effects are predicted for agriculture in northern regions. Throughout the world, climate change is exacerbating threats to biodiversity (UNEP, 2002: 3–4) (see Box 2.5). Furthermore, due to ozone-depleting substances (ODS), particularly chlorofluorocarbons (CFCs), ozone layer depletion has reached record levels, especially over the Antarctic and the Artic, though the thickness of the ozone layer over parts of northern Europe also declines by 50 per cent in winter and spring. This threatens human health through diseases such as skin cancer, eye cataracts and immune deficiency; it also affects flora and fauna, as well as the climate. Though by the year 2000 intergovernmental action had succeeded in reducing the production and use of ODS by 85 per cent, molecules can persist in the atmosphere for as long as 100 years and some trafficking and unlicensed use of new CFCs has been reported.

BOX 2.5   MASS EXTINCTION THREATENS

A comprehensive study showing an accelerating decline in the diversity of butterflies, birds and plants in Britain over the previous 40 years was published in the journal *Science* in March 2004. This showed that about 70 per cent of all butterfly species, 28 per cent of plant species and 54 per cent of bird species showed a decline over the period. Commenting on the findings, Jeremy Thomas of the Natural Environment Research Council, who led the study of butterflies, said that the findings add 'enormous strength to the hypothesis that the world is approaching its sixth major extinction event'. The previous five such events were triggered by cosmic events, such as the extinction of the dinosaurs and the loss of up to 70 per cent of all species in the last such event 65 million years ago. 'You could say this latest one is an organic event: that one form of life has become so dominant on Earth that through its over-exploitation and its wastes, it eats, destroys, or poisons the others', said Thomas. While the fossil record of 600 million years shows a pattern of continuous evolution and extinction, naturalists now think that current extinction rates are at least 100 times greater than the natural rate, due to pollution, habitat destruction, hunting, agriculture, global warming and population growth. 'We are going to lose a lot of species, there is no doubt about that', says Thomas. 'It is accelerating and we are going to lose more than we have lost in the last 20 years. And it is just going to go on and on' (Radford, 2004).

The increased threat of natural catastrophes affects all parts of the globe. However, while more than half of all the disasters reported between 1991 and 2001 occurred in countries with medium levels of human development, two-thirds of those killed were in countries with low levels of human development and just 2 per cent of casualties lived in highly developed countries. On average, 22.5 people die per reported disaster in highly developed countries, 145 per disaster die in countries with medium levels of development, and 1,052 die per disaster in countries with low levels of human development (UNEP, 2002). This illustrates graphically that increased risk alone does not cause vulnerability.

PERSONAL

No account of the riskiness of life in today's world would be complete without adverting to the impact of this on individuals themselves. Scholte mentions that, alongside the word 'globalisation', the word 'stress' has spread to countless languages (Scholte, 2000: 197). Beck describes why this is so:

> [T]he ubiquitous rule is that, in order to survive the rat-race, one has to become active, inventive and resourceful, to develop ideas of one's own, to be faster, nimbler and more creative – not just on one occasion, but constantly, day after day. Individuals become actors, builders, jugglers, stage-managers of their own biographies and identities, but also of their social links and networks. (Beck, 2001: 166)

Less bound by traditional ways of doing things, or by submitting to orders given by authorities, individuals have been thrown much more on their own resources (see Box 2.6). In this situation, life is experienced as a daily struggle constantly accompanied by the awareness that, no matter how much is achieved, one's life is also under threat. 'Even behind the facades of security and prosperity,' writes Beck, 'the possibilities of biographical slippage and collapse are ever present. Hence the clinging and the fear, even in the externally wealthy middle layers of society' (2001: 167).

A central feature of this individual riskiness is that people are no longer integrated into society as whole people. Touraine sees this taking place in the education of the young as they 'live several different temporalities – that of school, that of their peer groups and that of sexuality – and they usually do so without any principle that allows them to integrate their various experiences'. He adds that 'the idea of gradual submission to the norms of social life, or those of the world of work and the family, is fading' (Touraine, 2000: 53). For Sennett, the lack of integration derives from the fact that jobs are replacing careers since most young people graduating from university in the United States or Britain can now expect to work for at least twelve employers over the course of their working life. He asks: 'How can one expect to create a sense of personal continuity in a labour market in which work-histories are erratic and discontinuous rather than routine and determinate?' (Sennett, 2001: 183). All of this places additional pressures on the individual – not knowing how long one's job will last, fostering conformity and

BOX 2.6   CHILDHOOD AT RISK

Childhood itself has been transformed into a time of vulnerability and violence. HIV/AIDS presents huge new risks to many young people. UNAIDS estimates that 13.2 million of the world's children aged under 15 had lost their mothers or both parents as a result of the disease and that 90 per cent of these children live in Sub-Saharan Africa, though growing numbers are increasingly evident in Eastern Europe and in central Asia. The organisation's director, Dr Peter Piot, said that in these regions 'young people are at the core of the AIDS epidemic. In many places this is actually an epidemic among teenagers' (quoted in the *Irish Times*, 24 February 2004). Since in Africa the disease is mainly spread through heterosexual intercourse, teenage girls are most at risk since they are seen by men as being less likely to be infected; UNAIDS reports that between 20 and 48 per cent of girls aged 10–15 in a number of African, Latin American and Caribbean countries report that their first sexual encounter was forced. In Eastern Europe and central Asia, however, the disease is spread mostly through intravenous drug abuse, putting teenage boys more at risk. Those orphaned by the disease often struggle to subsist and to support siblings 'and are thus highly vulnerable to involvement in commercial or survival sex', while the pandemic also fuels a growth in demand for the sexual exploitation of children and a growth of child rape in the regions worst affected (O'Connell Davidson, 2004: 546).

Meanwhile, the Internet and mobile phones increase the risk of young people being sexually seduced. A report published by the British children's charity, Barnardos, documented how more and younger children are being sexually abused via the Internet, with some being 'advertised' online to paedophiles, through photographs taken by relatives or friends in their own homes. The Barnardos' report, *Just One Click*, published in February 2004, documented how Internet message boards and chat rooms are being used to sell children for sex, informing where and when abuse can be watched online. Barnardos found that the children being abused are getting younger, the abuse is more severe and the settings are more everyday while few of the victims are being traced or helped.

Another form of abuse suffered by growing numbers of young people around the world is their use as soldiers in armed conflicts. Human Rights Watch estimates that some 300,000 children serve in official, paramilitary or opposition armed groups in over thirty conflicts in all regions of the world. These include Colombia, Mexico and Peru; the Russian Federation, Turkey and the former Yugoslavia; Sierra Leone, Somalia, Liberia, Democratic Republic of Congo, Uganda and Sudan; Iran, Iraq, Israel and Lebanon; Indonesia, Myanmar and Sri Lanka; the Solomon Islands and Papua New Guinea. Many of these children are abducted from their homes or recruited by force and are compelled to obey orders under threat of death. Others join as a means of survival as society breaks down. Human Rights Watch has documented how children have witnessed and participated in atrocities against civilians such as beheadings, amputations, rape and burning people alive, while some were given drugs to overcome their reluctance to fight. Girls are subjected to sexual abuse and rape, and are sometimes given as 'wives' to commanders.

eroding loyalty, making long-term financial commitment risky. As well as taking personal responsibility for shaping one's life, and the heightened risks that go with it, this increased individualisation also absolves institutions from responsibility for failures. As Beck puts it, social crises such as poverty and unemployment 'can be directly turned into psychological dispositions: into guilt feelings, anxieties, conflicts and neuroses' leading people to turn against one another in violence rather than collectively mobilising to change society (Beck, 2001: 167). In this situation, social life is no longer experienced as a realm of solidarity and collective decisionmaking but as one of conflictual coexistence.

Touraine therefore writes of 'the breakup of both society and the personality': 'What we initially perceived as a crisis in the family or our schools, and therefore in education and socialization, is also a crisis in the shaping of individual personalities. Social norms and individual or collective identities used to complement one another, but this is no longer the case.' (Touraine, 2000: 53) He adds that 'this experience of being personally torn apart ... is not a pathological condition seen only in extreme cases; it affects us all' (2000: 55). In these ways, therefore, the very living of life itself has become more risky. Beck writes: 'Not only genetically modified food but also love and marriage, including the traditional housewife marriage, become a risk' (Beck, 2001: 170).

CONCLUSION

Life in today's world is therefore full of risks. While much commentary on globalisation, and on the liberalisation of markets that is driving it, emphasises the increased opportunities this opens up – for countries, for firms, for individuals – the survey in this chapter shows how such opportunities are accompanied by an increasing riskiness. Even for those who benefit in this situation, the benefits themselves are never secure and are always at risk. This was clear, for example, at the 2004 World Economic Forum in Davos, Switzerland – 'a unique barometer of elite attitudes and perceptions', as a report on the Forum published by *Foreign Policy* magazine put it. This report stated that 'risk cast a long shadow over the meeting's deliberations as a whole' (*Foreign Policy*, 2004: 25). Meanwhile, the many who lack such benefits face increasing pressures to survive. Violence – interpersonal, intra-familial, social, sexual, structural, environmental, communal, ethnic, terrorist and criminal – is a pervasive form of risk. Furthermore, the risks we all face are cumulative: they are both more frequent and they reinforce one another. Thus natural disasters cause poverty and migration, the growth of megacities results in greater social problems and interpersonal violence, civil conflict displaces populations and increases for women the risk of being raped, competitive pressures in the economy lead to the erosion of workers' rights and protection thereby increasing their insecurity. Yet the increase in risk does not in itself make us more vulnerable – this results from the coping mechanisms on which we rely to face and survive such risks. The question of what is happening to our coping mechanisms in today's world is the subject of Chapter 3.

3
Coping with Risk

People's vulnerability is generated by social, economic, and political processes that influence how hazards affect people in varying ways and different intensities. (Blaikie et al., 1994: 5)

Increased risks, of the kind described in Chapter 2, do not in themselves result in damage to individual or social well-being, though they certainly threaten such damage. To assess whether damage is likely to occur, we need to examine how well prepared people are to manage and survive the threats posed by increased risks. Though this applies to risks of all kinds – financial, economic, social, political, cultural, environmental, personal – it is in relation to environmental hazards that the understanding of the relationship between risk and people's coping mechanisms has been most developed. As Blaikie et al. write: 'In evaluating disaster risk, the social production of vulnerability needs to be considered with at least the same degree of importance that is devoted to understanding and addressing natural hazards' (Blaikie et al., 1994: 21). These authors are concerned to broaden the focus of attention away from the frequency and severity of natural disasters in themselves and towards the social systems which generate people's vulnerability to being damaged by such disasters. As they write, taking an extreme example: 'there is no risk if there are hazards but vulnerability is nil' (1994: 21). What is true for environmental hazards is also true for the many risks described in the last chapter – in themselves such threats as speculative financial flows, intensified economic pressures, urbanisation, or terrorist attacks do not necessarily damage individual and social well-being if states, communities, households and individuals have adequate resources, both physical and human, to withstand them, and are adequately protected by insurance cover and by welfare systems. It is for this reason that natural disasters have a disproportionate impact on the poor, because the poor have fewer of the resources necessary to survive and recover from such disasters. This chapter therefore takes the social production of vulnerability as its subject, examining how economic, political and social processes associated with globalisation are affecting the potential of states, communities, households and individuals to withstand, survive and/or recover from the increased riskiness of life in a more globalised world.

In its discussion of vulnerability, the Caribbean office of the UN Economic Commission for Latin America and the Caribbean (ECLAC) introduces the concept of resilience, which it sees as 'a critical factor in enabling units such as individuals, households, communities and nations to withstand internal and external shocks'. According to ECLAC, social vulnerability is 'the net effect of the competition between social risks and social resilience', where it views resilience as 'tantamount to an ability that is based on entitlement, enfranchisement, empowerment and capabilities' (ECLAC, 2003: 25). Use of the term 'capabilities' echoes Amartya Sen's concerns about how people translate goods or resources into well-being, drawing attention to the need to attend not just to people's levels of income but also to 'social arrangements and community relations such as medical coverage, public health care, school education, law and order, prevalence of violence and so on', all of which affect people's 'capability to lead the kind of lives we have reason to value' (Sen, 1999: 22–3; 285). While Sen's concern is not with vulnerability, his emphasis on what constitutes well-being highlights important dimensions of what we can call the social production of resilience.

Conceptualising vulnerability, therefore, requires establishing robust categories that capture as far as possible the different dimensions of resilience. In this regard, the four categories suggested by ECLAC – entitlement, enfranchisement, empowerment and capabilities – are more indicative dimensions of resilience than constitutive elements of it. This is because they lack precision and are not clearly distinct one from another. For these reasons, the approach of the World Bank is followed here. In discussing the elements needed to measure households' exposure to vulnerability, the Bank introduces the term 'assets', identifying physical assets such as income, human assets such as education, and social assets such as 'family-based networks, occupation-based groups of mutual help, rotating savings and credit groups, and other groups or associations to which a household belongs' (World Bank, 2000: 20). To these can be added a fourth form of assets, mentioned by the poor themselves in the Voices of the Poor survey (see Box 3.2).* These are environmental assets such as soil, trees and water which offer resources that help people cope

---

* The term 'capital' is also widely used to refer to what here are denoted as 'assets'. Strictly speaking, either term refers only to possessions such as wealth

with life's risks. Conceptualising the social production of resilience in terms of assets offers robust categories, distinct from one another yet mutually reinforcing, which together can be seen to constitute resilience. If employed as broad *social* categories (as distinct from categories referring to *individual* ownership or abilities as the World Bank tends to use them), they can also include the categories of entitlement, enfranchisement, empowerment and capabilities. This is the approach followed here.

PHYSICAL ASSETS

The word 'assets' is originally a legal term referring, as the *Oxford English Dictionary* puts it, to 'sufficient estate or effects for an executor to discharge a testator's debts and legacies'. Its core meaning, therefore, relates to the ownership of physical assets such as savings or property. However, as the World Bank makes clear 'what matters is not just the total value of the assets, but also their liquidity' namely the ability to realise them in money terms (World Bank, 2000: 20). Therefore, in examining the role of assets in providing security against risks, we need to examine not just the amount of assets owned but how the value of those assets is determined. As the World Bank puts it: 'Thus knowledge of the functioning of asset markets is needed to determine the usefulness of the assets as insurance' (2001: 20). Since most people's assets are in the forms of savings and property each of these is considered separately, beginning with savings.

A period of economic boom – such as happened in the United States and a small number of other countries (such as China, Ireland, Chile, Singapore and Mozambique) during the 1990s – provides real increases in income for many people. However, this does not necessarily mean that such people have more liquid assets available to them as a protection against risk. The availability of such assets will depend on how much of the increased income is saved, and on whether the means people use to save (investments in stocks, buying property) see such savings appreciating in value or not. Whether

---

and property so that their use to refer to human, social or environmental phenomena, as happens in this chapter, is a metaphorical usage. The term 'assets' is preferred to the term 'capital' in this chapter since the latter is derived from the world of business where it refers to activities related to profit-making, whereas assets is a legal term relating to protection against debts (and thereby risks). For this reason, assets seems more appropriate a term to use in a discussion of protecting against risks.

people save their increased incomes will depend on their levels of consumption, including the amount they have to pay for such major expenditures as owning or renting accommodation. If people choose to spend income on more extravagant consumption or if housing prices increase at a rate faster than incomes increase, people may end up with increased debts despite the fact that their incomes have increased. This would indicate a weakening in their ability to withstand risk, in other words an increase in their vulnerability (see Box 3.1).

Examining trends in the United States over the 1990s helps identify characteristics of asset ownership under the conditions created by globalisation. One of the characteristics of the US boom was low interest rates resulting from low inflation. This had two important consequences. Firstly, instead of keeping their savings in bank accounts, more and more Americans invested in the stock market. In 1990, stock funds attracted 29 per cent of the new money retail investors were putting into their mutual funds; by 2000, they were absorbing almost 80 per cent. As a result, stocks accounted for 60 per cent of the total mutual fund holdings of Americans in 2000, an increase from 23 per cent a decade earlier (Rapley, 2004: 155). As the stock market boomed, so did the value of these savings increase, stimulating a consumer boom. However, and this is the second consequence of low interest rates, what fuelled this boom was not increased incomes but credit, with the result that 'the savings rate dropped below zero by the end of the decade and debt levels reached record heights' (Rapley, 2004: 155). In early 2000, the stock market crashed. As Stiglitz puts it, 'stocks fell further, faster, than they had for years – S&P 500, which provides the best broad-gauged measure of stock market performance, had its worst annual performance for a quarter century' (Stiglitz, 2003: 6). Instead of reducing consumption, Americans responded to the lowering of interest rates and to the tax cuts introduced by President Bush by continuing spending, piling up more debt in doing so. In 2003, total US household debt increased by more than $900 billion, almost twice as much as in 1999, and total debt (public and private) increased by $6.5 trillion since 2000. Yet, as this is happening, wages and salaries stagnate: while wage income rose by barely 1 per cent in real terms in 2003, consumer spending growth reached an annual rate of 4.7 per cent at the end of that year (*The Economist*, 28 February 2004). As a result, even at a time of historically low interest rates, US households' debt-service payments as a percentage of their income are higher than at their previous peak

BOX 3.1   STIGLITZ ON 'MAKING RISK A WAY OF LIFE'

In his book on the 'Roaring Nineties', Nobel Prize winner in economics and former World Bank chief economist, Joseph Stiglitz, described the twin processes that generalised vulnerability among residents of the United States over that decade. He writes:

> We not only exposed the economy to more risk, we also undermined our ability to manage that risk. Changes in pension systems and employment policies meant that individuals were more exposed to the vicissitudes of the market: as the stock market went down, they saw their future pensions decrease; as the economy slowed, they saw a greater likelihood of being fired. At the same time, government policies too changed: unemployment insurance did not keep pace with the changes in the economy, and welfare was cut back. (Stiglitz, 2003: 180–1)

Paradoxically, the very conditions of success during the boom of the 1990s became a source of greater risk when recession hit. Stiglitz describes how increased productivity meant that fewer workers were needed, making it 'more profitable to fire workers'. As a result, 'job insecurity spread from blue-collar to white-collar workers' and 'worker anxiety increased'. As this was happening, safety nets were also eroded as 'unemployment insurance replaced a smaller fraction of earnings, and more workers were left uncovered' (Stiglitz, 2003: 183).

This is a situation in which people's lives are more and more affected by market volatility. Stiglitz writes that when the stock market was booming, many people were attracted to putting their savings in tech stocks rather than paying their Social Security contributions. However, this 'leaves individuals vulnerable to the irrational pessimism of the stock market, just as earlier it allowed them to benefit from its irrational optimism. ... Had they put their money into the typical tech stock, they would be looking forward to a bleak retirement. Social Security was designed to provide just that – *security*, not a gamble' (2003: 197; emphasis in original). Similarly, Stiglitz treats sceptically claims that in the 1990s capitalism managed to overcome its traditional cycles of boom and bust: 'For all the talk of the New Economy ending the business cycle, the changes of the Roaring Nineties actually may have increased our economic vulnerability, by making the economy more sensitive, more responsive to shocks.' The erosion of bonds of loyalty between employers and employees 'which insulated workers from some of the vagaries of the marketplace', and of defined pension programmes 'which insulated workers from some of the vagaries of the stock market' meant that 'as the bubble burst, the consequences not only for individuals but for the economy as a whole would be even greater – in spite of all the bravado about learning how to manage risk better' (2003: 200–1).

in the 1980s. Neither is this problem unique to the US: in Australia, credit card debt was at an all-time high in 2003, averaging nearly 2,500 Australian dollars per account, an increase of 71 per cent since 1999 (*The Economist*, 6 April 2004). In Britain, credit card debt has trebled since the mid 1990s and the national savings rate has fallen by half since 1993. As Hamilton writes: 'Young people (who spend almost half of their income on luxuries, including going out and recreational drugs) accept that they will remain in debt for most of their lives' (Hamilton, 2003: 5). In Ireland, which experienced a major economic boom in the late 1990s, the growth of personal debt has far outstripped the growth in average incomes with the result that debt-servicing costs as a percentage of after-tax income have risen from 18.2 per cent in 1998 to an estimated 29.3 per cent in 2004 (*Irish Times*, 16 April 2004). In this situation, the potential of assets to act as a protection against such risks as unemployment or serious health problems, is greatly reduced.

An important asset of many households that acted as a major protection against risks in old age was a defined-benefit pension, usually based on a worker's income and length of service. However, over the course of the 1990s many firms began to move to a defined-contribution pension, fixing the contribution employees made to the scheme but making the size of their final pension dependent on stock market performance. This was partly a response to a booming stock market but it also reflected a growing crisis affecting many large firms in both the US and Europe which faced mounting liabilities in their pension funds. For example, the British Telecom pension scheme, one of Europe's largest corporate funds, had a deficit of at least £1.4 billion in early 2004, while other exposed companies included Rolls-Royce, Sainsbury, Cable & Wireless, Whitbread, Lufthansa and Michelin (*Financial Times*, 29 March 2004). Whatever the causes, however, the result has been to force 'workers to bear more risk, not just on the job but in retirement' (Stiglitz, 2003: 185).

Despite the attention given to the stock market, property is by far the world's biggest single asset class with a lot more people owning houses than shares. In most of Europe and Australia housing accounts for 40 to 60 per cent of total household wealth, while in the United States it accounts for about 30 per cent. In the US, the typical household on an average income holds six times as much wealth in residential property than it does in shares. Furthermore, house prices have been booming in many countries, rising by more than 50 per cent in real terms since the mid 1990s in Australia, Britain, Ireland, the Netherlands, Spain and Sweden and by 30 per cent in the United States. In this situation, returns on property have been higher than have returns on equities. Rising property prices have helped to maintain consumer spending:

Since the IT and stockmarket bubbles burst, rising property prices around the globe have helped to prop up the world economy. Rising house prices have boosted consumer spending by making people feel wealthier, offsetting the effect of falling share prices. Consumers have also been able to borrow more against the higher value of their homes, turning capital gains into cash which they can spend on a new car or a holiday. For firms, property is the main form of collateral for borrowing, so swings in commercial-property prices can also influence corporate investment. (*The Economist*, 31 May 2003)

Owning property, therefore, gives people security against which they borrow. As a result, not only do they take out large mortgages but existing owners increase their mortgages to make capital gains. In the US, Britain and Australia, mortgage-equity withdrawal is running at record levels of 5 to 7 per cent of personal disposable income. *The Economist* points out that the consequences of a fall in house prices would be more severe than the stock market crash as more households own property and 'because home-owners are up to their necks in debt' (31 May 2003). Yet the magazine is predicting a fall of at least 20 per cent in house prices in most of the countries which have seen booms in such prices. This it bases on the ratios of house prices to rents and to incomes, both of which have risen to dangerous heights, according to the magazine. As returns to investors decline and as first-time buyers find it impossible to get on the bottom rung of the property ladder, *The Economist* predicts a change in sentiment, pushing prices lower. Similarly, the International Monetary Fund (IMF), referring to house prices in the same group of countries, warns of 'the likelihood of a sharp price correction' (IMF, 2004: 18). What concerns us here is not so much the accuracy of this prediction as the vulnerability built in even to the holding of what has traditionally been seen as a solid and secure asset. The threat of a collapse in housing prices in a situation of high levels of indebtedness signals that assets that previously hedged people against risk have now become sources of risk.

HUMAN ASSETS

If physical assets refer to possessions, human assets refer to something far closer to Sen's concept of capabilities, namely people's innate or developed abilities to make the most of a given situation. Chief among such human assets are health and education. The UNDP emphasises the synergies between education and health: education promotes better hygiene and increases the use of health services; improvements in children's nutritional status increases their learning abilities; higher educational levels are associated with better family planning and lower infant mortality. 'This notion of synergies among social investments is central to reducing hunger, malnutrition, disease and illiteracy – and to advancing human capabilities', it states (UNDP, 2003a: 85).

The situation of health in today's world presents a very mixed picture. On the one hand, most developed countries have reduced to negligible levels such threats as malnutrition, infant mortality and infectious diseases like TB; on the other hand, heart disease, smoking and cancer are major causes of death in these countries. Furthermore, affluence is giving rise to new threats to health such as obesity and allergies. In the US, between 1976 and 2000 the percentage of those who are overweight grew from 46 to 64.5 per cent of the population and of the obese from 14.4 to 30.5 per cent (Ritzer, 2004: 7). Scientists are predicting that by the year 2015 half of all Europeans may be suffering from some sort of allergy if present trends continue (Boseley, 2004). On the other hand, 18 per cent of the world's population, or 800 million people, went hungry at the beginning of the twenty-first century; over the course of the 1990s the numbers of hungry people had increased in 25 countries. Out of every 1,000 live births in the least developed countries, 100 infants died, while TB kills 2 million adults and malaria 1 million every year around the world. Furthermore, new sources of risk to health are emerging with globalisation (see Box 3.2). The sources of these problems are the lack of healthy living conditions and of adequate health care. In 2000, at least 1.1 billion people, or 20 per cent of the world's population, lacked access to safe water and over 2 billion access to improved sanitation. The 1990s saw some improvement in that situation, though due to rapid population growth the number of urban dwellers lacking access to safe water increased by nearly 62 million (UNDP, 2003a: 85–110). Yet for most people, health care systems exacerbate rather than resolve these problems. This is because 'the elite control of medical care in the developing world also creates problems of relevance, as the system is designed to meet the needs of a very small socio-political cadre rather than the general population' (Twaddle, 2004: 312). Spending on health remains low in many developing countries, with better-off urban dwellers benefiting most from it. Furthermore, the growing privatisation of health services under pressure from the IMF and the World Bank is resulting in a two-tier system, further disadvantaging the poor. Referring to the impact of these reforms in India, Twaddle predicts: 'It seems likely, but not proven, that infant and maternal mortality will increase and disability will become more prevalent' (2004: 310). Similar trends can be observed in developed countries. As Cockerham reports: 'Whereas communicable diseases killed off the poor in much greater numbers than the affluent in past historical periods, chronic diseases like heart disease and cancer now continue the same pattern. In fact, mortality from both acute and chronic diseases is now greater among the poor than the nonpoor' (Cockerham, 2004: 284–5). While more unhealthy lifestyles are one cause, problems of access, high costs and the lack of availability of high-quality health care is also a cause. In surveying health care reforms in 20 countries, Twaddle found a universal move towards a more market-led system since the 1980s and concluded: 'There is a growing consensus among health care researchers that market reforms have no documented benefits to patients and much is placed at risk. … Indeed, market reforms are primarily a mechanism for corporate interests to extract profits from the medical care system' (Twaddle, 2004: 311). One example of what is placed at risk in a more market-dependent health care system comes from the United States where 1.5 million people a year since 1993 have lost health insurance as they have moved out of full-time employment.

Education presents a similar picture. While the literacy rate among adults and youth in the developed world is touching 100 per cent, in the developing world the respective rates are 74.5 per cent and 84.8 per cent whereas in the least developed countries they are only 53.3 per cent and 66.3 per cent. Of the 680 million children of primary school age in developing countries, 115 million do not attend school, of whom three-fifths are girls. Furthermore, just half of those who do begin school actually finish it, a figure which rises to one in three in Sub-Saharan Africa. As a result, there are 879 million illiterate adults in the world, two-thirds of them women (UNDP, 2003a: 92–3). Apart from Latin America and the Caribbean, no region of the developing world in 2000 was on target to achieve the goal of universal primary education by 2015, one of the principal aims of the Millennium Development Goals (MDGs). Countries display different trends in spending on education: those in South Asia, West Asia and Sub-Saharan Africa doubled enrolment between 1975 and 1997 with only a modest increase in spending, while those in East Asia and Latin America increased spending sharply without a major increase in intake. This illustrates the dilemmas facing countries with

---

BOX 3.2   GLOBALISATION'S HEALTH THREATS: HIV/AIDS AND SARS

Though, as Berlinguer has written, the discovery of the Americas in the fifteenth century led to the 'microbial unification of the world' (quoted in George and Wilding, 2002: 63), it was the spread of HIV/AIDS which made this dramatically clear. Described by UN Secretary General Kofi Annan as the most globalised epidemic that humanity has ever known, HIV/AIDS is being spread by the mobility that globalisation fosters, especially along trading and migration routes, by the disruption of traditional patterns of work and kinship, by social dislocation caused by war, famine and poverty, by urban decay in developed countries, by social upheaval in the former communist countries of Eastern Europe, and by sex tourism (Lichtenstein, 2004: 319–20). First identified among gay men in the US in 1979, the disease has now become associated with heterosexual men and women in Sub-Saharan Africa (the rate among 15–24-year-olds in many African countries is six times higher among women than men), and is now emerging among injection drug users in Eastern European countries. UNAIDS predicts a 'new wave' of HIV/AIDS epidemics in Asia, while the UNDP predicts 100 million cases in India and 70 million in China by 2025 (UNDP, 2003a: 43).

Severe Acute Respiratory Syndrome (SARS) is an even more dramatic example of the swift global spread of disease. Analysts estimate that only in November 2002 did the original virus spread from animals to humans in China. By February 2003 it was being spread between humans and the first cases were reported in Asia where it quickly spread to Singapore and Hong Kong. From there it spread to Toronto and proved to be 'one of the most economically devastating disease outbreaks Canada has ever known' (*Globe and Mail*, 8 April 2004). By September 2003 more than 8,000 cases were recorded worldwide and deaths from the disease stood at 774. Diseases like SARS and HIV/AIDS show how health as a human asset is itself under threat in the context of globalisation.

---

very limited resources seeking to address educational deficiencies: the first group of countries concentrated on quantity whereas the second invested in improving quality. Yet ECLAC found a high level of under-utilisation of the human resources of those members of the workforce in Latin America with third-level professional or technical qualifications, estimating that a little over 4.5 million of the 19 million possessing such qualifications are either underemployed or unemployed (ECLAC, 2002b: 87). The move from elitist education to mass education in developed countries reflects similar tensions as data show high levels of functional illiteracy among the adult population: this reaches 48 per cent in Portugal, over 20 per cent in Ireland, Britain and the United States, and just under 20 per cent in Belgium and New Zealand (UNDP, 2003a: 248). These outcomes raise doubts about the degree to which increased educational provision is contributing to social mobility, fuelling fears that with the increased emphasis on economic competitiveness as a criterion for educational worth, equity may be becoming a residual issue (George and Wilding, 2002: 67).

In assessing human assets, therefore, attention needs to be focused not only on levels of achievement in health and education, especially in the developed world, but also on trends in the provision of these services. This highlights not only the shocking inequalities in the distribution of such assets but also the likelihood that such inequalities are deepening, in both the developed and the developing world.

SOCIAL ASSETS

In describing social assets such as 'family-based networks, occupation-based groups of mutual help, rotating savings and credit groups, and other groups or associations to which a household belongs', the World Bank adopts far too narrow a focus (World Bank, 2000: 20). It is too narrow because it presupposes the existence and strength of the support networks it mentions, especially the family which for most people in the world is still their most fundamental social asset. Secondly, and perhaps conveniently for the World Bank, it avoids any attention being given to the political dimension of social assets, namely the ways in which through joining collectively people contest the power of the market thereby protecting themselves from risks. For much of the twentieth century, trade unions (both urban and rural) and political parties were the main means through which this was done, though at the beginning of the twenty-first century social movements were emerging as perhaps more important collective actors. Finally, social assets also refer to means through which the state or the market offer forms of social protection against risks; the emergence of the welfare state was undoubtedly the most important of these in the twentieth century but forms of insurance such as health or accident insurance offered by the market also became a widespread means through which people protected themselves against risk. It is therefore through social assets that people's entitlement, enfranchisement and empowerment (as discussed in the opening paragraphs of this chapter) are primarily achieved. This section looks at some trends in social assets in today's more globalised world. It begins with the family, then examines forms of collective power, and finishes by looking at social protection.

For Manuel Castells, globalisation marks 'the end of the family as we have known it until now', though he emphasises that what is happening 'is not the disappearance of the family but its profound diversification' (Castells, 1997: 139; 222). A number of worldwide trends point in this direction. Foremost among these is 'a pervasive rise in divorce rates' around the world with a growing proportion of divorces involving couples with young children, therefore increasing the likelihood that marital dissolution will lead to single parenthood (Berardo and Shehan, 2004: 252). Castells finds that the proportion of single-parent households with dependent children (usually headed by a woman) increased between the early 1970s and the mid 1980s in developed countries and the upward trend continued in the US in the 1990s. He detected a similar trend in developing countries: over 20 per cent of households in Brazil were in this category in 1989, an increase from 14 per cent in 1980 (see Castells, 1997: 147–52). Furthermore, female-headed households are recognised as being at greater risk of falling into poverty. In this situation, the family is being eroded as a place of caring. As the percentage of women in the labour force increases, this puts pressure on caring roles within the family traditionally provided by women. This affects not only children but also the growing numbers of elderly people in many societies. Significantly, the proportion of elderly people residing with their adult children has declined significantly not only in North America and Europe but also in Japan, South Korea and Taiwan. While experts debate whether the family as an institution is in decline or merely adapting, clear trends worldwide point to the fact that, as the UNDP puts it, 'needs once provided almost exclusively by unpaid family labour are now being purchased from the market or provided by the state' (UNDP, 1999: 79). Far from being able to protect vulnerable people against risk, families themselves are 'experiencing considerable stress' and require assistance in dealing with this (Berardo and Shehan, 2004: 258).

Social capital constitutes a second form of social asset (see Box 3.3). While Putnam, whose work has popularised the term, distinguishes it from political participation, he acknowledges their close relationship. For him, the former refers to our relations with one another while the latter refers to our relations with political institutions (Putnam, 1995: 665). This, however, ignores the important political role played by social capital in that, through closer relations with one another, social capital constitutes a counterweight to other forms of power, especially the power of the state and of the market. Indeed, in including membership of trade unions and of political parties among those groups he surveys, Putnam implicitly acknowledges this political dimension. These forms of collective power, constituted through the self-organisation of members of society, played a decisive role over the twentieth century in bringing about a compact between state and market for the sake of the welfare of society. Both, however, are withering under the conditions of globalisation, mirroring the wider decline in social capital. Reporting trends in the membership of political parties in 19 European countries and the United States over the 1980s and 1990s, the UNDP found a decline of between 22 and 65 per cent in 13 cases while the only countries which had seen an increase were ones with dictatorial or communist governments in the recent past (Hungary, Slovakia, Portugal, Greece and Spain). In France, Italy, Norway and the US, membership of political parties is half or less of what it was 20 years ago, reports the UNDP (2002: 69). Furthermore, it reports opinion surveys from Latin America and Central and Eastern Europe which show political parties enjoy the lowest level of confidence among the population on a list of eight public institutions (including the Church, television, the armed forces and the police). Trade unions also have seen a decline in membership. As the International Labour Organisation's World Employment Report 1996–97 found, the proportion of union members in the labour force declined, sometimes sharply, almost everywhere over the previous decade. It reported: 'Out of a sample of 92 countries for which figures on union membership were available (calculated on the basis of the non-agricultural workforce), only 14 had a rate of more than 50 per cent in 1995; in 48 countries, more than half the sample, the rate was less than 20 per cent' (ILO, 1997: 3). It is not surprising therefore that analysts point to a significant weakening in the collective bargaining power of labour in all industrial countries (George and Wilding, 2002: 48–9). In this situation, social movements are emerging as a means of representing the voice of civil society, managing to capture the attention of the public through 'anti-globalisation' protests or the high-profile activities of Greenpeace. Though social movements have awakened immense hopes for some that they can deepen democracy, foster equality and mobilise the discontented against the abuses of both the market and the state, Radcliffe writes that 'the transformatory potential of social movements was often celebrated too soon' (Radcliffe, 1999: 214). This is because they do not have the same institutionalised presence in political systems as do trade unions and political parties: while they can mobilise huge numbers around a particular cause (for example, the war on Iraq in 2003), their political influence is easily undermined by co-option and fragmentation. As Scholte puts it in summarising the impact of civil society organisations on attempts to democratise global governance, 'the manifestations and modalities ... are so diverse as to inhibit precise pronouncements on – let alone predictions about – impacts and legitimacy' (Scholte, 2002: 164).

BOX 3.3   ERODING SOCIAL CAPITAL: 'MORE PEOPLE WATCH *FRIENDS* THAN HAVE FRIENDS'

Robert Putnam is concerned at the decline in social connections among Americans and identifies the increasing time spent watching television, in particular commercial entertainment television rather than public affairs, as being to a large extent responsible. Putnam uses the term 'social capital' to refer to features of social life such as networks, norms and trust 'that enable participants to act together more effectively to pursue shared objectives' (Putnam, 1995: 664–5). This is the reason for his comment about more people watching *Friends* than having them. He believes that 'the weight of the available evidence confirms that Americans today are significantly less engaged with their communities than was true a generation ago' and finds that, beginning in the 1960s and accelerating in the 1970s and 1980s, the fabric of American life began to fray (1995: 666). While his work is primarily on the United States, Putnam says such trends are not unique to that country and he observes them happening also in both Europe and Australia.

In his book *Bowling Alone* (2000), Putnam traces how in the first two-thirds of the twentieth century more and more people in the US were joining organisations. The 20 years after the Second World War witnessed a civic boom when most civic organisations doubled their share of the cohort of those who were their potential members. 'Then suddenly, silently, mysteriously, all of those organisations began to experience levelling market share, and then slumping market share, and then plunging market share' (Putnam, 2001: 4). This erosion of social connectedness includes declines in churchgoing, in picnics, in card playing and even in having dinner with one's own family. Putnam presents evidence that 'social capital makes us smarter, healthier, safer, richer, and better able to govern a just and stable democracy' (2000: 290), improving children's development and behaviour, making neighbourhoods safer, providing economic opportunities, promoting physical and psychological well-being and fostering active citizenship. Its decline, writes Putham, leaves a sense of civic malaise and affects schools, neighbourhoods, the economy, democracy and even people's health and happiness.

Finally, social assets are also provided by the state and the market through various mechanisms of social protection. Undoubtedly, the welfare states of Western Europe have been the most developed forms of social protection provided to vulnerable populations, though various states in other parts of the world have also provided rudimentary welfare benefits, usually for workers in the formal sector funded through social insurance. While there is no consensus among social policy analysts about the extent to which globalisation is eroding the welfare state, there is a recognition of the more hostile environment in which it now operates. As Scharpf puts it, 'the terms of trade between capital, labour and the state have shifted in favour of capital interests, national powers to tax and regulate have become constrained, and governments and unions wishing to maintain employment in the exposed sectors of the economy must seek ways to increase productivity rather than redistribution', which was a central feature of the most developed welfare states. 'At the same time,' he continues, 'welfare state revenue is constrained by international tax competition, by the need to reduce non-wage labour costs, and by the need to avoid public sector deficits' (Scharpf, 2000: 224). Mishra concludes that, under these pressures, the welfare state is at best a holding operation: 'True, many European nationals have inherited a large welfare state from the golden age and, for the moment, seem to be able to hold on to them. But can they hold out against global pressures?' (Mishra, 1999: 70). If this is true of some of the most developed states in the world, it is even more true of states throughout the developing world where 'the state is being subtly deformed as an instrument of human well-being by the dynamics of globalisation, which are pushing the state by degrees and to varying extents into a subordinate relationship with global market forces' (Falk, 1996: 14). As states give priority to global competitiveness over and above the welfare of their own citizens, people are forced to rely on the market for protection against risks. The situation of workers in Latin America illustrates this. In their overview of the region, Gwynne and Kay conclude that 'labour has become more vulnerable and insecure due to the growth of short-term contracts, the shift to more competitive labour markets and the decline of social security' (Gwynne and Kay, 2004: 255). However, as Stiglitz points out (see Box 3.1), this makes people's well-being more dependent on the vagaries of the marketplace. Even the provision of insurance is being withdrawn where the risk is considered too great. Already it is a routine practice of many insurance companies to refuse cover to those who are HIV positive. As environmental hazards grow, the insurance industry is now stating that it may have 'to withdraw from individual regions and zones that are regularly and almost predictably affected by weather-related natural catastrophes' (Munich Re Group, 2004: 17–18). In all of these ways therefore – family networks, social capital and mechanisms of social protection – the social assets available to people to reinforce social resilience in the face of increased risks are being eroded.

ENVIRONMENTAL ASSETS

Environmental assets often receive less attention than do physical, human and social assets, possibly due to the approach of neoclassical economics which gives priority to monetary value and which, by and large, treats environmental assets as 'externalities' in its theorising. However, the swift pollution and depletion of environmental assets such as soil, water, air and species, on which human life depends and which humankind has tended to take for granted, has focused attention not just on the threat to them but also on how the environment provides us with resources essential for survival.

While the number of people with access to clean water increased from 4.1 billion in 1990 to 4.9 billion in 2000, 1.1 billion still lack such access and 2.4 billion lack access to improved sanitation, most of them in Africa and Asia (see Box 3.4). Lack of such access results in hundreds of millions of cases of water-related diseases and an estimated 5 million deaths a year. The introduction of what the UNEP calls 'invasive species' is responsible for deteriorating water quality, the extinction of local species and the disruption of ecosystems in many lakes and rivers. The number of such aquatic introductions rose rapidly during the second half of the twentieth century. For example, nutrient pollution in the Danube and the Black Sea has had damaging effects on wildlife, human and animal health, ecosystems, biodiversity, economic activities and natural resources, affecting the 17 countries served by these waters. Human activities have also resulted over the course of the twentieth century in the loss of about 50 per cent of the world's wetlands, an important freshwater ecosystem influencing species distribution and biodiversity as well as human settlements and activities. About 60 per cent of the world's largest 227 rivers have been strongly or moderately fragmented by dams. The resulting damage to ecosystems reduces water quantity and quality, leading to a reduction in the effective availability of water for human use (UNEP, 2002: 7–10).

Land degradation had by the mid 1990s affected nearly 2,000 million hectares or some 15 per cent of the world's land area and was estimated to be worsening at a rate of 5 to 6 million hectares a year. Its main cause is deforestation as vast reserves of forests are cleared for farm and urban use or degraded by logging. Some

BOX 3.4   FACING A 'GLOBAL WATER CRISIS'

It may surprise many that the United Nations declared 2003 as the International Year of Fresh Water. For there is probably no resource in the world that is more taken for granted than water. Yet, as McDonagh writes, 'it is clear to any researcher that the human community is facing a global water crisis' (McDonagh, 2003: 14). At the beginning of the twenty-first century, about 1.2 billion people or one-third of the world's population, lived in water-stressed areas where water consumption exceeds renewable freshwater resources by at least 10 per cent. The UN Environment Programme (UNEP) estimated that some 80 countries, home to 40 per cent of the world's population, suffered serious water shortages in the mid 1990s. While the world's population tripled during the twentieth century, its consumption of water increased seven-fold with the demand for water doubling every 21 years. This is largely due to its increased use in industry and irrigated agriculture: it takes 400,000 litres of water to manufacture a car and 42,500 to produce a kilo of beef. It takes 52 million gallons of fresh water to move a ship through the Panama Canal and an average of 36 ships pass through each day. Furthermore, as with so much else of the world's resources, the distribution of water is highly unequal: Canada receives 26 times more than does Mexico while Asia receives only 36 per cent of the world's fresh water though it contains 60 per cent of the world's population. The average person in the US uses 600 litres of domestic urban water a day, in the EU 250 to 300 litres, and in Sub-Saharan Africa 10 to 20 litres.

Until recently people relied mainly on streams, rivers and lakes for their water supply. However, according to the UNEP, 2 billion people now depend on groundwater found below the land's surface, a finite resource which is fast being exhausted. By 2020 experts predict major shortages in California and the US southern Great Plains. In India, the number of wells used to draw groundwater has increased from 3,000 in 1960 to 6 million in 1990 and in many continents these sources of water, called aquifers, are being depleted ten times faster than they are being refilled.

Access to water is increasingly becoming a source of tension between countries. In 1989, Turkey threatened to cut the flow of water in the Euphrates to Syria because of the latter's support for Kurdish rebels. In 2002, a severe drought in Malaysia led that country to threaten to cut water supplies to Singapore. Of the annual yield of 362 million cubic metres of water in the Western Aquifer System under Israel and Palestine, Israelis use 340 million leaving only 22 million for the Palestinians. Tensions over the waters of the Nile, which supplies water to nine countries and on which 60 million Egyptians depend, has led to UN mediation on equitable access to the river. The decline in the volume of water in the Indus is exacerbating tensions between Pakistan and India and putting pressures on the 1960 Indus Water Treaty between the two countries. Thailand, Myanmar and China are in conflict over damming the river Salween between the three countries, while Cambodia, Laos, Vietnam and Thailand are seeking agreement over the future development of the Mekong river. Ismail Serageldin, the World Bank's vice-president for environmentally sustainable development, is quoted as saying that, as many of the wars of the twentieth century were over oil, many of those of the twenty-first century will be over water (McDonagh, 2003: 22–6).

94 million hectares were estimated to have been lost each year over the 1990s. Overgrazing, fuelwood consumption, agricultural mismanagement, and industry and urbanisation are also among the causes. Soil degradation involves water and wind erosion, chemical degradation and physical degradation, and can considerably lower the productive capacity of land. They also reduce the soil's ability to filter out pollutants and to act as a buffer for soil acidity or alkalinity as well as to maintain natural habitats and biodiversity. In the worst cases it leads to desertification which is an ever-present risk in almost 50 per cent of Africa's drylands, affects over 104 million hectares in Asia and the Pacific, is a pressing problem across Iraq, Jordan, Syria and the whole Arabian peninsula, and in Latin America is affecting Argentina, Brazil, Chile, Mexico and Peru. The UNEP concludes: 'Despite improvements in soil conservation techniques and general recognition of the urgent need to slow the rate of land degradation, there are no clear signs of progress' (UNEP, 2002: 16).

The conversion of land to cropland, cutting down forests and pressure on ecosystems such as coral reefs cause the extinction of species and the loss of biodiversity (see Box 2.5). These in turn erode human well-being. Plants and animals provide the raw materials for medicines and over 75 per cent of the world's people rely on traditional medicines extracted directly from nature. Furthermore, since resources such as energy, water and nutrients are retained in greater amounts by more diverse ecosystems, the loss of biodiversity is eroding such resources. Species diversity also acts as a coping mechanism for natural ecosystems against damaging impacts from human activity. The erosion of biodiversity coupled with climate change is therefore estimated to threaten food security. The Intergovernmental Panel on Climate Change reported the findings of studies that 'climate change would lower incomes of the vulnerable populations and increase the absolute number of people at risk of hunger', adding though that this requires further research. It is more firmly established, however, that it will worsen food security in Africa (IPCC, 2001: 11). Finally, despite having been banned in many countries, toxic chemicals accumulate over many years in the environment, affecting human and animal health. The UNEP reports that persistent toxic substances are transported by air masses to become long-distance contaminants. Reaching cooler regions they condense in snowflakes or on particles and so the Arctic is creating a sink for these substances. The health risks they pose include glandular and hormone imbalances, immune system breakdowns, birth abnormalities, developmental defects and neurological disorders (UNEP, 2002: 14). Increased environmental risks therefore themselves erode coping mechanisms, exacerbating the quality and supply of water, reducing food security and causing risks to health. Age-long constituents of human and community resilience are not only being eroded but in some cases are becoming threats to well-being.

CONCLUSIONS

Of the impact of globalisation on society over the 1990s, Joseph Stiglitz writes: 'Even many of those who are better off feel more vulnerable' (2003: 20). This refers not only to the increased risks they have faced but also to the erosion of people's ability to manage those risks. This chapter has outlined some of the principal ways in which people's coping mechanisms have been eroded, reducing their social resilience to risks. Stiglitz's comment highlights the fact that increased income is by no means sufficient to safeguard people against vulnerability, and may indeed go hand in hand with increases in vulnerability. The survey in this chapter also draws attention to the fact that people's resilience is affected in different ways – depending on their physical assets (ownership of assets and levels of indebtedness), their human assets (education and health), their social assets (belonging to supportive networks) and their environmental assets (the quality and resilience of the ecosystems they inhabit). It is no part of the argument here to claim that everyone's vulnerability is increased to the same extent nor, in fact, to claim that it is necessarily increased at all. As the epigraph to this chapter put it, people are affected in varying ways and different intensities according to how social, economic and political processes influence the impact of risks or hazards on them. One utility of the approach developed here is that it offers bases for measuring how vulnerability affects different social groups or different regions. One example of this, the 'Assessing vulnerability' table produced by the World Bank, was described in Chapter 1. The wider analysis of vulnerability developed in these two chapters offers a broader range of possible criteria for elaborating indicators, as is being pursued by the Caribbean office of ECLAC in their preparation of a Social Vulnerability Index (see ECLAC, 2003). Only when such measurements are made can grounds be offered for drawing firm conclusions about how people's vulnerability is being affected in today's more globalised world. However, if the analysis in this chapter captures anything of the forces shaping our world, it would be strange to claim that people are unaffected by these, even if their own physical, human, social and environmental assets remain as resilient as ever. For there is a strong collective dimension to vulnerability, affecting the fragile bonds that constitute society and thereby inevitably affecting the resilience of society itself to risks. From this social vulnerability, no one can remain immune.

This chapter completes Part I of the book, the purpose of which was to describe the two sides of vulnerability and show how the concept applies in our world. It has made reference throughout to our more globalised world, assuming rather than establishing a causal connection between global changes and the different ways vulnerability and violence manifest themselves in today's world. However, such a causal connection needs to be established rather than simply assumed. This is the purpose of Part II which examines globalisation to diagnose its links to the forces and processes described in these two chapters.

Part II

Diagnosis

4
The Political Economy
of Globalisation

[A]t some point in the 1990s, internationalization turned into
globalization. It got a momentum of its own, became less a consequence of
demonstrable human decisions, more self-contained and self-supporting.
The driving force was twofold: first, technological progress, enabling
full and fast information and communication everywhere, physically
and virtually; second, economics, the global market, linking production,
investment, transportation, trade, advertisement, and consumption
anywhere in the world to any other place. The result was a disregard
for national frontiers, the strengthening of global corporations, and the
erosion of nation-states. (Pronk, 2003: 27–8)

As this quotation from the former Dutch Minister for Development
Cooperation, Jan Pronk, suggests, the concept of 'globalisation' came
into widespread use in both the social sciences and in public discourse
over the course of the 1990s in an attempt to capture some of the
immensely complex changes that are reshaping our personal and
social worlds. Waters traces its usage since the early 1960s but states
that it was not recognised as academically significant until the early
or mid 1980s. He found that even by the mid 1990s the term was
relatively rare in the title of journal articles (Waters, 1995: 2). By the
early 2000s, however, there was an avalanche of social science books
with the word in the title, as a glance at the catalogues of leading
publishers would attest, and the term had found its way into everyday
public (and in some circles private) discourse. Scholte found that the
number of entries for 'globalization' in the US Library of Congress had
increased twenty-fold in the five years from 1994 to 1999 (Scholte,
2000: 14), while the newly built Bibliotheca Alexandrina in Alexandria,
Egypt, has enough writings on it to fill a whole room (Krizsán and
Zentai, 2003: 17). The importance of the concept as an interpretative
category is indicated by the fact that the prestigious US magazine
Foreign Policy began publishing an annual index of globalisation in
2001 using indicators based on economic integration, technological
connectivity, personal contact and political engagement to list the

world's 20 most globalised countries (Singapore topped the index in 2001 and 2005 while Ireland topped it in the three years in between) (see A.T. Kearney/Foreign Policy, 2001, 2002, 2003, 2004, 2005). As Held and McGrew put it, globalisation has become 'the leitmotif of our age' (2000: 1).

Since the purpose of this two-chapter part is to diagnose the vulnerability and violence described in the previous part, the burgeoning literature on how globalisation is changing our world seems a good place to begin. Sklair finds that researchers on globalisation have focused on two increasingly significant phenomena: the first is whether a more globalised economy is emerging based on new systems of production, finance and consumption; the second is the idea of 'global culture' (Sklair, 1999: 4). The chapters within this part examine each in turn. This chapter takes as its subject the political economy of globalisation, namely the shifts in the ways market, state and society interrelate that are caused by processes associated with globalisation. Chapter 5 examines the cultural worlds of globalisation. The purpose of each is to identify as precisely as possible the processes that result in the increased vulnerability and violence described in Part I.

Before beginning to examine the shifts in political economy associated with globalisation, however, the notion of globalisation as a leitmotif needs to be interrogated. For leitmotif simply means a recurrent idea. As such, it may be no more than a passing fad, of no particular utility in diagnosing society in our times and liable to fade as quickly as it has emerged. The lack of any consensus as to its meaning, even the questioning of its very existence, requires that it be subjected to some scrutiny before being adopted. This is the purpose of the first section of this chapter which arrives at a definition of what globalisation means as used throughout this book. The second section of the chapter looks at the technological innovations that have made possible the emergence of the contemporary form of globalisation, and how the application of these in the spheres of finance, production, trade and communications is reshaping the world's economy in fundamental ways. Having examined the market in section two, the third section looks at the state and how its relationship to the market is changing. Section four of the chapter takes society as its subject, in particular the changing social structures of informational capitalism. The final section draws conclusions about how the shifts in political economy associated with globalisation are a principal cause of growing vulnerability and violence.

DOES GLOBALISATION EXIST?

Globalisation has been described as 'an elastic concept that has been stretched in many directions' (Boli, Elliott and Bieri, 2004: 410). Those labelled as 'hyperglobalists' see its presence everywhere, either as a magical panacea to bring prosperity to all or as shorthand for the ills of our world, while others, the so-called sceptics, doubt that it exists at all. In between are the 'transformationalists' who accept globalisation's central role in reshaping our world yet who see nothing inevitable as to where, how or on whom it impacts (Held et al., 1999: 2–10). This illustrates the extent to which, as Scholte puts it, 'due to irreconcilable definitions, many globalization debates are stalemated from the outset' (Scholte, 2000: 17). Often, even in influential reports, the concept is given a very loose meaning, offering simply a convenient hook. A good example is the World Bank's research report on globalisation, growth and poverty, widely quoted as evidence that globalisation reduces poverty and inequality. Yet this equates globalisation with economic integration; all that is global about it is the strong prescription that such integration should be extended worldwide (World Bank, 2002). Given its manifold meanings, Scholte's five broad definitions of globalisation offer a useful mapping of some of the most common. These are:

- Internationalisation: the growth of international exchange and interdependence.
- Liberalisation: the process of removing government-imposed restrictions on movements between countries so as to create an open and borderless world economy.
- Universalisation: spreading objects and meanings to people throughout the world.
- Westernisation or modernisation: spreading the social structures of modernity (capitalism, rationalism, industrialism, bureaucratic organisation) to countries worldwide.
- Deterritorialisation or the spread of supraterritoriality: a reconfiguration of geography so that social space is no longer wholly mapped in terms of territorial places, distances and borders (Scholte, 2000: 15–16).

Obviously, these meanings are not mutually exclusive and all these processes tend to overlap with and reinforce one another. Yet Scholte himself dismisses the first four meanings, on the basis that they do not really tell us anything that might warrant the coining of a new category, and opts instead for his fifth meaning, what he calls 'the relative deterritorialization of social life', as expressing the essential meaning of globalisation (Scholte, 2000: 50).

In doing this, however, Scholte responds to the problem of a lack of definition by offering one that is too tight. For the concept of globalisation as it is commonly used does include the other uses he lists, since it expresses the interaction and intensification of these processes, including their local impacts; furthermore, the definition he offers obscures the power relations that drive the process (McGrew, 2001: 298). This tendency to treat globalisation as a process without a subject is rightly criticised by Hay and Marsh who seek instead to analyse globalisation not as a cause or explanation of social change but rather as something that needs to be explained in its own right (as an *explanandum* rather than an *explanans* as they put it) (Hay and Marsh, 2000: 6). They argue that globalisation 'cannot in itself explain anything' and urge the need to 'cut through the causal haze that tends to surround the concept', offering instead 'rigorous and precise accounts both of globalizing tendencies and of de-globalizing counter-tendencies as and when they can be identified' (2000: 10). However, in preferring to stress 'the highly complex, contested, contingent and political nature of global social, political and economic dynamics as well as the paucity of undifferentiated accounts couched at the level of the global system' (2000: 10), they run the risk of distracting from the task of identifying the underlying logic of these dynamics, a logic that today more than ever operates globally. While fully accepting that there is nothing inevitable about this logic, that it is promoted by very specific actors and resisted by others, that it is appropriated in very different ways in different locales, it is nonetheless the operation of a dominant market-driven logic that unites the different meanings identified by Scholte above (and, indeed, by the contributors to Hay and Marsh's collection on 'demystifying globalisation'). It is this common and global logic that has given rise to the need for a concept like 'globalisation' to allow analysts to capture the nature of today's global dynamics. This is not to deny that it itself needs to be explained or that the social forces driving it need to be identified, but it does highlight the utility of the concept. It is most accurate therefore to conceive of the concept in dialectical terms – it is a concept that can help throw light on the global dynamics of economic, political, social and cultural change, but it also requires careful specification of what exactly it means.

A concern with state agency manifests itself in the case of analysts who argue that globalisation needs to be distinguished from internationalisation since the latter implies a process still driven by nation states (for example, Sklair, 1999 or Hirst and Thompson, 1999). The argument of the present book does not deny the validity of this concern or of the distinctions being made, but rather cautions against tight definitions insofar as they elide the interlinked and cumulative nature of the processes that are implicated in the reshaping of our societies – processes that are *in principle* global in their reach even if in practice this may not manifest itself in particular empirical instances. For, as Cerny puts it, globalisation is an 'increasingly additive process, involving many and diverse levels of internationalisation and transnationalisation, without an overall shape or logic of its own, and without a readily identifiable or wholly credible set of political (or economic or social) "change masters" to give it coherence or stable values'. He concludes that 'its very complexity makes it a volatile and unpredictable process' (Cerny, 1999: 160).

In seeking a satisfactory definition of globalisation, therefore, these dimensions need to be borne in mind. For example, Held et al. identify a number of influential definitions, including 'accelerating interdependence' (Ohmae); 'action at a distance' (Giddens); and 'time-space compression' (Harvey) (Held et al., 1999: 15). The definition offered by the UNDP has the advantage of drawing explicit attention to the way in which the concept is used, both as description and as prescription: 'The description is the widening and deepening of international flows of trade, finance and information in a single, integrated global market. The prescription is to liberalise national and global markets in the belief that free flows of trade, finance and information will produce the best outcome for growth and human welfare.' This is presented 'with an air of inevitability and overwhelming conviction', not seen since the heyday of free trade in the nineteenth century, adds the UNDP (UNDP, 1997: 82).

However, these definitions all lack in some way or another the essentially additive, dynamic or multilayered dimensions that the concept entails. For this reason the following definition is to be preferred and is used in this book:

A process (or set of processes) which embodies a transformation in the spatial organization of social relations and transactions – assessed in terms of their extensity, intensity, velocity and impact – generating transcontinental or interregional flows and networks of activity, interaction, and the exercise of power. (Held et al., 1999: 16)

Offering a definition raises the issue of agency. Does globalisation effect anything? Is it correct to say that globalisation is a cause of either good or ill, as is often claimed? In fact, does it exist at all? These questions are important since some critics claim that globalisation is a convenient ideological tool used to convince states that they have no option but to deregulate and privatise their economies and dismantle laws and welfare systems that protect their citizens (Hirst and Thompson, 1996). In this context, it is important to bear in mind that globalisation is no more than a conceptual category to make sense of complex processes of social change. To this extent it can be said that it does not in itself exist. However, since the processes effecting change are multiple, interactive, additive and contradictory, we need a concept that captures these dynamics which may be missed if we limit ourselves to terms like those from Scholte listed above. In these ways, therefore, the concept 'globalisation' plays a role in social science discourse akin to that played by the concept of modernisation throughout most of the twentieth century. When employed as a causal category (as in Box 4.1 on globalisation and famines, for example) it is being used in a metaphorical or representative, rather than literal, sense, in which it stands for a complex set of causes rather than being proposed as a cause in its own right.

A final issue that arises when considering the meaning of globalisation is its history. When did these complex processes we label globalisation begin? Are they anything new? For, if we hold that globalisation has been evident since at least the nineteenth century if not before, why coin a new term for it? As with other issues concerning globalisation, there is no consensus on its history either. Held et al. (1999: 415–35) refer to four eras: premodern globalisation (from 9,000 to 11,000 years ago down to 1500); early modern globalisation (circa 1500–1850); modern globalisation (circa 1850–1945); and contemporary globalisation (since 1945). The World Bank speaks of 'three waves of globalisation': 1870–1914; 1945–80; 1980–present (World Bank, 2002: 23–51). ECLAC divides its three phases of globalisation slightly differently again: 1870–1913; 1945–73; 1974–present (ECLAC, 2002a: 4). What is common to all these is the recognition that there has been a growing process of interconnectedness linking different regions to one another at an uneven pace that goes back in human history. The European conquest

BOX 4.1   DOES GLOBALISATION MAKE FAMINES MORE LIKELY?

Famines have always been a feature of social life, though for much of human history people died quietly, unnoticed by the rest of the world. With the increase in instantaneous worldwide communications associated with globalisation, famines have become a telespectacle, viewed by the outside world from its armchair. But knowing more about them does not necessarily help prevent them, though if aid is sufficiently mobilised it may help to mitigate their worst effects. In fact, it draws our attention to the fact that famines are not exceptional or abnormal events but result from the same processes that affect all our lives, processes such as competition for scarce resources, civil conflict, exploitation and insufficient income, or marginalisation from social supports. Taken to an extreme, these processes can result in famine in certain situations.

Understanding famine in this way, Hall-Matthews poses the provocative question as to whether globalisation may make famines more or less likely. To answer it requires him to clarify that globalisation in this context refers to four processes of change in today's world: the increase in the volume and value of international trade; improved communication and transport facilities; the increased movement of people both from rural to urban areas within countries and also across borders; and the growing power of global institutions. He then offers an answer to his question by assessing the impact of these global processes on the conditions that give rise to famine.

While increased international trade may open up opportunities for improved livelihoods, it may also marginalise the more vulnerable who don't have the human or physical resources to compete in these markets and who may lose the one secure resource they have, namely the ownership of land. Furthermore, by switching production to cash crops for export, it may drive up the prices of local subsistence crops. Whether these risks materialise depends to some extent on the second feature of globalisation: access to improved communications and transport infrastructure. Infrastructure that will benefit the poor depends on governments to provide it, but in many parts of the world their capacity is being eroded and they are leaving it to private interests to provide such goods. The lack of opportunities that result is driving the third process, namely the increase in migration which is a manifestation of global inequalities. This may open up opportunities for some but it increases risks for many others. Finally, while global institutions like the World Bank, the IMF, the WTO and the UN organisations have more power, are they using this to ensure greater security and opportunities for the poorest?

Hall-Matthews concludes: 'To date, globalisation has been driven by profit and little has been done to ensure that it also addresses the quite different issue of welfare protection.' He points out that in famine-prone areas, there are no more roads, computers or reporters. As a result, there are few new opportunities for trade or democratic accountability that would force either local leaders or international donors to respond to crises. 'If anything, such areas are more marginalised, economically and politically, and more prone to conflict, increasing food insecurity', he adds (Hall-Matthews, 2003: 11).

of the Americas at the end of the fifteenth and beginning of the sixteenth centuries spurred this in important ways but it was the introduction of such technological innovations as the steamship, the railway and the telegraph in the mid nineteenth century that greatly intensified and extended it (after all, Europe's 'scramble for Africa' only began after this). This process received a setback with the First World War, and especially the retreat into protectionism following the Great Depression in 1929, but since 1945 it has been growing in pace and dynamism again. However, many recognise that a qualitative shift occurred in the 1980s and early 1990s that was significant enough to warrant coining the new concept 'globalisation' to try to understand it. What is common to each of the shifts in the story of globalisation is the intersection of technological innovation and state power. We cannot understand the most recent qualitative shift without understanding the technological revolution that has driven it and the changing nature of state power associated with it. These are the subjects of the next two sections.

THE SECOND INFORMATION REVOLUTION

When revising in 1999 his history of the digital revolution published in 1983, Howard Rheingold listed a few contemporary technologies which were not known when the first edition was published (Rheingold, 2000: 321). Among these were mobile phones, home fax machines, ATMs and civilian global positioning satellite receivers; to which he could have easily added the Internet, digital cameras, CD-Roms, DVDs, as well as the fact that the intervening period had seen dramatic changes in the speed, cost, size and variety of other technologies, such as computers and video games, making them virtually unrecognisable as the same products in use 16 years earlier. This highlights the fact that we live in the middle of a revolution in information and communications technologies (ICTs). The diffusion of these new technologies is the fastest in human history, much more rapid than electricity, the motor car, or even television (Webster and Erickson, 2004: 416). After all, the World Wide Web, a daily tool for tens of millions of people at the start of the twenty-first century, was only developed in 1989 and launched into general use in 1994 (Drori, 2004: 434). While technological innovation does not in itself change society, it produces tools that permit new ways of undertaking social activities. Therefore, just as the invention of the railway, the steamship and the telegraph played a major role in the first phase of globalisation that is usually dated to around 1870 (facilitating more dense flows of information, goods and capital around the world), so too the latest ICT revolution is providing the tools that drive the present phase and intimately integrate the lives of so many people into it (though, as Box 4.2 shows, this is by no means true for all).

Central to this revolution was the invention in 1959 of the microchip by Robert Noyce and Jack Kilby, working independently of one another. Noyce went on to found Intel, which in 1971 produced the microprocessor, combining on a single wafer-thin chip thousands of minute electrical circuits for storing and processing large amounts of information reliably and at high speeds. The invention transformed the computer industry and set the scene for the production of ever smaller, faster, cheaper and more reliable computers driven by ever more complex and capable microprocessor chips. The speed of microprocessors doubled every 18 months over the 1990s. By 2004, Intel was preparing its latest range of chips which would put 3 billion transistors into a tiny coin-size chip smaller than its predecessor. Developments in communications technologies happening at the same time opened up new possibilities for the transmission of information. The 1960s saw the launching into orbit of a number of communications satellites relaying both telephone and television signals across the Atlantic. This network was supplemented by other countries around the world over the following decade so that by the end of the 1970s more than two-thirds of all international telephone calls were routed via satellites. The development of the fibre-optic cable in the 1980s marked a major improvement on the copper or aluminium electric power cables that had been in use for over a century. This permitted the transmission of light signals through thin fibres of plastic or glass resulting in lower costs, greater security, higher transmission capacity and less interference. By 1988 a fibre-optic cable spanned the Atlantic. The net result of these major technological breakthroughs has been to allow the storage and processing of vast amounts of information, and its transmission to anywhere in the world virtually instantaneously, all at relatively low cost. A further feature of these innovations is their interconnectivity, thus stimulating the development of novel ways of linking technologies that previously operated more in parallel, such as the camera, the telephone, the television and the keyboard (witness the latest generation of camera phones).

As a result of these technological developments, information itself, and the tools which process and communicate it, have now become

BOX 4.2   BRIDGING THE DIGITAL DIVIDE OR E-IMPERIALISM?

For the UNDP, the digital divide – which it defines as the uneven diffusion of information and communications technology – has caught the attention of world leaders. 'Bridging this divide is now a global objective' (UNDP, 2001: 38). For others, however, the digital divide is simply another expression of longstanding social, economic and cultural divisions worldwide 'which further develops *with* new technologies' (Guichard, 2003: 76; emphasis in original). This raises fears that the attempt to bridge it 'is a vehicle for penetration of Western ideas and ideals', or 'e-imperialism' (Drori, 2004: 439). Debates on the digital divide, therefore, serve to illustrate key disagreements about the role of technology in global development.

There is little doubt about the reality of the digital divide. Taking the Internet as an example, only about 5 per cent of the world's people are online and over 75 per cent of these live in high-income countries which account for only 14 per cent of the global population. Of the half a billion people who live in the 35 least-developed countries, only 1 per cent are online. Unequal use reflects different infrastructural capacities. The whole of Africa has less bandwidth than the city of São Paulo, Brazil, while all the bandwidth in Latin America is equal to that of the South Korean capital, Seoul. Finally, costs vary greatly around the world, related to differentials in income. Differences are evident even among high-income countries. The number of Internet hosts per 1,000 people in 2000 was 200 in Finland, 193 in Norway and 179 in the US, but only 57 in the United Kingdom, 41 in Germany and 36 in France. Compounding the global divide are internal divides. Shanghai and Beijing, with 27 million people, account for 5 million Internet users in China, whereas the 600 million people in its least-connected regions account for only 4 million users. Among India's 1.4 million connections, 1.3 million are in the five most prosperous states. Not surprisingly, well-educated young men account for large percentages of users everywhere (Drori, 2004; UNDP, 2001).

Proponents of the new technology see it as having the potential to leapfrog the obstacles that keep people poor, allowing them to access information from anywhere in the world and, with that, to develop their human capital. Others, however, criticise the focus on technology use, pointing out that one needs high levels of economic capital to access it, of human or cultural capital to find what one is looking for and make use of it, and of social capital to access the services that allow one overcome problems with the hardware or software. Indeed, Castells points out that 'computer sex' is a major and fast-growing use of computer-mediated communications (Castells, 1996: 361). Furthermore, there is little evidence that the new technology is a means to national development or to social justice; even within the most developed and connected countries diffusion tends to be limited to 'hubs', thus widening regional inequalities. In this situation, the fear is that unequal access to the new technology perpetuates existing inequalities but 'also works to further expand inequality, adding dimensions of inequality (digital upon income and education) and of social differentiation (transnational upon urban/rural and male/female)' (Drori, 2004: 446).

high-value commodities in the world economy. Not only has the value of the cross-border sales of technological and office equipment overtaken that of agricultural commodities (Scholte, 2000: 120–1) but the software programmes which drive the equipment, and the content which is communicated through them (information, entertainment, statistics, pornography), have become highly profitable industries. Labels like 'information society', 'knowledge economy', 'network society' or 'new economy' seek to capture this dimension of today's economic and social order. However, such accounts have a tendency to concentrate on flows while paying little or no attention to the economic and social structures which channel these flows in certain ways; central to these structural features are the gross inequalities of wealth, technological knowledge and political power that characterise today's capitalist order more than ever before. They also tend to a certain technological determinism, seeing technology as inevitably resulting in certain economic or social outcomes. They therefore pay little careful attention to how these technologies are helping to transform the spatial organisation of social relations and transactions and to generate transcontinental or interregional flows and networks of activity, interaction and the exercise of power; as the definition offered in the previous section indicated, these are the features that help us decide how the latest ICT revolution is related to globalisation.

These new technologies can be identified as having a significant impact in four key spheres of today's economy and society – finance, production, trade and communication. Developments in telecommunications and information technology have 'transformed the financial services industries' making possible the global integration of financial markets and creating the potential for 'virtually instantaneous financial transactions in loans, security, and a whole variety of financial instruments' (Dicken, 2003: 446–7). Not only is the reach of their operations changed, but the medium of their operation is also transformed. As Susan Strange put it, 'computers have made money electronic', something evident not only in the vast sums that are transferred around the world electronically every day but also in such ubiquitous means of ordinary transactions as credit and debit cards. She identifies computers, chips and satellites as the three key technologies that have transformed the world of finance globally (Strange, 1998: 24). In the sphere of production, information and communications technologies (including advances in shipping and containerisation) have significantly improved companies' ability to organise production transnationally. Held et al. (1999) identify three main developments in the organisation of production to have emerged from this. The first is the shift from hierarchical control to more horizontal forms of networking, involving greater autonomy for subsidiaries and two-way flows of information with head office. The second involves greater subcontracting to small and medium-sized enterprises (SMEs) which 'may have lower costs and be more flexible, thus allowing MNCs [multinational companies] to pass on the costs of adjustment to changing market conditions' (Held et al., 1999: 256). The third they call 'alliance capitalism', as firms in the same industry increasingly cooperate in a range of ventures including subcontracting relationships and franchising, as well as cooperative ventures to develop particular products and enter specific markets. Many of these are not just cross-border but intercontinental. The information and communications revolution has also played a major role in facilitating greater flows of trade, in goods and also in services. National barriers to trade have been sharply reduced as transport costs have fallen, reducing the costs of trading. 'As tariffs and transport costs have declined they have become secondary or even negligible components of the price of traded goods. Under these circumstances global markets are evolving in so far as traditional barriers to trade no longer significantly limit foreign competition in national markets' (Held et al., 1999: 170–1). Finally, in the sphere of communications new technologies are having a major impact not only on the quantity of information flows but also on their form. Held et al. identify five main trends: an increasing concentration of ownership; a shift from public to private ownership; the structuring on a transnational basis of the corporations that emerge; corporate diversification across different types of media products (such as TV, film, books, music); and an increasing number of mergers of cultural producers, telecoms corporations, and computer hardware and software firms (see Box 5.2) (Held et al., 1999: 347).

It is the ways these technologies are being used to transform production and distribution that are driving the transcontinental or interregional flows and networks of activity, interaction and the exercise of power central to our definition of globalisation. In this regard, therefore, Scholte has got the direction of causality wrong when he writes that 'spurred largely by globalization ... information and communications industries have moved to the core of capitalism for the twenty-first century' (Scholte, 2000: 123). Rather, it is the information and communications industries that have spurred the globalisation of capitalism. As Cox has recognised, it is the global organisation of production and global finance that constitute the two principal aspects of globalisation (Cox, 1996: 259–60). They have also intensified the sorts of financial and economic risks identified in Chapter 2. However, the application of technologies to the production and distribution of goods and services is only a partial aspect of what drives globalisation. As Dicken reminds us when he writes of the application of new technologies to the sphere of finance, completely borderless financial trading does not exist 'for the simple reason that most financial services remain very heavily supervised and regulated by individual national governments' (Dicken, 2003: 447). Therefore, it is states that, on their own or in concert through intergovernmental bodies, create the regulatory conditions to facilitate or limit the application of these technologies. For this reason, the next section examines the ways in which states are being reconfigured under the pressures created by the application of new technologies in the spheres of production and distribution.

FROM THE WELFARE TO THE COMPETITION STATE

'Globalization does not bring about the disappearance of the state any more than *real socialism* brought about its "withering away". States have made the framework for globalization' (Cox, 2002: 76–7; emphasis in original). This reminds us that, despite discourse about the withering away of the state or the existence of a borderless world as claimed by hyperglobalists, the waxing and waning of globalisation since the mid nineteenth century has been intimately related to the way states have used their power. While technology may open new opportunities for production, distribution and communication, it is states that have created the frameworks of laws, norms and regulations that shape the ways these opportunities are used. This is no less true today than it was in the past; indeed, some would claim that the state now plays a more crucial role in shaping economic and social outcomes than it ever has before (Weiss, 1998: 209–11). However, while states remain key actors, the situation in which they operate presents them with new challenges and dangers due to the ways in which technologies are helping transform production and distribution. In other words, states are playing their key role in a new environment. How they are responding, how states are reorganising themselves and the ways they operate, is the subject of this section.

Rapley draws our attention to the fact that a focus on the institutions of the state runs the risk of minimising the extent of the changes that have taken place. Instead, he places emphasis on 'regimes', namely 'a prevailing way of doing things based on implicit and explicit norms'. In particular, he emphasises the importance of 'the norms of reciprocity that govern relations between governors and governed, and between dominant and subordinate classes', arguing that 'a stable regime corresponds to an implied contract that binds elites and masses in bonds of mutual obligation' (Rapley, 2004: 6–7). Three forms of such contract can be identified in the era of national capitalism that flowered in the second half of the twentieth century. The most successful was the Keynesian welfare state (KWS) through which the state intervened to sustain demand in the economy and to modify the impact of market forces through institutional welfare benefits. In the world's most industrialised countries (Western Europe, the US and Canada, Australia and New Zealand), broad-based agreement between the political left and right, and between labour and capital, sustained this regime (Pierson, 2004: 100). However, stable regimes of reciprocity were also provided during this period by communist states, in which the state completely controlled the economy, and by many developing states (few of which became coherent developmental states) which 'sought to manage capitalism in such a way as to produce rapid growth and modernization' and through this to maintain the loyalty of citizens (Rapley, 2004: 36). Each of these regimes was sustained by a perceived commitment on the part of the state to promote the welfare of citizens, what Rapley calls 'a mass perception of distributive justice' (Rapley, 2004: 7), derived from a close link between the regime of accumulation (broadly speaking the productive economy) and a regime of distribution (broadly speaking the ways in which the state helped channel economic benefits to citizens).

Focusing on this grand bargain between rulers and ruled helps identify the essence of what has changed in the nature and role of the state under the conditions of contemporary globalisation. But it is important to remember that globalisation is as much a result of this shift in the state as it is a cause of it. For, long before the term globalisation came into widespread use, each of the three regime-types identified above was under pressure. The most dramatic collapse was that of communism in the late 1980s, eroded both by the rigidities of its accumulation regime and the cost of its welfare benefits. Similarly, since the 1970s, throughout the developing world the state was finding it harder and harder to maintain the economic growth on which its legitimacy rested and, under the impact of growing indebtedness, succumbed to pressures to liberalise economically and slim down politically. By the early 1990s, few states around the developing world were still resisting this trend. Arguably, by opening up economies almost everywhere, these regime changes had further intensified the economic and financial interconnectedness of the world that is central to the nature of today's globalisation. For example, by integrating low-wage economies in production chains, liberalisation has increased competitive pressures on producers in more developed countries. Furthermore, such regime changes have undermined state capacity severely: 'As global deregulation has made certain types of capital more footloose, state functions have been cut back in order to pay back debt and attract international capital through low tax rates. In Africa, the cutbacks are sometimes so large as to leave the state a virtual entity' (Carmody, 2002: 54). In this situation, it is no wonder that severe breakdown seems to be a feature of an increasing number of states in Africa (Rwanda, Somalia, Sierra Leone, Liberia). In Latin America, the declining legitimacy of the state as it proves unable to satisfy citizens' demands is leading to a 'profound crisis of governability' (Kirby, 2003: 148).

The most sustained attention, however, has been paid to shifts in the nature of the welfare state, since it was the most successful and enduring of these three regimes. From the late 1960s, welfare states were being undermined by economic recession, by their expense and by a growing perception that they were acting as a fetter on economic success due both to their high cost and to their rigidities (protection for labour, high taxes, lack of incentives). While these pressures originally derived from within nation states, by the 1980s and 1990s pressures deriving from outside were also being recognised, such as those of international competitiveness, the mobility of capital worldwide and intensified international trade (Pierson, 2004: 100–2). As Ruggie has recognised, the globalisation of financial markets and production chains challenges the premises on which the grand bargain between capital and labour rested, since that bargain presupposed a world in which the state could effectively mediate external impacts through such tools as tariffs and exchange rates (Ruggie, 2003: 94). In this situation, welfare states have not collapsed in the way that communist and developing states did, but, as was stated in Chapter 3, they are under pressure to reduce both costs and the level and extent of protection they previously provided. Amid debates about the degree to which globalisation is eroding the welfare state and the ability of social democratic governments and strong trade unions to resist these pressures (Garrett, 2000; Mishra, 1999; Esping-Anderson, 2002; Scharpf, 2000; Kvist and Meier Jaeger, 2003), the focus on regimes allows an identification of the essential shift that has taken place, namely a shift in power relations. As Rapley puts it:

new communications technologies have made possible new forms of corporate organization, making the so-called global firm a reality in a few subsectors. This, in turn, has put both governments and the working class on the defensive. The result has been a shift in the balance of class power and a concentration of wealth on a global scale. (Rapley, 2004: 41–2)

The relations between citizens and their governing elites have been altered in fundamental ways, though this change expresses itself differently in each society according to such factors as the nature of its economy, the strength of social democratic parties, and the legacies it has inherited from the past. Yet, even in the most economically successful states, the links binding the regime of accumulation to that of distribution are being seriously weakened. As a result, vulnerability is increasing (see Box 4.3 on Ireland).

These fundamental changes in the state find expression in attempts to characterise the new regime that is emerging as a successor to the Keynesian welfare state. Jessop sees this 'new state form' as a Schumpeterian workfare state (SWS) which seeks 'to strengthen as far as possible the structural competitiveness of the national economy by intervening on the supply-side; and to subordinate social policy to the needs of labour market flexibility and/or to the constraints of international competition' (Jessop, 1994: 24). In his work, Cerny describes the ways in which state actors, both politicians and bureaucrats, react to the pressures of the global market by 'promoting the competitive advantages of particular production and service sectors in a more open and integrated world economy' (Cerny, 2000: 22). He sees a 'competition state' emerging out of the tensions between the demands of economic globalisation and the embedded state/society practices that characterised the national welfare state as the priorities of policy move away from the general maximisation of public welfare (full employment, redistributive transfer payments and social service provision) to the promotion of enterprise, innovation and profitability in both private and public sectors. In this situation, state actions:

are often designed to enforce global market rational economic and political behaviour on rigid and inflexible private sector actors as well as on state actors and agencies. The institutions and practices of the state itself are increasingly marketized or "commodified", and the state becomes the spearhead of structural transformation to market norms both at home and abroad.[As a result,] the actual *amount* or weight of government imbrication

---

BOX 4.3   THE VULNERABILITIES OF IRELAND'S SUCCESS

For long a laggard in development terms, in the 1990s Ireland achieved some of the highest economic growth rates in the world and became known as the 'Celtic Tiger'. Its success in winning high levels of US foreign investment in some of the leading-edge industrial and service sectors (information technology, software, pharmaceuticals, financial services) led to it being seen as a model of successful development in which the state had played a key role in availing of the opportunities provided by globalisation for a small, peripheral country (Sweeney, 2003). For many of the Central and Eastern European countries which joined the European Union in 2004, Ireland was the model they hoped to emulate.

Yet, in 2003, in its triannual strategy report on Ireland's economic and social policy, the state's National Economic and Social Council (NESC) drew attention to a range of economic and social vulnerabilities that threaten its success. Some of these derive from its small size and peripheral location but others derive from its 'type of economic development' (NESC, 2003: 133). As a small and open economy very dependent on high levels of inward investment, the NESC sees Ireland as being very vulnerable to changes in the international system and to 'extensive decline' through the out-migration of both people and enterprises (NESC, 2003: 54). Furthermore, its very openness makes it difficult to coordinate the actions of employers, unions and government. These economic characteristics 'contain undoubted social vulnerabilities', says the NESC (2003: 133). These include inequalities in opportunities, increased inequality in earnings and incomes, the emergence of 'two-tier' social services, and 'expensive and slow progress on some key infrastructural developments' (2003: 151). The NESC recognises that what it calls 'an internationalised economy' is only socially acceptable 'if a few key aspects of personal and social well-being – housing, education, health services, transport, enough income to live with dignity and, nowadays, training and life-long learning – are secured for everybody'. It adds that these are 'major challenges that must be met if Ireland is to secure its long-run social and economic well-being' (2003: 150).

What the NESC fails to examine is the extent to which Ireland's economic and social vulnerabilities result from the state having resituated itself so that it serves the needs of global capital over the needs of its own citizens. This alternative view sees the Irish success as being very ambiguous and the state's ability to translate economic success into a project of social development as very circumscribed, even if it wished to do so. It therefore offers a more sober reading of the lessons of the Irish case, indicating the limits of translating economic growth into social development under the conditions of real existing globalisation (see Kirby, 2002a, 2004).

in social life can increase … at the same time the power of the state to control specific activities and market outcomes continues to diminish [undermining the] overall strategic and developmental capacity [of state agencies]. (Cerny, 2000: 30–4; emphasis in original)

Cerny concludes: 'The crucial point … is that those tasks, roles and activities will not just be different, but will lose much of the overarching, macro-political character traditionally ascribed to the effective state, the good state or the just state' (2000: 23). In adjusting to the pressures presented by a more globalised economy, therefore, the state has itself become a key actor driving the process. As Rapley puts it:

Driven by the fractions that benefit the most from liberalization, and managed by political elites responding to these challenges, globalization has all along been a directed process. However, once globalization's ball got rolling it would prove very difficult to resist. Countries get into spirals whereby incremental integration into the global economy necessitates a subsequent further integration. (Rapley, 2004: 80–1)

As a consequence, and through the public action of states, 'those rules that favour global market expansion have become more robust and enforceable' (such as intellectual property rights or World Trade Organisation trade dispute resolutions) while, at the same time, 'rules intended to promote equally valid social objectives, be they labour standards, human rights, environmental quality or poverty reduction, lag behind and in some instances actually have become weaker' (Ruggie, 2003: 96–7). This marks a decisive shift in the nature of state regulation: from a regulation that sought to harness market forces for the welfare of society to one that seeks to impose competitive disciplines on society for the good of the market. This is just one example of how the grand bargain between rulers and ruled has been severely weakened if not entirely sundered as public authorities prioritise the well-being of market actors over the well-being of citizens. As a result, there is an increase in social, political and personal threats (see Chapter 2) and an erosion of human and social assets (see Chapter 3).

SOCIAL STRUCTURES OF INFORMATIONAL CAPITALISM

With its focus on the market and on the state, political economy analysis can pay less than adequate attention to the third constituent dimension of these interrelationships, namely society. Society is important, both because as an actor it affects the ways the state and the market interact (its potential for transforming today's form of globalisation is examined in Chapter 9) but also because it is the arena in which impacts on human livelihoods and well-being are most clearly manifested. It is in the latter sense that it will be considered here. Society is often negatively defined as that realm which is constituted by involvement neither in profit-making endeavours nor in formal state power. As such, it is both a vast arena and one whose boundaries are less than exact (are not-for-profit businesses part of the market or of society? Are public bodies such as universities part of the state or of society?). However, while society encompasses broad areas of human activity, it is characterised by structures, even if these social structures are often not immediately evident to those whose lives and prospects are so constrained by them. It is only by identifying these social structures and the ways they impact on individuals' and families' life chances, that we can when analysing social deprivation and similar problems avoid a tendency either towards reducing these to technical issues (levels of welfare payments or access to education) or towards blaming individual or group characteristics (ethnicity or race). When dealing with the multifaceted processes grouped under the label of globalisation, it is especially important that the social structures through which these processes impact on and help structure people's lives are identified. In other words, the impact of global processes is mediated to people through their position in the class structure. If this is not appreciated, there is a tendency to absolve globalisation from any implication in causing growing inequality and social polarisation; indeed, far from being a cause, globalisation is seen as the cure to these ills through linking regions and groups more closely to global flows of capital and trade. This view characterises the approach of the leading multilateral organisations such as the World Bank, the IMF and the WTO.

Examining data on income inequality worldwide, Sklair concludes that 'there is clearly a polarization crisis on a global scale' associated with globalisation. He asks, however, whether this is a class crisis and answers it by pointing to the fact that it is not people's gender, ethnicity or location that causes their poverty but their lack of access to education, to well-paying jobs, to land, to fair prices and to health care. In other words, lack of access to economic resources explains why the poor grow poorer, while access to such resources explains why the rich grow richer. 'It is their relationship to the means of production, to capital in its various forms, that locks most of the poor into poverty, thus it is at its base a class crisis' (Sklair, 2002: 52–3). During the era of national capitalism, debate raged among social scientists about definitions of social class. Marxists emphasised a division based on owners of capital on the one hand and those who sold their labour power on the other. Weberians elaborated a more complex hierarchical class structure based on occupational categories, from a managerial/professional category at the top to an unskilled manual category at the bottom. The benefit of the first was that it paid central attention to the issues of power involved in class structure, though its application to the growing complexity of occupational categories became less clear over time. The second analysis paid more adequate attention to occupational categories but tended to obscure the differential power relations involved. Similar divisions of emphasis are obvious in analyses of how globalisation is changing class structures and how such changes may impact on people's well-being, especially in relation to their vulnerability.

Sklair has introduced the concept of 'the transnational capitalist class' (TCC), as a way of identifying that group which furthers the interests of the global system. This, he clarifies, is not a capitalist class in the traditional Marxist sense of owning the means of production; rather, it is constituted by four fractions: a corporate fraction (TNC executives and their local affiliates); a state fraction (globalising state bureaucrats and politicians); a technical fraction (globalising professionals); and a consumer fraction (merchants and media). The members of this class share global as well as local interests, they come from many countries, and share similar lifestyles, consumption patterns and perspectives on global issues. They exert economic control in the workplace, political control through domestic and international politics, and culture-ideology control through the media and consumerism. 'The concept of the transnational capitalist class implies that there is one central transnational capitalist class that makes system-wide decisions, and that it connects with the TCC in each community, region, and country', writes Sklair (2002: 98–9). Its relative strength is linked to the relative weakness of transnational labour and its principal struggles are not with labour but with what Sklair calls 'localizing bureaucrats and politicians' who wish to protect their state and citizens against intensified global competition. Thus, the site of struggle has shifted from the workplace to the state (Sklair, 2002: 100–5).

Other attempts to identify the changing nature of the class structure focus more on how shifts in the nature of work associated with new technologies are changing occupational categories. Aoyama and Castells summarise their theory of the 'informational society' as involving a shift from the production of goods to services, the rise of managerial professional occupations, the demise of agricultural and manufacturing jobs, and the growing information content of work. Analysing trends in the G-7 countries (the US, Canada, Japan, Britain, France, Germany and Italy) between 1990 and 2000, they find that the informational economy has become a fully fledged reality, involving a growth both in managerial workers but also in semi-skilled service workers, characterised by being both part-time and temporary. However, the authors point out that this characterisation of service work derives either from one small sector (the wholesale and retail trade) or from the influence of gender (more female jobs are part-time), and cast doubt on how widely it characterises semi-skilled service work as a whole. While there was no overall decline in the level of wages in the 1990s, its distribution became much more polarised, though the decline in the share of the lower paid either slowed down or stopped entirely (the reference here is to the three lowest quintiles, namely the bottom 60 per cent of wage earners). However, the growth in wages of the top 5 per cent accelerated during the 1990s (Aoyama and Castells, 2002). Examining the case of Finland, regarded as an exemplar of the new informational economy, Blom, Melin and Pyöriä found a clear polarisation over the 1990s between 'informational workers' (those using information technology in a creative rather than routine way), automatic data processing workers (ADP, using computers in a routine way) and traditional workers who don't use information technology. This manifested itself not only in regard to income but also to work situation (the extent of creativity and learning involved, the extent of surveillance, physical and mental strain). They concluded that informationalisation has not had the same sort of egalitarian effects as did earlier phases of industrialisation and that, while it may increase wealth, 'it is far from certain whether it will foster equity and overall social well-being'. The authors warn that the risk of polarising workers into 'core' and 'disposable' segments of the labour force 'is a threat that needs to be taken seriously' (Blom, Melin and Pyöriä, 2002: 341). While any conclusions that can be drawn from such detailed examination of data are inevitably tentative, they do partially confirm the existence of categories of integrated and precarious workers as indicated in

Cox's outline of the world's changing social structure (see Box 4.4). For evidence of the excluded category, we need to broaden our analysis to focus on regions beyond the core countries.

BOX 4.4   COX'S INTEGRATED, PRECARIOUS AND EXCLUDED WORKERS

Robert W. Cox identifies the changing social structure of the world as consisting of a three-part social hierarchy that is worldwide in extent. While the proportions of population in each level of the hierarchy vary from country to country, the nature of the structure is uniform throughout the world.

At the top of the hierarchy are the *integrated*: this level is made up of those who are essential to the maintenance of the economic system, such as global managers in public and private sectors and the privileged workers who serve global production and finance in reasonably stable employment. These are relatively secure and well-paid workers though they constitute only a small percentage of the global population.

In the middle come the *precarious*: though these may at times have well-paying jobs, they are not essential to the system and are therefore disposable during periods of 'downsizing', 'rationalisation' or 'outsourcing'. This type of employment is expanding in industrialised countries as employment conditions are liberalised, while it constitutes most industrial employment in poorer countries. As Cox writes of this group: 'Its members are placed in an ambiguous position towards the social order: supportive in their concern to find and keep a job, but potentially hostile when insecurity strikes' (Cox, 2002: 84).

At the bottom are the *excluded*: those who are permanently unemployed or who eke out a living through forms of employment marginal to the productive economy constitute this group. Subsistence farmers or many workers in the informal sector are examples. While they may be a minority in industrialised countries, they constitute large percentages of the population in many low-income countries.

Cox points out that this emerging social structure challenges notions of a 'working class' as it divides wage labour between each level of the hierarchy with the result that they have very divergent interests. Yet, he argues that 'the concept of "class" retains vigour and calls for reformulation ... as a means towards the formation of a common front of resistance and movement towards an alternative to the future that is being prepared by globalization' (Cox, 2002: 85).

The UN Economic Commission for Latin America and the Caribbean has identified the changing occupational stratification of the region's workforce and concluded that, by the end of the 1990s, the Latin American workforce could be clearly divided into three relatively homogeneous groups:

- an upper group comprising 9.4 per cent of the workforce, made up of employers, high-level management in the public and private sectors, and high-level professionals, with average incomes almost 14 times higher than the poverty line and an average of over 11 years of schooling;

- an intermediate group, comprising 13.9 per cent of the workforce, made up of lower-level professionals and technical and administrative employees, with average incomes five times higher than the poverty line and an average of 11 years of schooling;
- a lower group, comprising 73.2 per cent of the workforce, made up of traders, manual workers, service workers and agricultural workers. Their average incomes are 2.8 times the poverty line and they have an average 5.3 years of schooling. ECLAC concludes: 'The great majority of workers at this level do not earn enough to raise an average-sized Latin American household out of poverty' (ECLAC, 2000: 66).

This stratification of the workforce reverses previous trends towards upward social mobility in many of the region's countries, a process described as the emergence of 'middle-class societies' as manual and rural occupations gave way to non-manual and urban ones. What ECLAC now finds is that in the 1990s the non-manual and urban occupations that are expanding offered, for the most part, low-productivity, insecure and low-wage employment. As a result, it concludes that 'there is every indication that the occupational structure has become the foundation for an unyielding and stable polarisation of income'. It estimates that whereas at the beginning of the 1990s some 66 per cent of households received incomes less than the average income, by the end of the decade some 75 per cent of households find themselves in this situation (ECLAC, 2000: 61–8).

This evidence, from a region well integrated into global flows of capital and trade, provides strong evidence to support Cox's category of excluded workers. As Pronk has put it: 'Globalization has changed the character of capitalism. There are more people excluded from the system than are exploited in the system. Those who are excluded are being considered dispensable. Neither their labour nor their potential buying power seems to be needed' (Pronk, 2003: 29). What is particularly worrying is that this exclusion appears to be a feature of the social structure of a globalised world. Rapley shows how this differs from the social structure of national capitalism since it transcends the nation state:

By driving up the wages of highly skilled professionals, who thanks to the communications revolution can now forge close bonds with counterparts around the world, globalization has created what some call the new global middle class. Nodes of wealth can emerge in the poorest lands. India, for example, has produced some of the planet's most advanced computing centres. But these herald few benefits to the poor cramped into the slums surrounding them. The rich have forsaken the poor. (Rapley, 2004: 88)

Through new ICTs, facilitated by the state, new global class alliances are being forged and new forms of precariousness and exclusion are emerging as characteristic features of a new global social structure, resulting in the increased economic and personal risks outlined in Chapter 2 and in the erosion of social assets outlined in Chapter 3.

CONCLUSIONS

Defining globalisation in terms of its growing extensity, intensity, velocity and impact in the spatial organisation of social relations and transactions, this chapter has traced how these transformations are manifesting themselves through the application of new information and communications technologies to the spheres of finance, production, trade and communications. The impact of these transformations on the ways in which states relate to the market was traced and the social structure emerging under the impact of the intensified regimes of global accumulation outlined. What has been done, therefore, can be likened to a kind of X-ray of the emerging world order, identifying the features that help structure that order and therefore explain many of the increased risks and the erosion of coping mechanisms covered in Part I of this book. However, these political economy features capture only a part of what characterises today's form of globalisation. Equally essential to understanding globalisation is its cultural dimension; indeed, it is this which gives it its meaning and, through its emphasis on consumption, helps reinforce its legitimacy. This is the subject of Chapter 5.

5
Globalisation's Cultural Worlds

*Since transnational capitalism also breeds isolation and anxiety,
uprooting men and women from their traditional attachments and
pitching their identity into chronic crisis, it fosters, by way of reaction,
cultures of defensive solidarity at the very time that it is busy proliferating
this brave new cosmopolitanism. The more avant-garde the world waxes,
the more archaic it grows.* (Eagleton, 2000: 63)

In today's globalised world, culture has become a site of struggle. As
Alain Touraine has perceptively put it: 'Our culture is no longer in
control of our social organization. … Culture and the economy have
become divorced from one another, as have the instrumental world
and the symbolic world' (Touraine, 2000: 2). Zaki Laïdi puts it even
more starkly when he argues that the end of the Cold War has 'buried
two centuries of Enlightenment' and ushered in 'a world without
meaning' (Laïdi, 1998: 1). A certain tension between meaning and
power lies at the heart of what is being recognised as a new form
of politics associated with globalisation, what Kaldor calls 'identity
politics', namely 'the claim to power on the basis of a particular
identity – be it national, clan, religious or linguistic' (Kaldor, 2001:
6). The tensions – between economic, political and cultural forces
that are fast integrating our world (including our personal worlds)
and forces using culture and identity to react against this integration
– are well expressed in the quote from Terry Eagleton that opens this
chapter. But if culture therefore warrants a treatment separate from
the political economy of globalisation, this is purely a matter of
convenience in presenting the argument, since culture (in the sense
of meaning, values and identities) is intimately interrelated with the
shifts of power between market, state and society analysed in the
previous chapter. Culture and political economy are the two sides
of the coin of a globalised world and one could not exist without
the other. Therefore, whether we follow Touraine in using terms
like culture and social organisation, or adopt Laïdi's terms, namely
meaning and power, the intimate connections between both need
to be emphasised throughout.

Before outlining the contents of this chapter, its use of the term 'culture' needs to be clarified. There are few concepts in the social sciences as slippery as that of culture and it is often used in ways that fail to understand the inherent tensions it embodies. In his survey of the concept's history and development, Eagleton identifies three distinct meanings. One very widely used meaning refers to artistic production, such as books, music, drama, film, dance, cuisine, dress – those elements that help refine and give meaning to our lives. A second meaning treats culture in the plural, namely features of life that distinguish nations (British culture, Ethiopian culture, Aymara culture) or social groups (gay culture, football hooligans' culture, working class culture). Finally, Eagleton emphasises culture's critical charge, namely its criticism of existing society in the light of its ability to envision a more humane social order (such as the Romantics' criticism of industrial society) (Eagleton, 2000: 1–31). He therefore emphasises the many tensions it embodies – between culture as description and as normative speculation, between culture as material production and as spiritual and intellectual freedom, between culture as controlled rationality and as exuberant spontaneity, between culture as refinement and as political contestation. But he also clarifies that culture is not divorced from nor superior to politics but rather that 'it is political interests which usually govern cultural ones, and in doing so define a particular version of humanity' (Eagleton, 2000: 7). As Eagleton puts it: 'Culture is not some vague fantasy of fulfilment, but a set of potentials bred by history and subversively at work within it' (2000: 23). In this way, culture is the site of struggle between meaning and power, as existing power elites seek to legitimise the social order over which they preside by presenting it as embodying perennial and superior values while those marginalised by that order contest its legitimacy through the use of alternative values and social imaginaries.

Distinguishing these different meanings helps structure discussion of the often quite distinct ways in which the concept 'culture' is employed in the social science literature on globalisation. For this reason, the chapter's title refers to 'globalisation's cultural worlds'. A central debate concerns whether globalisation fosters cultural homogenisation or cultural hybridity, and rests largely on the first two meanings of culture: are today's dominant artistic artefacts (such as films and music) resulting in a Westernisation or McDonaldisation of the world and eroding national cultures, or do they embody a cultural hybridity that reinforces national or local cultures? This debate is outlined in the first section of this chapter. But this debate may pay less than sufficient attention to issues of power, identified by Eagleton as being central to a fuller and more complete understanding of culture. For that reason, the second and third sections of this chapter examine two dimensions of how power moulds culture in today's world, dealing respectively with the power of the media and the resultant culture of consumerism, possibly the two central aspects of how the values and meaning of a more globalised social order are propagated and legitimised. Following this, the fourth section turns to culture as social critique, examining how tensions between meaning and political power that characterise today's world are finding an answer in the emergence of forms of identity politics, namely ways in which power is being refashioned and rearticulated through predominantly cultural categories with often violent outcomes. The final section draws conclusions to Chapters 4 and 5, arguing that contemporary globalisation is moulded by a dominant power structure and is best characterised as being a corporate, neoliberal globalisation. The implications of this argument are then highlighted.

GLOBALISING CULTURE?

There is probably no aspect of globalisation that more immediately impacts on our consciousness than does the cultural. Our senses are bombarded daily by sights, sounds, smells and tastes that we at least label as having distant origins, from the images on our TV screens to the music on our radios, and from the foods in our cupboards to the drinks in our bars. Without ever leaving our locality, so intermeshed are our lives in such an international array of products and messages that what used to be familiar distinctions between the indigenous and the exogenous, between the local and the foreign, no longer hold. Equally, we can travel to most places in the world and encounter similar foods and drinks to those we are familiar with at home, not just the ever-present emblems of US-led corporate globalisation, McDonald's and Coca-Cola, but Chinese, Italian or Mexican food or drinks such as Chilean wine, Danish beer or Irish stout. To this extent, our local neighbourhood has opened to the world and the world has become a global village, at least it has for those of us who are middle class, urban dwellers. There is, therefore, something very compelling about the argument that globalisation is leading to the swift emergence of a global culture. But is this really a culture or rather a superficial cultural homogenisation that, in fact, is highly destructive of distinctive cultures? Or, on the other hand, does it mark liberation from the imposition of a narrow imposed cultural straitjacket, offering people the freedom to fashion cultural values and practices that suit their needs?

In the debates on culture and globalisation, three principal positions can be identified (Hall, 1992). The first, Hall labels 'cultural homogenisation'. This is the view that 'within the discourse of global consumerism, differences and cultural distinctions which hitherto defined identity become reducible to a sort of international lingua franca or global currency into which all specific traditions and distinct identities can be translated' (Hall, 1992: 303). This view foresees local particularities progressively disappearing as a common Western consumer culture spreads its influence from metropolitan centres around the world. Countering this view are those who argue that globalisation is giving a new value to local cultures and strengthening them as they are now offered the possibility of global reach. Emblems of this tendency might be the worldwide appeal of the Irish dance troupe 'Riverdance' or the emergence to global popularity of many forms of local 'traditional' music. Furthermore, Hall also points to the strengthening of cultural identity among many immigrant communities in the West where younger generations often reaffirm what is distinctive about their cultures and resist assimilation into the dominant culture. This is sometimes called localisation, or alternatively, glocalisation, to capture the way it exists as a reaction to globalising processes and their impact on the local. A third position emphasises the cultures of hybridity that are emerging 'which draw on different cultural traditions at the same time, and which are the product of those complicated crossovers and cultural mixes which are increasingly common in a globalized world' (Hall, 1992: 310). While there is plenty of evidence to support each of these positions of how globalisation is affecting cultures, it may be more accurate to describe these not as different positions but as dialectical possibilities that describe the impact on individuals and groups of the intensification of cultural intermixing that we associate with globalisation. All these possibilities can manifest themselves not just in the same locales but even in the life of the same person at different times. Neither is it clear that these positions express anything that is particularly new about the world; certainly since the European conquest of the Americas if not before,* processes of cultural homogenisation, local resistances and the emergence of cultures of hybridity can be identified. The only thing that may be new about today's globalisation is that such processes are intensifying and extending their global reach.

But the debates about homogenisation and hybridity may be failing to distinguish clearly enough some of the most fundamental ways in which globalisation is affecting culture. For part of the problem with these debates is the very fluidity of the term 'culture' as used in them, covering both relatively ephemeral fashions (in dress, music and food, for example), but also more far-reaching changes related to shifts in power and threats to well-being. Deploying culture in the first and second senses outlined earlier in this section, they reduce it either to cultural artefacts or to rather well-defined notions of group culture (particularly national cultures). However, these meanings rest on a more fundamental meaning which is defined by Eagleton as 'the complex of values, customs, beliefs and practices which constitute the way of life of a specific group' or, more precisely, 'the domain of social subjectivity' (2000: 34, 39). The failure to be more precise in clarifying how the different meanings of culture relate to one another means that relatively ephemeral shifts in fashions can be equated to more fundamental threats to a people's social subjectivity such as their language. After all, throughout history fashions have been in constant change under the impact of new productive possibilities, access to new materials, and deeper underlying philosophical and theological shifts. Often these changes involved new interactions between the local and the foreign, and the creation of new hybrid cultures as a result (such as the coffee-house culture of eighteenth-century London that emerged as coffee became a fashionable drink amongst people with leisure time). All that seems new about today's globalisation in this regard is the speed and intensity of these changes in fashion.

However, the term 'culture' also encompasses far more fundamental, threatening and at times violent changes in power relations (such as the destruction of the Aztec culture by the Spaniards in Mexico in the 1520s). Here, obviously, far more is at stake for individuals and the collectivities to which they belong since what is changing is the organic coherence of a world that offers social solidarities and

* Hall's three positions describe well the long-term impact on culture in Ireland of the British conquest that first began in 1169 and reached a new level of intensity under the Tudor monarchs.

values which create horizons of meaning to underpin and secure well-being. In debates about the cultural impact of globalisation, what is important is not so much changes in fashion but rather the more fundamental threats to people's social subjectivity, the coherence of their cultural world.

More attention to the fate of languages might help focus on this dimension, as language is arguably *the* core feature of all our cultural worlds that resources, bonds and inspires the values, customs, beliefs and practices which constitute our distinctive ways of life. Often colonised peoples can be more attentive to this dimension as they have experienced the painful consequences of having the coherence of their cultural worlds destroyed. An example of the myopia that characterises much of the debate in this regard is offered by Peruvian novelist Mario Vargas Llosa's spirited defence of globalisation's positive impact on culture: 'The fear of Americanization of the planet is more ideological paranoia than reality. ... Globalization will not make local cultures disappear; in a framework of worldwide openness, all that is valuable and worthy of survival in local cultures will find fertile ground in which to bloom' (Vargas Llosa, 2001: 70). He goes on to illustrate his assertions by taking the example of the Spanish language which, taking advantage of the opportunities offered by globalisation, 'is dynamic and thriving, gaining beachheads or even vast landholdings on all five continents' (2001: 70). What is surprising is that he makes no mention of Aymara (2.2 million speakers) or Quechua (3.6 million speakers), not to mention the other 30 or more indigenous languages of his country. As with most languages, their fate in a globalised world is far less certain (see Box 5.1).

In the light of this evidence, it is hard to be as positive about the cultural impact of globalisation as is Vargas Llosa. For no matter how much hybridity may enrich aspects of our cultural worlds, the variety and richness on which hybridity draws is itself narrowed and impoverished every time a language dies. As McCloskey puts it:

Every language that succumbs to the economic, political, and cultural pressures being applied all over the globe today, takes to the grave with it an encyclopedia of histories, mythologies, jokes, songs, philosophies, riddles, superstitions, games, sciences, hagiographies – the whole cumulative effort of a people over centuries to understand the circumstances of its own existence. It is an enormously frightening thought that nine tenths of that accumulation of wisdom, speculation and observation is to be lost within the next century or so. The corresponding narrowness of the world-views that remain is equally frightening. (McCloskey, 2001: 36–7)

BOX 5.1   LANGUAGES UNDER THREAT

Obituaries are now being written for languages. On 5 November 1995 the Kasabe language died when its last speaker in Cameroon's Adamawa province died. On 8 October 1992 the West Caucasian language Ubuh died for a similar reason. Neither are these exceptional events. It is widely accepted by linguists that, of the 6,000 or so languages now estimated to be spoken on earth, at least 3,000 of them will die over the next 100 years, or one language on average every two weeks. Some linguists regard this as too conservative and predict that 90 per cent of languages will die over this period.

The birth and death of languages is nothing new. When people lived in small communities, largely isolated from the outside world, far more languages were spoken, probably over 100,000 on some estimates. Even today, 1,529 languages are spoken in Papua New Guinea and Indonesia alone, a quarter of the world's languages. Greater interaction between human communities has inevitably led to language change, adaptation, creation and extinction. None of the languages spoken in today's Caribbean region when Europeans first arrived in 1492 now survives. Of the 187 indigenous languages identified in North America, it is estimated that 149 are moribund, meaning they lack intergenerational transmission.

In today's world a growing polarisation is evident in language use, with eight languages having nearly 2.4 billion speakers between them (Mandarin, Spanish, English, Bengali, Hindi, Portuguese, Russian and Japanese) while 1,782 languages (55 per cent of the world's total) have fewer than 10,000 speakers and another 1,075 (25 per cent) fewer than 1,000 speakers. In 2000, there were 51 languages with just a single speaker alive (Crystal, 2000). The emergence of English as *the* global language in the worlds of business, communications and technology, is adding to these pressures. In this context, Ostler fears globalisation 'may pose the biggest threat of all'. As he explains: 'As the world becomes more intertwined, many of those who speak minority languages, especially the young, often begin to regard their native tongues as economic and social liabilities and stop using them' (Ostler, 2003: 30).

The loss for the racial descendants is even more devastating. As the Australian author, David Malouf, expresses it: 'When I think of my tongue being no longer alive in the mouths of men [sic] a chill goes over me that is deeper than my own death, since it is the gathered deaths of all my kind' (quoted in Crystal, 2000: 25). For 'language is our organic connection with our cultural past, the living root through which the sap of that past can rise into, enrich and diversify the growing plant of the future' (Brennan, 1969: 79). If lost, then so also is lost 'the cohesion, the continuity, the consciousness of belonging and the sense of personal and national worth that is the basis of all significant achievement' (Brennan, 1969: 76).

These are the issues at stake in the impact that ever more intense interconnectedness is having on culture, issues that are often missed in the debates on homogenisation and hybridity. As argued above, the differences between the positions may not be as great as sometimes appears. Steger expresses better the more fundamental differences that are emerging in this new situation, when he writes:

> The contemporary experience of living and acting across cultural borders means both the loss of traditional meanings and the creation of new symbolic expressions. Reconstructed feelings of belonging coexist in uneasy tension with a sense of placelessness. Cultural globalization has contributed to a remarkable shift in people's consciousness ... characterized by a less stable sense of identity and knowledge. (Steger, 2003: 75)

The remarkable shift in people's consciousness, with its new symbolic expressions and reconstructed feelings of belonging that characterise the cultural words of today's globalisation, is best understood through examining what are its distinctively new features, namely the role of the media in mediating reality and the culture of consumerism. These are the subjects of the next two sections.

MEDIA MEDIATION

It is a constant in human culture that consciousness of reality is always mediated and structured through a variety of filters that help order people's perceptions of the world around them. Throughout human history, the primary filters were provided by the myths, histories, values and solidarities passed on from generation to generation through the family, the clan and religious and political authorities. Of course, these were never frozen but changed and adapted over time; but there was a sense of continuity even if that was achieved by some generations revolting against their inheritance (during periods of cultural and political revolution, as 'modernising' authorities replaced 'traditional' authorities, for example). So there is nothing new in saying that reality is mediated in today's world. Rather, what is new is the *form* of this mediation, namely that it happens more and more through electronic media of communication and that these are more and more owned and controlled by private commercial interests. Each of these dimensions will be dealt with in turn.

It is estimated that in the United States a television set is on for seven hours every day in the average household and that individual family members watch it for about three hours a day, with children and older people watching the most. Television, and other electronic media like the Internet, have now become the principal source for the stories that the young in particular hear about the world:

> Our children are born into homes in which, for the first time in human history, a centralized commercial institution rather than parents, the church, or the school tells most of the stories. The world of television shows and tells us about life: people, places, striving, power, and fate. It presents both the good and the bad, the happy and the sad, the powerful and the weak, and it lets us know who or what is a success or a failure. (Weimann, 2000: 8)

In doing this virtually from the day we were born, day in, day out, its combined force is 'unprecedented and overwhelming' (Weimann, 2000: 9). The way in which electronic media mediate the world to all of us, and particularly to the young generation as they negotiate the process of socialisation into society, profoundly influences human culture. This derives from its epistemological and psychological impacts, namely how it affects our knowledge of and psychic orientation towards the world around us. The former relates to the world (or worlds) that we know, while the latter has to do with the way our socialisation into the world helps construct our identity.

While virtually limitless access to electronic media appears to offer us the ability to educate ourselves more about the world and to break out of the limitations imposed by family, tradition or even social class, many viewers are often very unaware of the ways in which the images and messages they receive are structured for them, 'filtering out many of the complexities of reality' to adapt them to mass audiences and to the preconceived views of media producers (and, at times, owners). In the ever more intense battle for ratings, the black-and-white assertion of the soundbite replaces nuanced presentation and argument, dramatic and larger-than-life events and spectacles replace more accurate portrayals of the range of human experiences, ever more graphic and heightened portrayals of violence and sexual encounters replace sensitive and contextual treatment of the horrors or the tenderness of what is being shown. Furthermore, over a typical period in front of a TV one will switch in quick succession from fiction to news, from entertainment to documentary. Without us realising it, 'an important element of the mass-mediated world is the integration of news and entertainment, facts and fiction, events and stories – into a symbolic environment in which reality and fiction are almost inseparable' (Weimann, 2000: 5). The characters in soap operas can become more real and better known to us than our next-door neighbours while the horrors of war or famine can come to seem more fictional than prime-time dramas. In this situation, the lines between fact and fiction become blurred in real life, as when US Vice President Dan Quayle attacked the values of the main character in a TV soap, Murphy Brown, during the 1992 presidential election only to find his speech being viewed by Brown in the soap who then went on the offensive against the Vice President. As Castells says of the outcome, the soap increased its audience share 'while Dan Quayle's outdated conservatism contributed to the electoral defeat of President Bush' (Castells, 1996: 373). Weimann tells us that during the first Gulf War he watched on CNN from a bunker in Haifa Scud missile attacks on the next street from him only to find out afterwards how 'distorted, manipulated, and censored the pictures, the numbers, and the facts transmitted to us were' (Weimann, 2000: 10). In these ways, we are being socialised into 'second-hand worlds' (Weimann, 2000: 10), created and mediated to us by ever more commercialised filters.

But the ways we are socialised into these worlds are also affecting our psychological orientation towards the world. When engaging with electronic media, we may be seated in one place but, as Bauman reminds us, by zapping through cable or satellite channels, we are 'jumping in and out of foreign spaces with a speed much beyond the capacity of supersonic jets and cosmic rockets, but nowhere staying long enough to be more than visitors, to feel *chez soi*' (Bauman, 1998: 77). This is probably the most commonly experienced instance of the 'space-time compression' that some theorists see as being the essence of globalisation, namely the erosion of a sense of place and distance through the ability to communicate instantaneously and have the sensation of being present in distant places. While this appears to liberate us from the constraints of space, it does so by breaking down the natural connection between identity and the physical world, place and received meanings. Thus, as Schirato and Webb (2003) put it, it seduces and threatens our sense of identity by continuously confronting us with images, narratives, information, voices and perspectives from all over the world that challenge whatever meanings we have received from our own culture. For the young, it undermines what has been the normal form of socialisation which happened through the establishing of boundaries by adult authority figures and the passing on of basic value orientations towards society within these boundaries. Through today's media saturation, boundaries are continuously being challenged, not just geographical boundaries but also boundaries of value systems, with the result that the socialisation into stable identities is replaced by having to 'make do', improvising and borrowing identities from various sources (Schirato and Webb, 2003: 151–2). Since identity involves a sense of belonging to a community (see the penultimate section later in this chapter for a fuller discussion of identity), what media seem to offer is the possibility of choosing or indeed even fashioning communities that suit our individual tastes. In the world of digital TV, we can subscribe to the channels that we choose, whether for sports, news, porn or history, and never be confronted by what we don't want to hear about. Similarly, some newspapers allow subscribers to construct their own version online, choosing those news items that interest them and discarding the rest. In these ways, we can filter out those realities of the world that might challenge us, constructing our 'imagined communities' to which to belong. At its more extreme, the Internet provides the opportunity of identifying and creating imagined communities whose purpose is to damage and destroy, whether these be communities of paedophiles, the racist right, al-Qaeda or homophobes. As Touraine starkly sums up the psychological impact of this fragmentation and individualisation of social experience in today's world: 'The ego has lost its unity. It has become multiple' (Touraine, 2000: 3).

Adding to, and greatly defining the impact of, media mediation is the fact that more and more media are owned and controlled by private commercial interests. This marks another major change associated with globalisation. For up until the 1980s much of the world's electronic media was publicly owned, and seen by states as a crucial tool to create a strong sense of national identification among their citizens, a national 'imagined community' with a strong public sphere. While most of the print media was privately owned, it was firmly regulated by public authorities who sought both to ensure that its content served the public interest and to avoid excessive concentration of ownership so that no particular private interests could dominate media output. Of course, in many authoritarian states, dominance by commercial interests was replaced by political domination. However, following the example of the United States and Britain in the 1980s, country after country began to deregulate its media, allowing private media corporations to compete with or take over public broadcasters. Structural constraints on broadcasting such as restricting ownership or requiring licences were modified. Public service requirements were removed as were restraints on advertising and programming. Similarly laws against dominant control of the print media have been weakened; as recently as 2003 President George W. Bush allowed corporations to own a higher percentage of local media while, in Britain, the House of Lords tried to prevent the Blair government from further deregulating media ownership. Kellner summarises the major changes that have taken place:

> In the era of intensifying globalization of the 1990s and into the new millennium, market models of broadcasting generally emerged as dominant in many parts of the world, and a series of global mergers took place that consolidated media ownership into ever fewer hands. The result has been that a shrinking number of giant global media corporations have controlled a widening range of media in corporate conglomerates that control the press, broadcasting, film, music, and other forms of popular entertainment, as well as the most accessed Internet sites. Media have been increasingly organized on a business model, and competition between proliferating commercialized media have provided an impetus to replace news with entertainment, to generate a tabloidization of news, and to pursue profits and sensationalism rather than public enlightenment and democracy. (Kellner, 2004: 216)

As a result, the media mediated world into which we are socialised is increasingly being constructed by a small number of giant media conglomerates (see Box 5.2).

BOX 5.2   MONOPOLISING THE MEDIA

In the various editions of his book *The Media Monopoly*, Ben Bagdikian has traced the growing monopolisation of the US media by an ever smaller number of corporations – from 50 in 1983 to six in 2000 (Bagdikian, 2000). Furthermore, whereas in the past the trend was towards concentration of ownership *within* different sectors of the media such as newspapers, television, books and films, the deregulation of the media in the 1990s has spurred growing concentration *across* these sectors with corporations seeking to control all parts of the media chain, from the creation of content to its delivery to audiences. As Alger writes: 'Increasingly, the megamedia giants have become multimedia owners – owners of various combinations of broadcast and cable TV networks, TV and radio stations, cable TV distribution systems, satellite TV systems, movie and TV entertainment programme production companies, book and magazine publishing, and Internet operations, as well as newspapers' (Alger, 1998: 31). In this situation, 'no content – news, entertainment, or other public messages – will reach the public unless a handful of corporate decision-makers decide that it will' (Bagdikian, 1997: x).

▶

Who are these giant corporations whose media influence is now global in reach? The top ten can be listed as follows:

- AOL/Time Warner: worth $36.2 billion with interests in magazines (including *Time* and *Life*), television (including CNN), cable, television and film production, Internet (America Online, CompuServe, Netscape), music, books and sports.
- Disney: worth $25.4 billion with interests in television (ABC network), films (Miramax, Buena Vista International, Touchstone), radio, magazines, books, resorts, sports, theatre and videos.
- Liberty Media: worth $42 billion with interests in television (Discovery and the Learning Channel), Internet, radio, music, sports, films (USA Films), magazines, cable and satellite, and TV production.
- Viacom: worth $20 billion with interests in film (Paramount Pictures, Nickelodeon Movies, MTV Films), books (Simon & Schuster, The Free Press), television (CBS, MTV, Nickelodeon, the Movie Channel, Sundance Channel), magazines, theme parks, advertising, radio and Internet.
- Vivendi: worth $37.2 billion with interests in television (USA Network, Sci-Fi Channel), cable and satellite, TV and film production (Universal Studios, PolyGram Films), Internet, magazines (*L'Express*), books (Houghton Mifflin), music (MCA, Mercury), newspapers (in France), theme parks and cell-phone services.
- Bertelsmann: worth $16.5 billion with interests in television and film (Europe's largest broadcaster and film producer), books (Random House, Knopf, Vintage, Bantam Doubleday), magazines, radio, music (over 200 labels in 54 countries), newspapers (11 dailies in Germany and Eastern Europe) and Internet.
- News Corporation: worth $11.6 billion with interests in television (Fox, National Geographic), newspapers (*The Times, Sun, News of the World, Australian, The New York Post*), film production (Twentieth Century Fox), books (HarperCollins), sports, music and Internet.
- Sony: worth $53.8 billion with interests in film (Columbia Pictures, Screen Gems, Revolution Studios), television (Telemundo and more than 25 channels in Spain, India, Japan and Latin America), broadcast and electronics equipment (including tapes, batteries, semiconductors, floppy disks), games (PlayStation), music (labels include Columbia, American, Epic and Sony) and Internet.
- AT&T: worth $66 billion with interests in television (networks, stations and network providers), films, radio, music and telephone networks.
- General Electric: worth $129.9 billion with a wide range of interests in electronics, military industries, nuclear and electrical power, financial services and aircraft engines, but it also has interests in television (NBC), cable (AT&T Cablevision), TV production and the Internet.

Many of these have overlapping ownership: AT&T owns 8 per cent of News Corporation, Liberty Media owns 4 per cent of AOL/Time Warner (The Nation, 2001). Furthermore, as Sklair reminds us, Bertelsmann, Vivendi, NewsCorp and Sony originate respectively in Germany, France, Australia-UK and Japan, while many so-called American media are subsidiaries of these: Houghton Mifflin publishers, Universal Studios, Fox, and PlayStation (Sklair, 2002: 184).

In this situation, culture in the sense of the complex of values, customs, beliefs and practices which constitute each society's way of life is being more and more colonised by private interests whose reach and influence is ever more global. Diversity is narrowed as a similar consumerist worldview finds expression through the media. Debate about issues of public importance is all too often replaced by a passive consumption of entertainment products. And our children are being intensely socialised into this culture virtually from birth. Schirato and Webb summarise its implications:

> [T]he media and communications now occupy a hegemonic place with regard to the social, precisely because their role is to transform the social into something else – a kind of simulation of the capitalist system of production. In other words, everything that is considered inalienable within society – sporting teams, artistic production, human body parts, children and childhood – is to be reformulated and rethought as alienable, as being subject to the market. The imperative, then, is to produce subjects disposed to see and understand the world almost exclusively through capitalist eyes and categories. (Schirato and Webb, 2003: 137)

In these ways, the most intimate spaces of our personal and family lives are being made vulnerable to market forces. In saying this, however, it is important to stress that there is a difference between media content and how that content is appropriated by viewers and listeners. For example, as Thompson reminds us, Western films and pop music circulated in Iran as part of a popular cultural underground 'taking on a subversive character' and helping to create an alternative cultural space within what many experienced as a repressive regime (Thompson, 1995: 175). However they are designed, therefore, media messages are always appropriated in different ways by different audiences according to their material and symbolic resources.

CONSUMERISM

If a global culture is emerging through the incessant flows of images, sounds, goods and services around the world, especially those that bombard our senses through the media, then it is a culture of consumerism. For, as Goodman puts it, 'our central shared values have to do with consumption. … Indeed, it seems that every human expression from art to sex to outrage, is either sold as a commodity or used to sell a commodity. It is this consumer culture that is now spreading over the entire world' (Goodman, 2004: 235). This culture promotes heterogeneity in that it is happy to adopt indigenous cultural forms (including symbols of protest) in its constant creation of ever new and alluring commodities. Yet it simultaneously homogenises since all this rich variety is incorporated into a common culture of consumerism. Thus, its products are endlessly heterogeneous but its processes homogenise since consumption becomes 'our model for dissent, our model for freedom, our model for political activity. All alternatives to consumer culture – the simple life, the spiritual, the traditional, the local – become variant consumer fantasies' (Goodman, 2004: 242).

The central value of this culture as well as its novelty is not consumption but consumerism. Consumption has always been a central feature of all human cultures; indeed, in some of them it has been given a core ritual significance (for example, the place of the Eucharist in Christian culture). What is new about the culture of consumerism is that consumption is now elevated to the predominant value and central activity of human culture, so that it is no longer an activity whose primary purpose is to satisfy needs (either biological or spiritual) but rather an activity driven by induced wants; for this reason, it never satisfies since new wants are all the time being created by the culture. The fundamental change in values being wrought by this culture of consumerism is expressed well in Bauman's question: do we consume to live (as has happened throughout all of human history) or do we live to consume (the characteristic of this new culture)? (Bauman, 1998: 80–1). Commodities are therefore being consumed not for themselves but rather for the meanings associated with them, as is well illustrated by the central role played by branding in this culture (Klein, 2000). One can speak therefore of the 'consumption of the symbolic meaning of goods' (Elliott, 2004: 135), meanings such as success, freedom, sexiness, prosperity and power. Though the culture of consumerism is sometimes seen as being quintessentially American, this is to confuse the origin of much of the culture with its essence. For the same values find expression in the highly successful TV soap operas produced in Latin America or Asia while global chains such as Benetton (Italian), the Body Shop and Pret a Manger (both British) are as much part of this globalised culture as are McDonald's or Starbucks.

The symbolic meanings attached to consumption are created by a powerful transnational advertising industry. This is now one of the most globalising industries with a small number of global companies having interests in countries throughout the world. These concentrate on promoting a relatively small number of consumer goods such as soaps and detergents, tobacco, drugs, perfumes, deodorants, toothpaste, processed foods, alcohol, soft drinks and cars, all products characterised by high profits, high spending on advertising as a ratio of sales, and a high penetration by transnational companies (Sklair, 2002: 180–3). However, far more important than the goods being sold, what this industry sells are the values of consumption itself, 'engineering social, political, and cultural change in order to ensure a level of consumption that is the basis for a global consumer culture' (Sklair, 2002: 181). This change reaches far beyond our patterns of consumption, changing social institutions and practices so that they are made compatible with the values of consumerism. So, for example, religion has for some become a consumer choice. 'People still have religion, but increasingly, they "shop around" for the right religion and choose one that fits their lifestyle. Religion is not a tradition that we are inextricably embedded in; instead it is chosen, consumed, and sometimes discarded, returned, or exchanged like any other commodity' (Goodman, 2004: 235). In similar ways, education, news, politics and sex have become consumer commodities to be bought and sold. In the process, fundamental values are promoted such as individualism and impermanence. As Bauman puts it:

> Ideally, nothing should be embraced by a consumer firmly, nothing should command a commitment till death do us part, no needs should be seen as fully satisfied, no desires considered ultimate. There ought to be a proviso 'until further notice' attached to any oath of loyalty and any commitment. It is but the volatility, the in-built temporality of all engagement, that truly counts; it counts more than the commitment itself, which is anyway not allowed to outlast the time necessary for consuming the object of desire (or, rather, the time sufficient for the desirability of that object to wane). (Bauman, 1998: 81)

But the values promoted are not just personal ones. Consumerism also holds out the prospect of satisfying social values such as choice, equality and democracy. After all, in entering a shopping mall one enters a realm which makes no distinctions and which offers anyone who can afford it the promise of consuming. Yet, as Baudrillard recognises, far from satisfying these values, what consumerism does is to conceal the absence of them (Baudrillard, 1998: 50). Indeed, the only choice that consumerism does not offer is the choice not to consume: in this way, the apparent array of endless choices conceals the lack of choice between different value systems about what matters in life. And, paradoxically, in imposing consumption as the ultimate reason for working, it forces many people to work harder in order to maintain their levels of consumption. Ultimately, therefore, what advertising sells is the view that our happiness depends on consuming, leaving 'little space for competing conceptions of the good life' (quoted in Goodman, 2004: 230). Its remarkable success lies in its ability to conceal what it is ultimately doing – imposing a homogenising culture throughout the world that profoundly penetrates all spheres of human life with market values.

As with all cultures, the culture of consumerism creates its own infrastructure to facilitate its cultural practices. This includes the changes in retailing which have seen large self-service supermarkets, some of them huge transnational companies like Wal-Mart, Sears and Marks & Spencer, replace small, local shops; in doing this it has often displaced the location of consumption (and of much social life) from town centres to their edges. More and more these supermarkets are located in what is perhaps the primary institutional creation of the consumer culture, the shopping mall, what Chilean sociologist Tomás Moulian calls 'the cathedral of consumption … a place conceived to eroticise' (Moulian, 1998: 55, 56). In the United States, over one billion square feet of total land area has been converted into shopping malls, or 16 square feet for every man, woman and child (Gini, 2000). And there are now few large cities in the world where such malls do not exist, testaments to the homogenising processes of consumerism. Associated with the growth of the shopping mall has been the growth in franchising chains. While such chains have long been associated with fast-food outlets, in the 1990s they extended to clothing stores, car dealerships, specialised stores and services. These spaces become not just places to buy but centres of leisure and relaxation; in the United States shopping is now the chief cultural activity after watching television (Gini, 2000). Indeed, so ubiquitous has consumption become that the home has now been turned into a virtual retail outlet with cable shopping channels on TV, mail-order catalogues delivered unsolicited, and ever more extensive facilities to buy goods and services over the Internet. But how do people, many of them on modest incomes, actively participate in such leisure activities? This question is especially acute since these outlets serve to create new dependencies on imported goods, such as foods, clothes and household products, which in many cases may be more expensive to buy than their locally produced equivalents. This requires the extension of mechanisms of credit, especially the ability to buy goods through paying by monthly quotas or multiple credit cards (actively marketed by stores to their customers), each of which has its own limit but without there being any limit on the number of cards an individual consumer can have (see Box 5.3).

Consumerism is now a global culture offering the poor of the developing world three things, as Sklair puts it: cheap imported

---

BOX 5.3   CHILE'S 'CREDIT-CARD CITIZENSHIP'

In its report on the cultural identity of Chileans today, the Chilean office of the United Nations Development Programme (UNDP) wrote that, 'for many Chileans, consuming has a similar meaning to that held by work in the past. It is the physical expression of individual identity, while at the same time being a new material anchor to social belonging' (PNUD, 2002: 98). It found that the number of credit cards held by Chilean consumers has grown steadily from 1.35 million in 1993 to 7.05 million in 2000, or about one card on average for every second Chilean.

Sociologist Tomás Moulian writes that the pervasive culture of consumerism that has resulted from the thorough neoliberalisation of the Chilean economy by the military dictatorship (1973–90) is leading to a new form of citizenship which he calls 'credit-card citizenship' (Moulian, 1997: 102). Through the use of multiple credit cards, people can achieve levels of consumption beyond what their incomes would permit. By this means, they achieve their social identity and sense of belonging, thereby replacing an earlier practice of citizenship through belonging to political parties, trade unions and other collective organisations oriented to social change.

Credit-card citizenship results in a conservative and conformist culture, writes Moulian, since it leads to high levels of personal indebtedness and therefore long hours of work. As self-esteem results from the ability to consume, people seek to avoid anything (such as political action or social critique) that might interfere with this ability. 'Alienated by the individualistic illusion of consumerism, it is difficult to rediscover the lost practices of collective action', Moulian writes (1997: 103).

In its survey of Chileans' attitudes towards their country, the UNDP found 'a hollowing out of a sense of collective identity' (PNUD, 2002: 64). The report identifies three experiences of being Chilean: the proud Chilean, made up of older and better off people who are proud of the country's history and customs; it comprises 32 per cent of the population. The second is the insecure Chilean, made up of middle-income educated people who feel a sense of confusion about what it is to be Chilean and a disillusion about all that has changed in Chile; it comprises 38 per cent. The final one is the angry Chilean who does not feel part of society. This is composed of lower class and less well-educated people and comprises 30 per cent of the population. The UNDP concludes: 'The lack of a sense of a future means that people experience change as an erosion of identity and security' (PNUD, 2002: 70–4). This is the consequence of consumerism and credit-card citizenship.

goods, a veil to obscure the difficult material conditions in which they live, and symbols of a different life (Sklair, 1993: 32). Indeed, for so many of the world's people, its potency derives from the lack of choice (both of goods to buy and of wider social and political opportunities) that has always characterised their lives. For what consumerism appears to offer is the prospect of sustainable prosperity. This exercises a particularly strong influence on the young to whom consumerism provides 'a symbolic vocabulary and resource for identity construction and maintenance' (Elliott, 2004: 129) through the incessant bombardment of images and sounds. This is most clearly seen in youth culture as young people create a meaning and a sense of belonging through adapting styles of dress and self-presentation, codes that distinguish them in the eyes of their peers. For example, Kjeldgaard reports the various styles and sub-cultures through which young people in Copenhagen identify themselves: hip-hop, pop-girl ('the Britney Spears look'), the techno-types, pop-boy, the skater-look (Kjeldgaard, 2002: 389). Though highly influential and all-pervasive, the culture of consumerism is also inherently volatile, as its constant novelty leads to what Kjeldgaard calls a 'globalization of fragmentation' as it increases the flows of symbols and meanings to the consumer (2002: 387). Furthermore, for so many of the world's people, their lack of income prevents them from realising its promise, thereby fostering a sense of alienation. For example, the UNDP estimates that only a quarter of Chileans can participate in consumer culture while another 20 per cent base their identity on being seen to participate but do not have adequate means to do so. The remaining 55 per cent cannot participate and feel losers and impotent as a result (PNUD, 2002: 100–1). For some, this situation can foster new modes of resistance. Through such resistances, people seek to claim back forms of power that have been lost in the transformations we label globalisation. This tension between power and meaning is the subject of the next section.

IDENTITY, BELONGING AND VIOLENCE

The power of the media and the culture of consumerism it helps propagate are central features of the economic system that has emerged from the application of new information and communication technologies to the spheres of production and distribution, as was outlined in Chapter 4. Just as the technological and institutional features of this system cannot be separated from one another, so also must the cultural features outlined so far in this chapter be seen as an integral dimension of today's globalised system. These various dimensions – the economic, the political, the cultural – all constitute the power of that system. But no system is all-powerful and, as already mentioned at the beginning of this chapter, culture is also a sphere of social critique where meanings subversive of the dominant social order find expression. Indeed, as was briefly outlined there, for some analysts there exists a greater gap today between the power of the dominant system and the meanings that give value to people's lives. This section examines the origins and nature of this gap and the ways in which culture is being used as a means to contest the system's power over people's lives.

The concept of identity brings us to the heart of these issues. For up to this point the present chapter has discussed culture as a force that impacts on the lives of people and communities from the outside, as it were. Identity reminds us that we also generate our own values and meanings to live by; that we use the raw materials available in our wider culture to fashion our individual identities. These identities give us a role in society, a sense of belonging. While all identities are necessarily multiple (one takes identity from one's place of birth, one's occupation, one's family status, one's recreation activities, etc.), these multiple elements are incorporated into an overriding and more fundamental identity, what Castells has called 'a primary identity' that frames the other elements of identity and that is self-sustaining (Castells, 1997: 7). For much of human history, individuals were socialised into quite a restricted identity intimately related to where they came from, their family and their role in society. Few people had many opportunities to change that in any fundamental way. With the emergence of more modern and mobile societies, however, the state became ever more important in fostering a strong sense of national identity, through the development of national educational systems, mass media and democratic politics. As Tomlinson puts it: 'Since the eighteenth century, national identity has been the most spectacularly successful modern mode of orchestrating belonging' (Tomlinson, 2003: 274). Central to this national identity was the role of citizen, combining a sense of meaning and belonging with a sense of having some modicum of power in society. Through widespread and determined popular struggles such as nationalist movements, the workers' movement and movements for liberal democracy, power was wrested from oligarchic elites and gradually democratised, though of course the distribution of that power still remained highly unequal.

At least, however, a system emerged that combined meaning with power; in other words, people's active involvement in the structures of their society could make a real difference to how power was used in that society. Citizenship, a sense of belonging to a national community, mattered to most people and helped integrate people into society.

Contemporary globalisation, by contrast, has been characterised by:

> the weakening of former national identities and the emergence of new identities – especially the dissolution of a kind of membership known as 'citizenship', in the abstract meaning of membership in a territorially defined and state-governed society, and its replacement by an identity based on 'primordial loyalties', ethnicity, 'race', local community, language and other culturally concrete forms. (Friedman, 1994: 86)

The reasons for this shift are not hard to find. Rapley reminds us that, during the period of state-led national capitalism, 'regimes bound citizens in relationships of vertical loyalty to the state, which looked after many and often most of their material needs', so that 'loyalty and a sense of collective identity were bound to be strong' (Rapley, 2004: 63). In this situation, collectivism and self-sacrifice for the common good were seen as virtues and greed as a vice. As the state withdrew from this role, however, and as it left individuals to survive more and more on their own, individualism came to be valued more highly. 'Greed would come to be celebrated as a virtue, and self-sacrifice as a folly' (Rapley, 2004: 63–4). For Castells, the new flexibility and impermanence associated with conditions of work 'blur the boundaries of membership and involvement, individualize social relationships of production, and induce the structural instability of work, space, and time' (Castells, 1997: 66). Globalisation has also been associated with 'a growing cultural dissonance between those who participate in transnational networks which communicate through e-mail, faxes, telephone and air travel, and those who are excluded from global processes and are tied to localities even though their lives may be profoundly shaped by those same processes' (Kaldor, 2001: 69–70). Touraine summarises the effects of these changes on people's identities: 'As it becomes more difficult in this globalized society to define oneself as a citizen or a worker, it becomes more tempting to define oneself in terms of a cultural community such as an ethnic group, a religion or belief, a gender or a mode of behaviour' (Touraine,

2000: 31). Castells highlights the essence of what happens: 'The search for meaning takes place then in the reconstruction of defensive identities around communal principles' (Castells, 1997: 11). Discussion of identity, therefore, needs always to be placed in the context of changes in people's material conditions. For identity refers not only to establishing a 'source of meaning and experience' as Castells puts it (1997: 6), but this meaning derives from people's sense of belonging to a wider collectivity through which their material interests are secured. The erosion of a strong sense of national identity has come about because this no longer provides many people with a secure way of ensuring a decent livelihood; instead, people give priority to particular ethnic (for example, Hutus or Tutsis in Rwanda), religious (for example, identification with Islam, Hinduism or fundamentalist Christianity) or sub-national (Kosovar or Chechen) identities as a way of protecting themselves against what they see as threats from others, or struggling for more local autonomy based on ethnic grounds. What is important here, of course, is not some 'objective' assessment made in conditions where people have access to a wealth of information on different options to choose. What is important are people's perceptions that identifying with a particular cultural community is 'functional to their personal material interests' even if that may not turn out to be true or may not be understood by those outside that community (Rapley, 2004: 52). For what it offers is a sense of individual security rooted in a collective identity, a sense of belonging to a wider group. The essential point about shifting identities is made by McSweeney: 'We can be led to perceive ourselves differently – to choose a different position on the continuum of identities – by the opportunities which may be offered to satisfy new interests' (McSweeney, 1999: 167).

It is for this reason that one dominant form of politics in a more globalised world is called 'identity politics', namely 'the claim to power on the basis of a particular identity – be it national, clan, religious or linguistic' (Kaldor, 2001: 6). In a situation of struggle over scarce resources, often associated with the collapse of states or the neoliberal restructuring of economies, 'new forms of power struggle may take the guise of traditional nationalism, tribalism or communalism, but they are, nevertheless, contemporary phenomena arising from contemporary causes and displaying new characteristics' (Kaldon, 2001: 70). Four such characteristics of this form of politics are identified here. Firstly, being based on particularistic identities that, by definition, are exclusive to some, this politics serves to fragment rather than to integrate. This is obvious in the disintegration of a number of states (Yugoslavia, USSR, Czechoslovakia, Ethiopia), and the breakdown of others (Somalia, Rwanda, Liberia, Sierra Leone, Democratic Republic of the Congo) in the 1990s. Secondly, identity politics introduces a new volatility into social life as the relationship between interests and identities becomes more provisional and less secure. This is evident, for example, in the growth of the 'new right' in the politics of many Western European states. Thirdly, identity politics tends to be conflictive, at its most extreme leading neighbour to turn against neighbour in brutal savagery, as happened in Rwanda, Bosnia, Kosovo and East Timor. But even in more intimate domestic spheres, concerns with identity are associated with violence, as for example in discussions of male violence and identity (see Box 5.4). Finally, identity politics can often be defensive and reactive, as expressed in the epigraph with which this chapter opens. In this way culture breeds resistance to what is perceived as a system that cuts off and excludes large parts of humanity. Instead of seeking benefits and a future within this system, therefore, people turn against it and seek to resist it, in extreme cases fuelling support for what has come to be called 'the new terrorism' (see Chapter 2). Neither is this reaction limited to those in developing regions. It must not be forgotten that a sense of threat to their way of life has also motivated groups in the United States – sometimes associated with fundamentalist Christianity – to take up arms and support a politics of resistance (see Castells on the American militia (1997: 84–97)).

No easy judgements can be made about identity politics. While some may lament the erosion of what Kaldor calls the 'politics of ideas' (2001: 77), with its liberal secular character and its integrative function, others welcome the emergence of a form of politics that seems to be more effective in challenging the destabilising inroads of market forces which benefit some but marginalise many more. For example, the uprising in 1994 by the Zapatista Army of National Liberation (EZLN) in the Chiapas region of southern Mexico won widespread international support. While identity politics has won new recognition and rights for women, indigenous peoples, gays and lesbians, people with disabilities and speakers of minority languages around the world, it has also fuelled highly destructive forms of political action such as terrorist and communal violence, and mafia gangs. Its emergence is linked to the vulnerability and violence that arises from the resituating of the state and the growing polarisation in the world's social structure, both processes intimately associated with globalisation (see Chapter 4). It is therefore unlikely to disappear soon.

BOX 5.4   MASCULINITY IN CRISIS OR IDENTITY POLITICS?

At the beginning of the twenty-first century, one identity under attack is the masculine. 'Serious commentators declare that men are redundant, that women do not need them and that children would be better off without them' (Clare, 2000: 3). Anti-social behaviour – such as violence, the sexual abuse of children, illicit drug use, alcohol misuse, and gambling – is predominantly a male activity. Indeed, men are also much more likely than are women to inflict violence on themselves through suicide. 'When it comes to aggression, delinquent behaviour, risk taking and social mayhem, men win gold' (Clare, 2000: 3).

Two principal reasons are given for this so-called 'crisis of masculinity'. One relates to the erosion of their monopoly of power in both public and private spheres, as women challenge the dominant roles played by men. As this happens, values that were seen to be 'manly' virtues (courage, strength, will, virility) are increasingly seen as vices (aggression, violence, detachment, coldness). The second main reason relates to the changing nature of work as the secure identity men received from their role as workers has been eroded by flexible conditions, the increasing number of women in the labour force, technology and the decline in traditional male jobs. Taken together, these result in 'a deep sense of uncertainty and instability' for many men (Beynon, 2002: 89).

And yet, what is a crisis for some men may be a liberation for others, as men are freed from the more restricting roles of previous generations and adopt a more varied 'bricolage style of masculinity than did their fathers' (Beynon, 2002: 95). Instead, the crisis may be class-specific, affecting men of lower social classes and of ethnic origins who bear the brunt of unemployment or low-status jobs. In this situation, McDowell reports that 'in circumstances of high youth unemployment and low-paid, casualized work, young men may cling even more firmly to outmoded versions of hegemonic masculine identity', further exacerbating their relative disadvantage in the labour market and jeopardising their personal relationships with women (McDowell, 2000: 207). On this reading, the crisis of masculinity turns out to be a typical case of ethnic politics: when one's interests are under threat resist by emphasising all that makes one different.

CONCLUSIONS

This chapter has surveyed the changing nature of culture in this more globalised world and, through making explicit some of the principal ways in which the term culture is used in the social sciences, attempted to identify as precisely as possible the key changes wrought through the application of new information and communications technologies. In doing this, emphasis was placed upon what is distinctively new about this situation, and the novelty was found to lie not so much in the much rehearsed arguments about homogenisation or hybridity but, rather, in the culture of consumerism that is the principal characteristic of the cultural worlds of globalisation. In this situation, marked by 'a less stable sense of identity and knowledge' (Steger, 2003: 75), cultures of resistance are flourishing as power is claimed, or resisted, on the basis of particularistic identities. As the chapter's opening quote expressed so well, the more avant-garde the world waxes, the more archaic it grows, at least in the sense of referring to cultural reference points from the past. But there is nothing archaic about identity politics as it becomes perhaps the principal means through which the destabilising impact of globalisation is being resisted and responded to. It all adds up to a volatile mix, leaving many with no secure sense of what lies in store.

   In concluding this part entitled 'Diagnosis', a final word of clarification is necessary. For what has been diagnosed here are the causes of the growing vulnerability and violence described in Part I of this book. Through examining the political economy of globalisation and its cultural worlds, the wider contemporary context which explains these outcomes has been analysed. If there is one major conclusion, it is that vulnerability and violence are not accidental side-effects but rather inextricable features of a world in which the state (namely those institutions that embody public authority) facilitates market forces and indeed imposes them on society while eroding or failing to reinforce coping mechanisms against the onslaught of the market. While, as was made clear in Chapter 4, new technological innovations have facilitated enormously global flows of finance, goods, services, messages and images, the role of the state has been crucial in creating the institutional context that shapes the way these impact on society. A clear example of this interaction is found in the way in which government deregulation combined with technological innovation to create the conditions for the emergence of media monopolies, as covered earlier in this chapter. It is therefore very important to make one final distinction before closing this part. This relates to the term 'globalisation' itself. For it is no part of the argument being advanced here to claim that the growing economic, cultural, political or social interconnectedness that characterises today's world is *in itself* the cause of growing vulnerability and violence. Rather, it is *the particular form* that this globalisation is taking, characterised by its relationship of state and market, that is responsible (Schmidt and Hersh, 2000). This is often called *neoliberal* or *corporate* globalisation since it is driven by a neoliberal understanding of the respective roles of state and market, and it prioritises the interests of global capital over those of citizens, workers or the environment. It is this form of globalisation that has been analysed in these two chapters and it will be remedies for this form of globalisation that will be examined in Part IV. Before that, however, Part III interrogates the implications for society (Chapter 6) and for the individual person (Chapter 7) of growing vulnerability and violence.

Part III

Interrogation

6
Society and Market

Questions and doubts are everywhere. The ever-increasing problems that contemporary economic theory has encountered since the high point of its confidence in the 1950s lead us back to the most fundamental questions about the economy and its functional relation to society. One need not any longer catalogue all the critical problems that policies based on conventional economic theory have failed to resolve or even to confront. But it is important to emphasize that these problems are not only the traditional ones of employment, price levels, and growth in the economy. ... They are also the much more fundamental problems of the market economy's capacity to meet the generic needs of the society it is supposed to serve. Basic questions of the allocation of resources, and of the total effect of the economic system on the quality of our lives and habitat, are involved. It is the contemporary importance of this functional relation between economy and society, both in theory and policy, in Western and non-Western societies, in industrial as well as nonindustrial economies, that demands we return to a fundamental examination of what we mean and what we want when we speak of the economy and its role in society. (Pearson, 1977: xxvii)

The diagnosis of vulnerability and violence undertaken in Part II concluded that they derive not so much from the new information and communications technologies (ICTs) that have been shrinking our world (thereby rejecting a technological determinism) but rather from the conditions created by public authorities that have shaped the ways these ICTs impact on society. Central to these conditions is the key role played by the market in deciding how these technologies transform the four spheres of finance, production, trade and communication. As was argued in Chapter 4, public authorities (states and intergovernmental bodies) have for the past decade or so been systematically strengthening those rules and regulations that favour global market expansion while neglecting or even weakening those rules and regulations that put limits on the activities of market actors in order to protect society and the environment. In this situation, the state has ceded power to market actors so that these latter have become more crucial determinants of social outcomes than they were previously. The social outcomes that are the subject of this book, vulnerability and violence, are therefore intimately related to the role of the market in society, which for this reason is the subject of the present chapter.

While social scientists devote much attention to the relationship between the state and the market (it is the central concern of political economy analyses), the relationship of the market to society receives less attention. This is surprising, since it is the economy that generates the material resources that permit society to reach a higher standard of living. Yet, largely derived from the split between the academic disciplines of economics and sociology, most analyses of the economy are devoted to the internal workings of the market system (often conducted in a highly abstract and mathematical way), while society, and the many spheres into which it is divided, is analysed as a self-contained entity. The relationship between the two is treated in very cursory ways, focusing largely on the extent to which the economy generates resources for society, and based on benign assumptions about how economic growth is good for society. Yet, as Pearson reminds us in the epigraph to this chapter, the relationship of the market to society raises more fundamental questions concerning 'the total effect of the economic system on the quality of our lives and habitat', questions that are central to the analysis of vulnerability carried out so far in this book.

The investigation pursued in this part, therefore, questions some key assumptions about the relationship of the market to society that widely influence social analyses. This is required if the causes and implications of vulnerability and violence are to be more fully understood. Similarly, if it is accepted that vulnerability and violence are increasing, it is far from clear what the implications of this are for society or the individual person. The two chapters in this part, then, seek to situate the concept of vulnerability in social theory, interrogating theory in the light of the concept and interrogating the concept in the light of theory. In so doing, the intension is to offer a more robust substantiation of the concept and its importance. This chapter focuses on society while Chapter 7 focuses on individual well-being and its relationship to society. As already outlined, the concern of this chapter is to interrogate more fully the influence on society of the market. To do this, it draws extensively on the work of Karl Polanyi, a social theorist to whom we are indebted for his ground-breaking work on this important topic. The chapter opens by outlining Polanyi's analysis of what he variously calls 'our obsolete market mentality' (Polanyi, 1968: 59), 'the liberal economic outlook' (Polanyi, 2001: 158), or 'economistic thinking', which he regarded as 'the central illusion' of our times (Polanyi, 1977: 5). It then goes on to trace the creation of the market system and its impact on society, before turning to examine the influence this has had on people's livelihoods. The chapter concludes by reintroducing the concept of vulnerability, arguing that this gives contemporary expression to the social impact of the market which was a central theme of Polanyi's analysis.

MARKET MENTALITY

'Nothing obscures our social vision as effectively as the economistic prejudice', wrote Polanyi in his best known work *The Great Transformation*, first published in 1944 (Polanyi, 2001: 166). By this he meant that equating the economy to a market system, and making the welfare of society depend upon this system, resulted in an 'ingrained habit of thought' that presents 'a formidable obstacle' to attaining 'a more realistic view of the general problem posed to our generation by man's [sic] livelihood' (Polanyi, 1977: 5). While Polanyi's analysis of the socially destructive role of the market system will be presented in the next section, in this section the focus is on the restricted or, to use Polanyi's term, 'warped' (1968: 63) view of society and the human person that was one result of that system. Paradoxically, Polanyi undertook his analysis at a time when he believed the market system was on the wane, following the catastrophe of the Second World War and the subsequent attempts to regulate and restrict markets through Keynesian demand management and the extension of the welfare state. What he was analysing therefore was, in his terms, the legacy of 'oversimplified views of the function and role of the economic system in society' and 'novel notions about man and society [that] became current and gained the status of axioms' during the period of the market economy (1968: 60). For this reason, he regarded the market mentality as 'obsolete', to use the title of an essay first published in 1947 (1968: 59–77). Therefore, if Polanyi viewed the market mentality as being an obstacle to addressing effectively the challenges of social well-being in his own day, how much more important is it to focus critical attention on this restricted mindset at a time when the market economy has been reinstituted as the central organising principle of society throughout the world?

Writing in the wake of the collapse of 'real existing socialism' in Eastern Europe, Altvater highlighted the impact of this on social theorising:

While planning is thought to have foundered as a means of accelerating economic development and achieving a human society, the market is awarded an extraordinary capacity to solve problems relating to income distribution and optimum allocation of the factors of production. In the contest between rival conceptions, the market is thus supposed to have borne off the palm of victory. The movement of history now follows its procedural constraints; there no longer seems any room for substantive alternatives or morally grounded principles of action in the 'technological-scientific civilization'. And as the critique of existing reality becomes superfluous, so does the theory of society itself, not to speak of the devising of realistic utopias. (Altvater, 1993: 2)

This describes well the central elements of what is often referred to as a 'market fundamentalism', since it involves not just a belief in the superior efficacy of the market as the central mechanism of economic organisation but also, by extension, a denial of the importance or even validity of social critique because the dominance of the market principle allegedly makes alternative principles for organising society marginal or even irrelevant. As such, it echoes Polanyi's perceptive comment that the imposition of the market system on society also 'cast our thoughts and values in the mould of this unique innovation' (1968: 59). In our times, so pervasive has this market fundamentalism become that we take it largely for granted (see Box 6.1); we lament the rise of various forms of religious fundamentalism but fail to recognise that they are reactions against this more endemic and influential form of fundamentalism (see, for example, Nussbaum, 2004). It is by far the most dominant influence on our thinking about society and has largely motivated the policies that have resulted in today's form of neoliberal or corporate globalisation. It therefore urgently requires that we make explicit the 'thoughts and values' that we derive from it.

For Polanyi, a warped view of society and of the human individual results from 'equating the human economy in general with its market form', namely with what he calls 'the supply-demand-price mechanism' (1977: 6). He explicitly identifies two central features of 'our practical philosophy ... overwhelmingly shaped by this spectacular episode': firstly 'the heresy' that human motives can be

BOX 6.1   THE POWER OF THE MARKET

Anthropologists have generally examined so-called 'primitive' or non-Western societies to find out why people and groups act as they do. For long, they have recognised that in economic matters such societies differ from the Western market-based economy. Taking the Western as the norm, they have treated these as primitive or exceptional forms of economic activity (Roseberry, 1997: 251). In examining the market in developed capitalist societies, however, anthropologists have found that it is based on an idealised conception of buying and selling which 'bears a questionable relationship to the world it seems to describe' (Carrier, 1997: 14). For, in observing market actors, they find they do not act with clear-headed calculation but that moral, cultural and social considerations influence their decisions. Yet the idealised notion of society being composed of free individuals fulfilling their desires by buying and selling, and influenced by nothing more than value for money, is proving remarkably enduring and is capturing the popular imagination all around the world. As Carrier puts it, representations of the market 'affect how people in the West understand their world, affect the symbols people invoke to persuade each other, affect how people act in the world, and those representations have these effects because people adopt, espouse and respond to them, not because they are true' (1997: xi).

This conception of the market became dominant again in the 1980s, associated with the influence of President Reagan in the US and the British Prime Minister, Margaret Thatcher. But it also responded to the shift from manufacturing to services, as people begin to define themselves more as consumers than as producers, more as individuals than as workers. The collapse of Eastern European socialism in 1989 seemed to confirm the superiority of a market model. But its appeal worldwide may have more to do with the promise it evokes of consumer plenty and freedom from the tyranny of government regulation. As an idealisation of economic activities 'it is also an idealisation that itself idealises the modern West' (Carrier, 1997: 31); an undoubted part of its appeal in places like Latin America, Eastern Europe and China. Despite its associated notion of individual freedom from vested interests, powerful corporate interests actively promote the market and resist attempts to restrict its operations. Finally, once adopted as the common sense of the age, all are under pressure to accept it. 'Failure to do so is to risk being treated as parochial and hence of not being taken seriously' (Carrier, 1997: 54).

distinguished as being either 'material' or 'ideal' and that the former are the incentives on which everyday life is organised and, secondly, that the institutions of society are determined by the economic system. He accuses both liberals and Marxists of sharing these views (1968: 60–1). For Polanyi, however, elevating the market to such a determinative place in human life is severely to restrict our understanding of the human person and of society. Yet such an 'economistic outlook' has become so generalised as to constitute 'a philosophy of everyday life comprising criteria of common sense behaviour, of reasonable risks, and of a workable morality', indeed 'the seeds of a whole culture – with all its possibilities and limitations' (1977: 10). He wrote: 'It was almost impossible to avoid the erroneous conclusion that, as "economic" man was "real" man, so the economic system was "really" society' (1977: 12). This social philosophy, therefore, has reduced society to 'an agglomeration of human atoms behaving according to the rules of a definite kind of rationality', namely an economic rationality based on the calculation of how scarce means can be employed to achieve self-interested ends. Polanyi regarded such an economic rationality as highly defective since it avoids philosophical questions about ends, and moral questions about what means should be chosen; indeed, he wrote that such rationality is 'the antithesis of the aesthetic, the ethical, or the philosophical'. In elevating the needs of the individual to primary status while ignoring the complex ways in which individuals are embedded in social networks, such an economic rationalism eclipsed an earlier political rationalism and was 'totally blind to the sphere of state, nation and power', so that justice, law and freedom, as values institutionalised in society, 'wore thin'. Furthermore, none of the social disciplines could escape the influence of this economic rationality and were unwittingly turned into 'strongholds of economistic modes of thought' (1977: 12–17). Indeed, Polanyi described the separation of economics and politics as 'this outstanding characteristic of market society', since it allowed economists treat of economic issues divorced from considerations of political power or social consequences (2001: 204).

A more detailed consideration of why Polanyi singled out human motivation and economic determinism as the two great fallacies of the market mentality will help illustrate how, in his view, they serve to restrict a more adequate understanding of the human person and of social processes. The market mechanism, Polanyi wrote, made a distinction between the motives of hunger and gain, regarded as essential for economic production, and more ideal motives, such as honour and power. Therefore, 'fear of starvation with the worker, lure of profit with the employer, would keep the vast establishment running'. As a result, these so-called 'economic motives' came to occupy a predominant position as 'the individual was made to act on them under pain of being trodden under foot by the juggernaut market. Such a forced conversion to a utilitarian outlook fatefully warped Western man's [sic] understanding of himself'. In societies before the advent of the market system, such as those of ancient city-states, feudalism, thirteenth-century urban life, the sixteenth-century mercantile regime or eighteenth-century regulationism, invariably the economic system was merged in the social and incentives sprang from a wide variety of sources such as 'custom and tradition, public duty and private commitment, religious observance and political allegiance, judicial obligation and administrative regulation as established by prince, municipality, or guild. Rank and status, compulsion of law and threat of punishment, public praise and private reputation, insure that the individual contributes his share to production'; among such motives also ranked fear of privation and love of profit, but not as predominant ones. Indeed, Polanyi's study of early societies convinced him that 'the productive or economic system was usually arranged in such a fashion as not to threaten any individual with starvation', giving the person a secure place in society. For this reason, he regarded these societies as more humane than modern market society (1968: 62–7). Though capitalism is based on motives of starvation or gain, for Polanyi, 'in actual fact, man [sic] was never as selfish as the theory demanded' (1968: 69). He wrote that elevating starvation and gain to predominant motives 'is at the root of the "sickness of an acquisitive society" that Tawney warned of. And Robert Owen's genius was at its best when, a century before, he described the profit motive as "a principle entirely unfavourable to individual and public happiness"' (1968: 72).

The second great fallacy Polanyi identified was the idea that the economy determined society, since his anthropological studies of societies prior to early nineteenth-century Britain convinced him that the opposite was true, namely that the economy was always embedded in social relations. In previous societies, markets were isolated institutions in which goods were traded and which were hedged around by laws and customs. What happened in nineteenth-century Britain for the first time was that these isolated markets became transmuted into a self-regulating system in which 'order in the production and distribution of goods is ensured by prices alone' (2001: 72). The second element of this new market *system* is that not only are goods traded but that labour, land and capital are also treated as if they are commodities to be bought and sold in the market, though for Polanyi 'no more thoroughly effective fiction was ever devised'. By setting prices for labour (wages) and for the use of land (rent), 'the commodity fiction handed over the fate of man [sic] and of nature to the play of an automaton running in its own groves and governed by its laws'. As a result, an 'economic sphere' sharply delimited from other social institutions came into being which had the effect of making the rest of society dependent on that sphere and the market system became determinative for the life of society. What emerged is an economic society, 'to a degree previously never even approximated' (1968: 62–3) which offers individuals the illusion that they can 'repudiate the reality of social responsibilities in the name of ... imaginary freedom'. As Polanyi put it: 'By ignoring this limitation of man's meaningful wishes, the marketing view of society reveals its essential immaturity' (1977: 74).

If we accept Polanyi's view of history and of the human person, therefore, elevating the market to be the key principle for social organisation is to base society on a theoretical fallacy. Yet the power of that fallacy lies in 'its staggering capacity for organizing human beings as if they were mere chunks of raw material and combining them, together with the surface of mother earth, which could now be freely marketed, into industrial units under the command of private persons mainly engaged in buying and selling for profit' (1977: 9). It therefore brought about in practice what the economistic outlook had recognised as an ideal, namely the identity of market and society. How this happened is the subject of the next section.

FROM MARKET ECONOMY TO MARKET SOCIETY

In speaking of a market society, it is useful to remind ourselves of just how ubiquitous market conceptions of important social activities have become. For example, when students are described as 'customers' or when we are thanked for choosing a certain airline or telephone operator, what are being expressed are economistic views implying that we are individual actors who freely choose between different suppliers of education or services on an open market, being largely determined in our choice by the prices at which these are offered. Not so very long ago such conceptions would have been anachronistic, since such services were, by and large, not supplied through market mechanisms but were seen as public services to be supplied by agents largely controlled and even funded by the state for the purpose not of profit but of servicing human needs. Debates rage about the balance between efficiency, quality and equity involved in these different forms of provision; it suffices here to draw attention to the fundamental shifts that have taken place in our understanding of how essential social activities are increasingly entrusted to the market.

I suspect that, for Polanyi, this resurgence of the market system at the end of the twentieth century would have come as a great shock. He presumed that market society was a 'utopian experiment' (2001: 258) of the early nineteenth century (he dated its emergence to the period 1815–45 in Britain) which, by making social needs subservient to the market, 'produced the typical strains and stresses which ultimately destroyed that society' in the first half of the twentieth century, hastened by the two world wars (2001: 257). Yet Polanyi also knew that the emergence of the market system was essentially an initial response to the challenges of the Industrial Revolution and that, while this system was on the wane when he was writing in the aftermath of the Second World War, it only served to focus attention on the essential challenge still facing humankind. This is how he expressed it:

> How to organize human life in a machine society is a question that confronts us anew. Behind the fading fabric of competitive capitalism there looms the portent of an industrial civilization, with its paralyzing division of labour, standardization of life, supremacy of mechanism over organism, and organization over spontaneity. Science itself is haunted by insanity. This is the abiding concern. (1968: 59)

While we might today wish to broaden the conception of industrial civilisation to emphasise such elements as its corporate nature and scientific, reductionist rationality, Polanyi's point is very timely and urgent. For in the triumphalism following the so-called 'victory' of liberal capitalism over collectivist communism in 1989–91, the more fundamental challenges of our time have often been lost sight of, namely how to elaborate social structures into which to integrate technologies in a way that enhances human well-being (rather than making society subservient to technologies used to make profits for the few). Essentially, this is the issue that lies at the heart of debates about globalisation. But Polanyi's work does more than draw our attention to the fact that this challenge is not a new one; he also alerts us to the dangers of repeating the 'utopian experiment' that was the first attempt to elaborate such a structure. For this reason, his account of the creation of a market society in early nineteenth-century Britain, and of its fate, offers a framework of analysis absolutely pertinent to any critical understanding of today's experiment in neoliberal and corporate globalisation.

Polanyi took issue with classical economics which claims that economic activity derives from some natural propensity of the human person to 'barter, truck and exchange one thing for another', to use Adam Smith's words. From this was derived the view that markets had always played a central role in societies' efforts to provide themselves with sufficient material resources for their livelihood, the 'paradigm of the bartering savage' as Polanyi dismissively put it. He went on:

In retrospect it can be said that no misreading of the past ever proved more prophetic of the future. For while up to Adam Smith's time that propensity had hardly shown up on a considerable scale in the life of any observed community, and had remained, at best, a subordinate feature of economic life, a hundred years later an industrial system was in full swing over the major part of the planet which, practically and theoretically, implied that the human race was swayed in all its economic activities, if not also in its political, intellectual, and spiritual pursuits, by that one particular propensity. (2001: 45–6)

The fundamental confusion that resulted from this particular misreading of history was to equate economic activity with a particular system of market exchange. Economics became reduced to the study of market exchanges, something that is still by and large true. Instead, Polanyi focused attention on the substantive meaning of the word 'economic' which he defined as 'bearing reference to the process of satisfying material wants' (1977: 20). According to Polanyi, in all societies previous to that of nineteenth-century Britain, economic production took place not for the purpose of gain but for the purpose of use and was organised for the satisfaction of social needs. He argued that the economic systems of all such societies were organised on the basis of reciprocity, redistribution or householding, or on a combination of all three. These ways of distributing material resources co-existed with markets on which goods were exchanged, though such markets never formed a market system nor did they direct production or income as they do today. Therefore, 'the orderly production and distribution of goods was secured through a great variety of individual motives disciplined by general principles of behaviour' (2001: 57). However, in the nineteenth century, this substantive meaning of 'economy' became confused with an entirely different and unrelated meaning: the formal meaning of 'economising' or 'economical', that is, the use of scarce means to achieve desired ends. As a result, the distinction between both meanings of economic has become lost and the study of economics became reduced to making choices between the uses of scarce means, though for Polanyi the substantive meaning of economics implies neither choice nor insufficiency. 'The current compound concept of economics, in fusing the satisfaction of material wants with scarcity, postulates no less than the insufficiency of all things material', he wrote (1977: 28). Even more significantly, in establishing the market as the means whereby material wants are supplied, economics restricted its attention to those wants and needs that could be satisfied through the purchase of things offered in markets: 'Therefore, by definition, no wants and needs other than those supplied in the market were to be recognized, and no person other than the individual in isolation was to be accepted as a human being' (1977: 29).

Conceiving economic activity in this way then led to the creation of an economy that was equated with a market system, namely a market economy regulated and controlled by the 'supply-demand-price system' which Polanyi regarded as 'a comparatively modern institution of specific structure, which is easy neither to establish nor to keep going' (1977: 6–9). In other words, there is nothing natural about the creation of a market system; rather, it has been 'the outcome of a conscious and often violent intervention on the part of government which imposed the market organization on society for non-economic ends' and required 'an enormous increase in continuous, centrally organized and controlled interventionism' to keep the free market operating (2001: 258; 146). For an essential feature of the creation of a market economy was the treatment of labour, land and money as if they were commodities that could be allocated a price and traded between suppliers and buyers. In his book *The Great Transformation*, Polanyi describes in detail how such a commodification happened in early nineteenth-century Britain. Thus was born the self-regulating market system. Polanyi described this system as follows:

> All incomes must derive from the sale of something or other, and whatever the actual source of a person's income, it must be regarded as resulting from sale. ... But the most startling peculiarity of the system lies in the fact that, once it is established, it must be allowed to function without outside interference. Profits are not any more guaranteed, and the merchant must make his profits on the market. Prices must be allowed to regulate themselves. Such a self-regulating system of markets is what we mean by a market economy. (2001: 44)

For this reason, he described it as an automaton governed by its own 'economic law'. But the creation of a market economy made necessary 'a more extreme development, namely a whole society embedded in the mechanism of its own economy, a *market society*' (1977: 9; emphasis in original). For treating human labour, nature or money as commodities 'means no less than the running of society as an adjunct to the market'. This resulted in a form of relationship between economy and society that was entirely new: 'Instead of economy being embedded in social relations, social relations are embedded in the economic system' (2001: 60). It was what he called 'a sociological enormity' (1968: 68). This same understanding of the subservience of society to the needs of the economic system lies at the heart of the objections made by many critics of today's globalisation who interpret the changing relationship of the market to society over the 1990s in a similar light (see Box 6.2).

For Polanyi, the creation of a market society was inherently destructive. He drew attention to one of the 'baffling paradoxes' of the new industrial society: 'the seeming contradiction of an almost miraculous increase in production accompanied by a near starvation of the masses'. The harmonious self-regulation that characterised the market system 'required that the individual respect economic law even if it happened to destroy him' (2001: 84–9). For 'the commodity fiction disregarded the fact that leaving the fate of soil and people to the market would be tantamount to annihilating them' (2001: 137). To counter this inherently destructive impact of the market on society, a spontaneous countermovement emerged to check the action of the market. This took the form of more restrictive or regulative legislation in relation to such areas as public health, factory conditions, municipal trading, social insurance, shipping subsidies, public utilities and trade associations. Using arguments that remind one of today's proponents of neoliberal globalisation, economic liberals decried these restrictions, saying 'all protectionism was a mistake due to impatience, greed, and shortsightedness, but for which the market would have resolved its difficulties' (2001: 148). However, Polanyi countered that this was no left-wing conspiracy but rather a pragmatic response to the destructive inroads of the market, happening not only in Britain but also in France, in Austria, and in Germany in the last decades of the nineteenth century through the actions of politicians of all political outlooks. He saw this pragmatic self-protective response as 'conclusive proof of the peril to society inherent in the utopian principle of a self-regulating market' (2001: 157).

This, then, is Polanyi's essential contribution to our understanding of the relationship of society to the economy. It draws our attention

BOX 6.2   WAXING AND WANING OF 'EMBEDDED LIBERALISM'

In 1982, Harvard professor John Gerard Ruggie published an influential article in which he coined the term 'embedded liberalism' (Ruggie, 1982) to describe the reconciliation of market efficiency with the values of social community as described in what he elsewhere called 'Polanyi's classic and still unsurpassed account of these wrenching struggles' (Ruggie, 2003: 118, note 1). For Ruggie, political authority rests not on power alone but on 'a fusion of power with legitimate social purpose' (1982: 382), and it was the combining of both in the institutional features of the post-war international order that marked it out as being 'different in kind from that which had been known previously' (1982: 392). Ruggie described the essence of embedded liberalism as follows: 'unlike the economic nationalism of the thirties, it would be multilateral in character; unlike the liberalism of the gold standard and free trade, its multilateralism would be predicated upon domestic interventionism' (1982: 393). The balance achieved within this new international regime meant that 'movement toward greater openness in the international economy is likely to be coupled with measures designed to cushion the domestic economy from external disruption' (1982: 398). The term 'embedded liberalism' has therefore been widely used to refer to the sort of social order that would embed the economy in society, as envisaged by Polanyi.

Yet, as Mark Blyth has written, 'just as labour and the state reacted to the collapse of the classical liberal order during the 1930s and 1940s by re-embedding the market, so business reacted against this embedded liberal order during the 1970s and 1980s and sought to "disembed liberalism" once again' so that by the 1990s 'a new neoliberal institutional order had been established in many advanced capitalist states with remarkable similarities to the regime discredited in the 1930s'. Polanyi 'had been put into reverse gear' (Blyth, 2002: 6). Returning to his theme in 2003, Ruggie also saw that 'the globalization of financial markets and production chains' is putting the 'grand social bargain' of embedded liberalism at risk (Ruggie, 2003: 93–4). He identifies three factors which may provoke a backlash against embedded liberalism: firstly, the fact that the benefits of globalisation are distributed so unequally; secondly, the growing imbalance in global rule-making as rules favouring global market expansion are strengthened while those protecting society and the environment lag behind; and thirdly, the greater vulnerability brought by globalisation as it brings economic instability and social dislocation, sometimes at lightening speed. Ruggie writes that 'the long struggle that ultimately resulted in the embedded liberalism compromise suggests that disparities of this sort are socially unsustainable' (2003, 97). Yet the task of embedding the market within shared social values and institutional practices 'represents a task of historical magnitude', since it now has to be achieved at a global level and no forms of global government or public authority yet exist that are sufficiently strong to carry it out. His hope is that 'a global public domain is emerging, which cannot substitute for effective action by states but may help to produce it' (2003: 95).

to the way in which a market economy tends inherently to make society subservient to its economic laws, and offers a highly insightful framework of analysis through which to interrogate how today's market economy is impacting on society. Yet, bearing in mind the concerns of this book with social vulnerability, a further examination of the nature of the destructive impact on society of market forces, as seen by Polanyi, may yield further insights that will help guide us through contemporary debates on the nature of poverty. For this reason, the next section examines human livelihood.

HUMAN LIVELIHOOD

Although a book of his writings entitled *The Livelihood of Man* was published posthumously, Polanyi's treatment focuses much more on threats to livelihood and mechanisms for securing it (as outlined in the previous section) than on its actual nature. Despite this, there are sufficient hints throughout his work that alert us to the fact that Polanyi had a broad conception of what constitutes human and social well-being, echoing some contemporary debates on these issues. Indeed, his very choice of the term 'livelihood' to express his interest in well-being is itself one of these hints as it is a broad term encompassing all that we require to sustain life. For example, one contemporary definition sees livelihood as comprising 'the capabilities, assets (both material and social resources) and activities required for a means of living' (Carney, in Rakodi, 1999: 316). Indeed, an extensive literature in development studies now focuses on the livelihood strategies of the poor themselves, to counter what since the 1970s has been a predominant focus on poverty measured in income terms, a focus that has distracted attention from wider questions of social well-being and what constitutes it (see Box 6.3). Yet, as Ruggeri Laderchi et al. remind us: 'Each of the different approaches to poverty derives from a different perspective on what constitutes a good life and a just society' (Ruggeri Laderchi et al., 2003: 26). Polanyi's use of the term 'livelihood' implies such a perspective. The purpose of this section is to interrogate what that perspective might be and what it contributes to contemporary debates on poverty and livelihood.

At the heart of Polanyi's perspective on the good life and the just society is an explicit ontology or view of the human person. He wrote that the human person is not an economic being

but a social being. He does not aim at safeguarding his individual interest in the acquisition of material possessions, but rather at ensuring social good will, social status, social assets. He values possessions primarily as a means to that end. His incentives are of that 'mixed' character which we associate with the endeavour to gain social approval – productive efforts are no more than incidental to this. (Polanyi, 1968: 65)

BOX 6.3   POVERTY: DO WE KNOW WHAT IT MEANS?

While poverty reduction has become a major focus of political attention at national and international level throughout the world, there is growing debate among experts about what exactly poverty means. Surveying the present state of that debate, Ruggeri Laderchi et al. identify four different approaches to defining and measuring poverty, each with its distinct understanding of what constitutes poverty, each identifying different individuals and groups as being poor, and each recommending different policy solutions (Ruggeri Laderchi et al., 2003):

1) The monetary approach: this is the most common approach and identifies poverty with falling below a minimum level of resources (called a 'poverty line') defined in terms of income or consumption. While this approach can regularly employ very sophisticated tools of measurement, it is based on numerous value judgements that are often well hidden. For example, it equates poverty with lack of material goods and overlooks social, cultural or political aspects of poverty, thus embodying 'a narrow vision of human well-being' (Ruggeri Laderchi et al., 2003: 19). It is fundamentally individualistic in approach and emphasises the need for economic growth to improve the income of individuals.

2) The capability approach: based on the work of economics Nobel Prize winner, Amartya Sen, this emphasises not just income but rather how that might be used to expand human capabilities. It therefore shifts the focus away from monetary resources and focuses on indicators such as health, education and employment for evaluating well-being and deprivation. The UNDP's Human Poverty Index, contained in its annual *Human Development Report*, is one well-known example. While it encounters difficulties in defining a list of basic capabilities, it does focus attention on the provision of social goods such as education and health.

3) The social exclusion approach: the focus here is on exclusion from full participation in society and so it devotes attention not just to poverty at any one point in time but also to the dynamics of groups falling into and out of poverty. Its concern with exclusion makes it a much more social approach than the two previous approaches, examining such dimensions as unemployment, access to housing, minimal income, citizenship, democratic rights and social contacts. It is now a central aspect of EU social policy but is more difficult to apply to developing countries where exclusion may be the experience of the majority. It emphasises the need for redistribution and for overcoming obstacles to full participation (such as anti-discrimination legislation).

▶

4) The participatory approach: in contrast to each of the other approaches which makes judgements about the poor based on data and evidence, this approach goes to the poor themselves and involves a wide range of techniques to help them express what poverty means to them. Originally used more by NGOs, it is now used by the World Bank. While seeking to empower the poor through such involvement, concerns have been expressed about how well it deals with differences among the poor themselves. Like social exclusion approaches, it focuses attention on the need to address social problems such as class barriers and racial discrimination.

Ruggeri Laderchi et al. conclude that there is 'no unique, or "objective" way of defining and measuring poverty. There is a large element of "construction" involved in each of the poverty measures' while, in practice, the monetary approach retains its dominance (2003: 34).

In this view therefore, what is of primary importance to people is a secure sense of belonging to society. However, this essential social nature of the human person goes unrecognised in a market society because, 'since market situations do not, in principle, know wants and needs other than those expressed by individuals, and wants and needs are here restricted to things that can be supplied in a market, any discussion of the nature of human wants and needs in general was without substance' (Polanyi, 1977: 29). In this, Polanyi echoes contemporary critiques of the narrowness of dominant approaches to understanding and measuring poverty (see Box 6.3). But he goes much further in highlighting the implications of this view for social institutions. Institutionalising an economic system on such material needs as hunger and gain, writes Polanyi, is akin to basing the institution of marriage on sex. As a result, he wrote: 'Our humiliating enslavement to the "material", which all human culture is designed to mitigate, was deliberately made more rigorous' (1968: 72). Polanyi's critique of the market mechanism, therefore, was based on its narrow conception of human wants and needs which, institutionalised in a market society, fatally damaged and even enslaved the individual and society itself.

If poverty is a central concept used to express the damage to human livelihood caused by social processes, it is not surprising that Polanyi had a very distinctive conception of it. He identified as a characteristic of the Industrial Revolution in Britain 'the incomprehensible fact that poverty seemed to go with plenty', recognising 'two seemingly contradictory effects of manufactures, namely, the increase in pauperism and the rise in wages' (2001: 89, 98). Here Polanyi's understanding seems closer to contemporary debates on social inequality. However, his discussion in *The Great Transformation* of the debates about the social impact of the Industrial Revolution is where he most cogently outlines his distinctive view. For he takes issue with those who claim that the Industrial Revolution actually improved people's living standards, though he does so not by disputing the claim that wages increased but rather by arguing that poverty is primarily not an economic but a cultural phenomenon: 'Not economic exploitation, as often assumed, but the disintegration of the cultural environment of the victim is then the cause of the degradation.' The essence of this disintegration 'lies in the lethal injury to the institutions in which his social existence is embodied … loss of self-respect and standards, whether the unit is a people or a class, whether the process springs from so-called "culture conflict" or from a change in the position of a class within the confines of a society' (2001: 164–5). In this latter comment, he is equating the impact of the Industrial Revolution on Britain's 'labouring classes' with that of colonialism on African peoples at the time he was writing or on India in the nineteenth century. His view of poverty, therefore, is derived from his view that, for the individual, economic interest is rarely paramount but the 'maintenance of social ties, on the other hand, is crucial' (2001: 48). Sudden social dislocation and its impact on the coherence and sustainability of the lives of the majority is for Polanyi the essence of poverty, which manifests itself as a form of violence destroying individuals and communities. Purely economic progress, achieved through the impact of the market mechanism on society, is the cause. In this discussion, Polanyi makes two major contributions to contemporary debates on poverty. Firstly, in identifying the value of social belonging as being much more important to the individual's well-being than income alone, he offers an understanding that is close to some emerging currents within scholarship on poverty (see Boxes 1.3 and 5.3). Secondly, in identifying market liberalisation as the cause of such social dislocation, he directly challenges dominant approaches to addressing poverty through providing market opportunities for the poor.

None of this should be taken as implying that Polanyi was opposed to progress. He emphasises the need for a 'common-sense attitude towards change', by which he means that 'a process of undirected change, the pace of which is deemed too fast, should be slowed down, if possible, so as to safeguard the welfare of the community' (2001: 35). His comments about the market mechanism eroding humanity's institutional creativity and paralysing its social imagination implies that change could be organised more imaginatively and creatively (1968: 71, 73). Further, he argues that change should serve not just the interests of particular classes but the interests of the whole community, and that it is the responsibility of the government to ensure that this happens (2001: 158–63). So Polanyi's perspective on what constitutes a good life and a just society is far from being a romantic primitivism. Instead, he identifies very concretely what are the institutional mechanisms needed to ensure that the economy is embedded in society, that the generation of wealth serves the good of society. These, for Polanyi, are the essential features of a just society. He identified three such mechanisms, or forms of integration as he called them. These serve to create interdependence between the different elements of the economic process, from material resources and labour to the transportation, storage and distribution of goods, submerging economic processes in social relationships. They are reciprocity, redistribution and exchange. These he had identified as being present in all societies before the Industrial Revolution which he studied. Reciprocity refers to mutual relations of gift-giving between groups based upon notions of duty and honour and not economic self-interest. These tended to be uppermost in societies which lacked strong institutional power, such as tribal societies, though Polanyi points out that trade between early empires was organised on the basis of reciprocity. Where centralised power was present, this permitted institutional redistribution to occur as, for example, through the vast storage systems of ancient Egypt, Sumeria, Babylon or Peru. But Polanyi also emphasised that the extended household (the Central African kraal, the northwest African kasbas, the Hebrew patriarchal household, the Greek estate, the Roman familia, the medieval manor) was based on the principle of redistribution. Finally, exchange was based on the two-way movement of goods in local markets. The main difference between these and the modern-day market system is that exchange on such local markets was not dominated by the medium of prices and, of course, neither land nor labour was traded on them (1977: 35–43). Such institutional mechanisms fostered attitudes of mutuality and cooperation, integrating rather than undermining society. As Rotstein put it, Polanyi's understanding was that the authentic form of society involved the human person's 'dependence on his fellows and his habitat' (Rotstein, 1990: 99).

While Polanyi emphasised the essentially social nature of the human person, personal freedom was also of major concern to him. Indeed, he feared the threat industrial civilisation poses to the freedom of the individual. But he was also critical of the illusory notions about freedom promoted by liberal philosophy which 'can lead the individual to repudiate the reality of social responsibilities in the name of his imaginary freedom'; and he explicitly rejected the view, promoted by supporters of the market system (Polanyi mentions Friedrich Hayek, regarded as a father figure of neoliberalism), that saw the market as the guarantor of individual freedom. Indeed, for Polanyi, the market enslaves the individual by elevating material interests above higher and more humane motives and values. He was confident that 'we will have just as much freedom as we will desire to create and to safeguard. There is no *one* determinant in human society. Institutional guarantees of personal freedom are compatible with any economic system' (1968: 76; emphasis in original).

Polanyi's view of human livelihood, therefore, lies somewhere between the capability and the social exclusion approaches. His emphasis on the deeper needs of the human person echoes Amartya Sen's point that the goal of development is to allow people 'to live the kind of lives that people have reason to value' (Sen 1999: 295). However, his emphasis on society and the individual's fundamental need to belong places him much closer to the social exclusion approach with its central focus on participation. Furthermore, he shares with both approaches a criticism of the monetary approach for its individualism and its focus on material resources only. In focusing on the impact of larger macro-economic shifts on human livelihoods he shares common ground with those who work within the livelihoods approach to development (see Bebbington, 2004). However, Polanyi goes much further than any of these in elaborating a robust analysis of what lies at the heart of the 'baffling paradox' of poverty amid plenty which is clearly a characteristic of our times. While he derives this from historical and anthropological analyses, his central point about the destructive impact of market forces on society finds much supportive evidence in contemporary empirical literature on poverty and vulnerability around the world (see, for example, Moser, 1998). Indeed, while poor households might be managing to fend off destitution, Chant reminds us that they are doing so 'at the cost of unprecedented self-exploitation and self-denial' (Chant,

2004: 212). Polanyi's major contribution is to distinguish clearly the principles of the market and of public authority, identifying the market mechanism as itself generating poverty and drawing attention to the fact that the social (and indeed environmental) stresses and strains it generates can only be effectively addressed through public authorities re-embedding the market in social institutions. This therefore directly contradicts the wave of market liberalisation being promoted ceaselessly by the major states, intergovernmental organisations and large corporations that dominate power in our world. Yet the importance of Polanyi's analysis is that if the market is not re-embedded it will lead to social and environmental destruction of ever greater proportions, doing violence to individuals and society. Polanyi draws attention therefore to that fact that, whether it is called poverty, capability, social exclusion or livelihood strategies, the great social challenge of our time requires action of a fundamental and radical kind to create forms of public authority to ensure the market serves social well-being.

CONCLUSIONS: MAKING SOCIETY MORE VULNERABLE

Though he does not use the concept as an analytical category, vulnerability is at the heart of Polanyi's *oeuvre*. His central concern is with the damage, indeed violence, caused to society by the inroads of the market mechanism, deriving both from the threats which this unleashes for the human person, society and nature, and from the erosion of the norms, values and practices, and their various institutional expressions, through which nature, society and ultimately human livelihood were protected throughout history. Polanyi therefore provides an analytical framework through which to interrogate more deeply the sources of the growing vulnerability and violence identified in Chapters 2 and 3. This framework identifies the relationship of the market to society as the central causal mechanism at work. In doing this, it underlines the significance that economic liberalisation has in the growing vulnerability of the financial, economic, social, cultural, political, environmental and personal spheres and the violence that results, as described in the chapters of Part I and analysed in the chapters of Part II. The unique value of Polanyi's framework, however, is that it offers an explanation that identifies *how* and *why* the market has these effects, through his central categories of the market economy and the market society, identifying specifically the ways in which both the economy and society are made dependent on the self-governing market mechanism. In Polanyi's writings we therefore find an explanation as to how liberating the market from the restraining bonds of public authority (mostly but not exclusively the state) results in allowing market forces, motivated by the need for private gain, to determine more and more of how we think and what we value, of what is produced and by whom, of how it is distributed, and of how all these affect society, livelihoods and quality of life. Furthermore, in offering an historical reading of the destructive consequences in the late nineteenth and early twentieth century of this 'utopian experiment', as he called it, Polanyi provides a sobering reading of our own future if we persist in allowing the market mechanism to run society. It is an audacious contribution of immense contemporary significance.

One of the many original features of Polanyi's work, that marks it off for example from conventional Marxist accounts of exploitation, is that it rests unashamedly on a view of the human person as a social being motivated by much more than material needs. It is because the market mechanism bases itself on motivations that are so narrowly based, and destroys the fragile bonds of social belonging on which the human person's well-being depends, that it is so destructive. It is for this reason that Polanyi can write: 'we are faced with the vital task of restoring the fullness of life to the person, even though this may mean a technologically less efficient society' (1968: 73). Such a statement turns on its head the priorities of today's global order and involves a challenge, the order of magnitude of which Polanyi was well aware. For he wrote in 1947 that the task of adapting life in this Machine Age to 'the requirements of human existence must be resolved if man [sic] is to continue on earth. No one can foretell whether such an adaptation is possible, or whether man must perish in the attempt. Hence the dark undertone of concern' (1968: 60). Half a century later, the urgency of this task and its uncertain outcome are, if anything, even more pronounced.

In surveying Polanyi's work, this chapter has served to situate the concept of vulnerability in social theory, highlighting its importance as a concept that helps elucidate fundamental challenges facing human society. But if Polanyi's work has offered a theoretical framework that helps explain why vulnerability and violence are on the increase and why we should take this seriously, introducing the concept of vulnerability helps highlight the contemporary significance of Polanyi's core insight into the vital need to embed the market in social relationships. In these ways, this chapter has interrogated vulnerability in the light of social theory but also interrogated that theory in the light of this concept. Polanyi's work is, of course, but one reading of the relationship of the market to society. Very different accounts of markets exist in social theory (for an overview, see Lie, 1997). The historical accuracy of Polanyi's account of the role of the market in earlier societies has also been the subject of debate (see, for example, that between Silver (1983 and 1985) and Mayhew, Neale and Tandy (1985)). However, Polanyi's analysis remains an influential one, even if it is by no means a dominant one. The attempt to substantiate its validity here will not be through establishing its historical accuracy but rather through interrogating the accuracy of its view of the human person in society, drawing on recent developments in psychology and psychotherapy. As disciplines that interrogate what constitutes human well-being, the relationship between the individual and society, and the impact of vulnerability on the individual person, their findings are too often neglected by social scientists. Interrogating Polanyi's analysis in the light of debates within these disciplines will serve to establish just how authoritative it may be. This is the task undertaken in the next chapter.

7
The Individual and Society*

We go on shaping our individual destinies – many of us in greater comfort and contentment than human beings have ever known before – within the context of disaster. (Stevens, 1996: 343)

The disjuncture between individual and collective destinies is one of the great dramas of our times. Part of the world's population has a higher material standard of living than ever before in human history and, due to the pervasive influence of the media and the emblems of a consumer culture, a significant proportion of the rest of humanity aspires to the same goal. Yet, while individually our eyes are fixed on the lures of consumption, collectively we know that were most of humanity to achieve this goal the planet's biosphere could not sustain it for very long. Already, the destructive impacts caused to the natural environment by our levels of consumption (through climate change, the erosion of the ozone layer, loss of biodiversity) are damaging in sudden and unpredictable ways the lives of more and more people. Those of us whose desires, values and lifestyles are increasingly shaped by the insatiable demands of consumerism are at times stopped short by the tragic plight of people who live on the edge of survival, whether in our so-called 'developed' societies or in distant countries where they often make up the majority of the population. This awareness of the scandalous inequalities of our world motivates some to radical lifestyle change; the majority of us, however, live with the contradictions of personal affluence in a world where glaring basic needs go unmet. These contradictions are becoming ever starker. For example, the UNDP estimates that the 20 per cent of the world's people in the richest countries had 30 times the income of the poorest 20 per cent in 1960 but that this had grown to 74 times their income by 1997 (UNDP, 1999: 36). Yet, the greater the contradictions grow, the more we seem to seek to avoid them. Or at least there are pitifully few signs that, referring to the quotation opening this chapter, the scale of the disaster facing us all if present trends continue is being addressed with any adequacy

---

* Written with Toni Ryan.

by our decision makers, either political or economic, at national or at international level.

At the heart of this disjuncture between our individual and our collective destinies is a split between the individual and society. We somehow imagine that as individuals we can close ourselves off from, protect ourselves against, the plight of so many of the world's population and the plight of the natural environment itself. We can conceive of ourselves as individuals isolated from others and from nature rather than as beings who are deeply and inextricably interconnected with and interdependent upon both. This fundamental distinction operates within the social sciences also. As Polanyi put it, referring to Aristotle as his authority, the human person 'is not an economic, but a social being' (Polanyi, 1968: 65). If this is true, it challenges the methodological individualism which increasingly pervades large areas of the social sciences and finds its most elevated expression in neoclassical economics, namely that 'abstraction is inevitably made from systematic interconnections of a social or ecological character' (Altvater, 1993: 69). In the mindset of the market, so influential in the shaping of today's world, only individual beings and things exist. Yet, despite resting a whole science of economics on such a dubious premise, its adequacy is little interrogated by social scientists. This is the purpose of the present chapter.

In interrogating the relationship of the individual to society, recourse will be had to psychology and psychotherapy, disciplines that specialise in issues relating to human well-being and wholeness. The first section draws on debates within these disciplines to examine the relationship of the individual to society in a more informed way than is usually done in the social sciences. However, more is at stake here than simply establishing that the human person is inherently social. For one's view of the human person provides the basis for more adequately establishing the social conditions required for human well-being, the task that Polanyi referred to as 'restoring the fullness of life to the person' (1968: 73). This is the subject of the second section. Attempts to resolve the contradictions between the individual and the collective through closing ourselves off or protecting ourselves return us to the distinction between the concepts of 'security' and 'vulnerability', first raised in Chapter 1. The third section examines these concepts in the light of the discussions in the previous two sections, elucidating the implications of each and thereby refining the understanding of vulnerability being employed throughout this book. The objective of this chapter is to draw on recent research in psychology and psychotherapy to interrogate Polanyi's analysis of the primacy of social belonging for human well-being as outlined in the previous chapter. Polanyi himself wrote of the need for 'a more realistic vision of the human world' and 'a total view of man [sic] and society very different from that [of the] market economy' (1968: 60, 77). It is hoped that the discussion here may contribute to a more realistic vision, a fuller view of the human person and her interconnectedness with nature and with others.

'THERE IS NO SUCH THING AS SOCIETY'

Margaret Thatcher's statement negating the reality of society has become one of the great defining dictums of our neoliberal age, regularly referred to in social scientific texts. Made in an interview published in *Woman's Own* magazine on 23 September 1987, the then British prime minister was in fact lamenting the tendency of people to look to the state to resolve their problems rather than accepting their own responsibilities. Responding to those who say 'If children have a problem, it is society that is at fault', she then uttered her memorable statement 'There is no such thing as society' but followed it by affirming: 'There is living tapestry of men and women and people and the beauty of that tapestry and the quality of our lives will depend upon how much each of us is prepared to take responsibility for ourselves and each of us prepared to turn round and help by our own efforts those who are unfortunate' (Keay, 1987). Paradoxically, the policies of the governments led by Thatcher helped spur a worldwide transformation of this 'living tapestry' that may have forced more and more to take responsibility for themselves but also undermined their responsibility for, or even links to, 'those who are unfortunate'. It is this 'transformation of collective life – of social, economic and political relations' (Jordan, 2004: 26) that has further deepened the split between the individual and society, exacerbating the disjuncture between our personal and collective destinies.

At the heart of this transformation lie the new possibilities for exercising personal choice over our lives that resulted from the revolution in information and communications technology, coupled with the shift to the free market championed by Thatcher and Reagan. Increasingly it has become possible to live life as a 'project of self' as we grasp the multiple opportunities for self-advancement, wealth and new relationships that the market seems to offer. No longer limited by territorial boundaries, the whole world has been opened to us so that we can source goods and services wherever we find them at the price that suits us. Even more importantly, choice is increasingly being extended to such services as schools and hospitals, previously monopolised by the state. This greatly extended arena of choice leads to what Jordan calls 'hunter-gatherer social relations' as individuals gather the elements together for their lifestyle of choice, independence and self-direction, increasingly aping the *Homo economicus* of abstract economic theory (see Box 7.1). 'Many have made frequent changes of employers; others seek shifts of department and branch within the same organization. All are aware of the need to arrange their resource-holdings and lifestyle choices so as to allow movement and adaptation' (Jordan, 2004: 119).

While Thatcher might rejoice that she has helped open up new areas of freedom and self-responsibility for individuals, her concern for 'those who are unfortunate' prompts consideration of how this new arena of individual choice erodes the links that previously connected the private to the public worlds. Here what is being considered are not the many instances of generosity or charity through which individuals contribute to the lives of those less well-off but, rather, the structural basis on which society ensures a more equitable distribution of income, resources, opportunities and responsibilities across the rich–poor divide. There are two major grounds for concern here, one relating to the welfare state and the other to social values. The dynamic of choice through which individuals choose the communities to which they belong (neighbourhoods, schools and hospitals, sports and recreation clubs) has been eroding the supply and quality of public services and infrastructure which had helped reinforce the basis for solidarity across society. But the values of individual independence, value-for-money and choice are also eroding the cultural bases for such solidarity. As the lives of the well-off are more and more lived within bounded communities of choice to which the less well-off cannot gain access, the basis for social solidarity is severely eroded: 'Exclusion is automatic, and accomplished in tactfully low-key ways. The logic of variable university fees, foundation hospitals, league tables of schools and social care facilities, toll roads and private pension plans becomes the dominant dynamic of social organization' (Jordan, 2004: 130).

Even though political leaders like Tony Blair or institutions like the World Bank can speak of the need for eradicating poverty and spreading opportunity, the cultural and structural basis on which the claim of the world's poor for a more equitable share in resources and opportunities rested has been so eroded that the hope for such a

BOX 7.1   *HOMO ECONOMICUS* MAKES A COMEBACK

Though not often alluded to, and even more rarely justified, the whole edifice of mainstream or neoclassical economics rests on a particular conception of the human person, *Homo economicus*. This is the human person as a rational, economic individual, motivated in her actions by seeking to minimise costs and maximise gains for herself. Influenced originally by the utilitarian philosophy of Jeremy Bentham which sought a scientific means of calculating the maximisation of pleasure for individuals, *Homo economicus* has, according to Bowles and Gintis, been reintroduced by economists since the 1970s:

> The new economic man is not a Victorian gentleman: he is uncompromisingly thorough in pursuing objectives, and often he is less benign. Not satisfied with calculating marginal rates of substitution while shopping for groceries, he now optimizes while deciding how hard to work for his employer, how truthfully to transmit information to his exchange partners, and whether the benefits exceed the costs of defaulting on a loan. (Bowles and Gintis, 1993: 84)

This economic man is an asocial being who relates to others only through market exchange and who therefore extends the values of the market throughout society. As Anderson has put it: 'Every extension of the market thus represents an extension of the domain of egoism, where each party defines and satisfies her interests independent of the others' (quoted in Tsakalotos, 2004: 142). Marginalised from her activities are non-market values and priorities, particularly those relating to the collective good of society. Writing on Britain's New Labour, Hall makes the point that 'Economic Man or as s/he came to be called, the Enterprising Subject and the Sovereign Consumer, have supplanted the idea of the Citizen and the Public Sphere' (quoted in Tsakalotos, 2004: 155). For, if individuals continue to act as self-interested maximising agents, 'why would they bother to organize an economy dedicated to radical fairness and equality?' (Albert and Hahnel, quoted in Tsakalotos, 2004: 143).

Yet, despite its widespread influence, this *Homo economicus* 'turns out to be an odd and perhaps impossible construction', writes Turner. This is because it is based on a notion of rationality (activities and options arise from individuals' rational choices indicating their preferences) which fails to account for many of the most visible and central activities in society, such as collective action. Turner goes on:

> The problem may be ignored, as it is by economists, in the limited context of the market. At the level of the person, these preferences pose a deep problem: either the model is inapplicable to individuals treated as such, and the model of the person is a predictively useful but false abstraction, or the model is simply false and needs to be revised. (Turner, 1991: 193)

While economists debate, this narrow notion of the human person, akin to Marcuse's 'one-dimensional man', dehumanises people as they are constrained to act as if they were self-sufficient individuals while it erodes the fragile bonds of belonging that constitute our social networks.

grand social contract is, in Jordan's words, 'wishful thinking' (2004: 168). The connections between the lives of the affluent and mobile with their 'projects of self' and those of the majority of the world's people increasingly thrown back on 'archaic collective institutions of community, ethnicity and faith' are tenuous in the extreme. In this situation, 'polarization is more massively structural' (Jordan, 2004: 132) and the poor and excluded are thrown on their own resources and opportunities to survive, including drug smuggling, people trafficking and terrorism. As society, at both a domestic and a global level, becomes ever more atomised, fragmented and hostile, Thatcher's statement takes on a chillingly prophetic significance.

The erosion of the links that bind the human person to wider collectivities has, however, deeper origins. It derives from the dominant Western psychology of the self, still based on a Cartesian mechanistic worldview, where the whole is separated into parts. This separation and dualism has many implications.

The mind is separated from the body; the disease from the person who has it; the specific pathogen from the disease process as a whole; the parts from each other; the symptoms from the source of the ailment; and the patients from their self-responsibility and self-power. ... This division has made us susceptible to an inversion of process whereby the means (technological, industrial and scientific innovation) governs our ends (human values) and people become the 'objects' rather than the 'subjects' of their own activity. (Beinfield and Korngold, 1991: 26)

This dominant Western psychology of the self which sees the individual as primarily an autonomous being, independent of the living systems that surround him or her, has led to the emergence of a psychotherapeutic model that is largely based on individualistic assumptions. In such a schema, 'individuation' and a strong separate ego are seen as the key to mental health. This constricted sense of self highlights our divisions from one another, and allows for an objectification of others and of ourselves.

Individual humans are seen as separate from each other, and some humans are thought to be superior to others. Most of us describe ourselves by our occupational, family, gender, racial or ethnic roles. ... This way of describing ourselves emphasizes our separateness, our boundedness, fixedness, reification, non fluidity. We think we can locate ourselves as a 'thing' in space and time, separate from other 'things' in other spaces and times. This is the dominant version of reality: the world is a collection of separate entities that are related mechanically if at all. (Conn, 1998: 181)

The ideological framework informing much of the psychological treatment given to those who are labelled 'mentally ill', identifies their behaviour as 'abnormal'. Treating the person as a self-sufficient separate entity, the moral and political dimensions of the deviant behaviour are not addressed. Illness in such a worldview is an individual matter. There is no language of social suffering that can speak to the moral and political experience of both the sufferer and the suffering community. Even when attention is widened to include family dynamics, the family is usually seen as the source of its own dysfunction while the social, economic, political and ecological systems in which the family lives are ignored. This distorts the image of what the world is and who we are within it.

When people are like machines, modern medicine becomes obliged to keep the machine running. Its purpose is defined as avoiding death rather than enriching life. Bodies must be kept alive at all costs because to die is considered intrinsically evil – death is the enemy to be conquered. Life and death are no longer part of the continuous cycle. (Beinfield and Korngold, 1991: 26)

This Cartesian view of the world also created a split between nature and human life, whereby these two worlds are not just separate but are seen as being opposed to one another. Our control of nature has allowed us to exploit it for our own benefit, to the point where the dangers facing life on earth from massive consumerism, resource depletion and pollution are unprecedented. So it is not just our increasing technological ability to rob the earth of its resources that is at the heart of the crisis, but more our loss of deep connection to the Earth. Our belief in a separate self has numbed our innate response to the danger – a response that has been an essential feature of life through our evolution, allowing the human species to adapt to new challenges. As Joanne Macy (1995) points out, it is hard to credit our pain for the world, if we believe we are essentially separate from it. Thomas Berry calls this a crisis of cosmology: 'We have a mechanistic sense of the natural world, not a sense of an inherent sacred quality' (Berry, 1999: 12). A narrow definition of self, therefore, which disconnects us from nature, is not only at the heart of the environmental crisis but also leads to an increasing impoverishment of the psychological self. Denial of the desire to live in harmony with the natural world and its rhythms is just as damaging as the denial of other vital human needs. It also leads to alienation, numbness, anxiety and depression. The idea of the self-sufficient and supreme individual, whether in the version of *Homo economicus* or of Thatcher's denial of society, turns out therefore to be a dangerously truncated and atomised understanding of the human person.

'FULLNESS OF LIFE'

Again and again in his writings Polanyi returns to the hold on our psyches of 'the traditional picture of an atomistic individualism' and laments that 'the new knowledge has not produced a vision of society comparable in popularity' (1968: 116). These concerns, written half a century ago, take us to the heart of what is now being identified as a fundamental crisis of our times, namely the split or disconnection between individuals and society and between the human species and the biosphere.

> Ultimately the task is to integrate what has been split within each of us; within our families and between the generations; in our culture; in our way of life, which has discarded or harmed so many people and creatures, and in our collective relationship with the Earth. (Glendinning, 1994: 132)

Our new scientific understanding of how the universe came into being, and the knowledge that everything has a purpose, is helping towards healing this illusion of separateness. New insights from quantum physics and system theories are creating a paradigm shift from a reductionist, materialistic, quantifiable worldview to a more holistic, spiritual and qualitative one.

> On the level of quantum mechanics, everything is interconnected, not a hierarchy but in a vast, interconnected and far-reaching network. ... Regardless of where we look, the most progressive leaders in the field are talking the language of virtual reality, neural networks, system theory, cybernetics, the global village, cyberspace. (Bloom, 1998: 153)

It is leading to a return to a holistic approach to health, one that has always been recognised in Eastern and indigenous cultures. Here the root of the word 'health' – being whole or making whole – gives rise to an understanding of health and wholeness as 'being in tune with one's soul and the spirit of nature'. We can also see the beginnings of a redefinition of sanity and mental health within psychology that include an increased awareness of the interdependence between individual health and the health of the environment and between traumatic behaviours and the social conditions that support them. As we now understand in a new way 'the relatedness of social justice, psychological trauma, and cultural habitability' (Bloom, 1998: 18), psychology is searching for a larger context for the theory and practice of healing.

There are also those within the psychological field – ecopsychologists like Sarah Conn, Allen Kanner, Mary Gomes and Ted Roszak and depth psychologists including James Hillman and Stephen Aizenstat – who believe that our pain and neuroses are intrinsically connected to what is happening to the biosphere and that our well-being is conditional on the well-being of the ecosystem of the planet. For example, Roszak asks: how can the soul be saved while the biosphere crumbles? Conn refers to consumerism as 'materialistic disorder' and sees it as a serious signal of a culture's disconnection from the earth: 'Because we are cut off from our roots, we have forgotten how to hunt for and gather up its treasures, either concretely or imaginatively. Our only current way of hunting and gathering seems to be shopping and accumulating merchandise' (Conn, 1995: 162). The depth psychologists refer to the 'psyche of nature' and see our essential psychological spontaneities as being rooted most deeply in the natural world. Hillman likens modern psychotherapy to working in the below cabin of a sinking ship like the *Titanic*. He sees the cut off between the self and the natural world as being arbitrary: 'So long as we cannot ascertain where the "me" ends (is it with my skin? with my behaviour? with my personal interfacing connections and their influences and traces?) how can we establish the limits of psychology?' (Hillman, 1995: xviii).

An individual's harmony with his/her deep self requires therefore both a journey to the interior and a harmonising with the environmental world. It requires an examination of thoughts, feelings and behaviours to find new ways to develop a more ecocentric rather than egocentric worldview.

Human behaviour is responsible for quickly deteriorating ecosystems. … Solutions to environmental problems will require more that just technological answers. We will also have to make psychological changes: changes in the way we behave, the way we see ourselves, the way we see our relationship to nature, and even, perhaps, the way we see the meaning of our lives. (Winter, 1996: 2–3)

For transpersonal psychologists, who see the root of the psyche as being spiritual, these psychological changes involve a journey in spiritual awakening. 'We are more than psycho-physical-emotionally wounded and conditioned selves but spiritual beings' (Cortright, 1997: 243). While modern psychology has pointed to this in, for example, the idea of the 'real self' and of the 'authentic self', transpersonal psychology says that this wisdom is our spiritual nature and it is the ground that supports the psychological self. As we 'reoccupy the spiritual-ecological dimension of existence', recognising ourselves as a dimension of the earth rather than separate from it, we can begin again to develop a compassion for all things (Fisher, 2002: 190).

This compassion may bring us out of what Macy calls our 'psychic numbing' – like the individual who numbs or dissociates in the face of trauma we have been numbed in the face of the spiralling destruction of our world (see Box 7.2 on trauma). Many writers speak of our need to deal with this pain, both individual and collective, by providing a context for holding the pain (Fisher, 2002) and for rituals of grieving as a form of 'empowering' (Macy, 1995). Joanna Macy has with John Seed created the Council of All Beings, a collective mourning ritual and workshops that encourage people to work through their feelings of disbelief, denial, terror, rage, guilt, sorrow and despair at the possible loss of the planet. These workshops attest to the benefit of facing our pain, as unblocking our pain leads to a reconnection with the larger web of life and a shift to new levels of social consciousness and empowerment. 'By recognising our capacity to suffer with our world, we dawn to newer dimensions of being. In those dimensions there is still pain, but also a lot more. There is wonder, even joy, as we come home to our mutual belonging and there is a new kind of power' (Macy, 1995: 253).

The earth as a living soul is indeed a challenge to a worldview that has lost sight of the idea of the Great Chain of Being where everything is connected and has a purpose. The enormity of the ecological crisis, however, demands a deep reworking of basic patterns of thinking to ones that are 'holistic, systemic, symbiotic, connective and participatory' (Spangler, 1993: 78). Fisher speaks of the need for new myths, since myths are rich and nourishing as they are stories about forces larger than us. The modern myth of serving good by a rise in GDP (of which the pro-globalisation myth alluded to at the

BOX 7.2   TRAUMA: SOCIETY HAS BECOME EMOTIONALLY NUMB

Although the traumatic effects of war, violence and natural disasters have been recorded in literature, art and medicine throughout history, the study of trauma and its effects on people's minds and bodies is relatively new. According to Judith Lewis Herman, the research that led to the definition of trauma was largely based on studying the experiences of soldiers who fought in the Second World War and the Vietnam War, and more recently the experiences of women survivors of sexual abuse. Only since 1980 has post-traumatic stress disorder (PTSD) been recognised and defined in the *Diagnostic and Statistical Manual of Mental Disorders* (DSM). According to the manual's definition of trauma, the person 'experienced, witnessed or confronted an event or events that involved death or the threat of death, a serious injury or an attack or threat to the person's physical integrity or that of other people, and in that situation the reaction was intense fear, powerlessness and/or horror' (quoted in Cane, 2000: 14).

Trauma is also social. Herman (1992) shows how, while every trauma that occurs is an individual trauma perpetuated by individuals and experienced by individuals, every trauma is also social with roots in social institutions and with implications for society at large. This systemic view of trauma recognises that it has become an organising principle in the formation, development and maintenance of society as a whole. Bloom describes how the symptoms of trauma are lived out in modern societies: how society has become emotionally numb, overwhelmed by daily accounts of wars, hunger and violence so that we have become capable only of responding to massive and life-threatening stimulations. Anger fails to serve the purpose for which it was designed – the protection of boundaries, but leads to violence in all its manifestations.

> The voices of protest that should be organising and vociferously countering forces of intolerance, hatred, and repression are largely quiet or absent. Instead the forces of rage are left to go on a rampage, attacking the sick, the injured, the poor, women, children, homosexuals, non-Caucasians and anyone who fails to conform to rigid and repressive expectations. (Bloom, 1997: 216)

Diminished awareness leads to dissociation. We feel so little personal control over massive social problems. 'The hallmark of dissociation is the ability to tolerate marked incongruity as witnessed in our attitudes and behaviours to violence. We are concerned with violence yet buy arms at an alarming rate. Child abuse continues to rise' (Bloom, 1997: 219). One way of coping in such a traumatised situation is through multiple addictions. This includes not just addiction to alcohol and drugs but to all destructive behaviours that are beyond the individual's ability to control by acts of conscious will. Like individual victims of extreme terror who tell the story of their unresolved past through behaviour in current relationships, as a society we are caught up in cycles of violence, abuse and poverty. 'How much of our national discontent, anxiety and ongoing angst is related to an underlying knowing without knowing – an awareness of guilt for acts of perpetration which we have actively engaged in or passively allowed?' (Bloom, 1997: 224). Alienation

▶

from self and others leads to emotional isolation or dissociation, a state of estrangement between the self and the objective world or between different parts of the personality. There is a loss of meaning and purpose. 'Like traumatised people we avoid the pain of confronting real horrors and deny whole segments of our experience because we lack a clear vision of a different world, a different way of being' (Bloom, 1997: 225).

beginning of Chapter 1 is a version) is a defective myth that provides no spiritual satisfaction. Fisher says we need satisfying myths 'that sing a more-than-human world' (2002: 176). Berry finds such a myth in today's scientific discoveries about the universe:

This story that we know through empirical observation of the world is our most valuable resource. ... This story as told in its galactic expansion, its Earth formation, its life emergence, and its self-reflexive consciousness, fulfils in our times the role of the mythic accounts of the universe that existed in earlier times, when human awareness was dominated by a spatial mode of consciousness. (Berry, 1999: 163)

Finally our new understanding of our deep interconnection to one another, to society and the universe calls us to live more mindfully and differently. Aware of our intimate connection to all of creation, we are drawn to make creative contributions and responses to stopping the destruction of our planet: 'As the pain of the world is rooted in our interconnectedness with all of life, so surely is our power. ... Here power means openness, vulnerability and readiness to change' (Macy, 1995: 256). Macy writes of the Great Turning – the revolution needed to save our world from destruction and ourselves from despair. She says it is happening in three areas: actions to slow the damage to the earth and its beings; analysis of structural causes and the creation of structural alternatives; and a fundamental shift in worldview. Ignacio Martin-Boro, a Salvadorean Jesuit priest and psychologist who was assassinated by the US-trained government soldiers in 1989, wrote about a 'liberation psychology' – where victims of violence would be encouraged to see the connection between their individual problems and the oppressive political structures under which they lived so as to be encouraged to 'speak out to power'.

There is an urgency to meet this challenge not just in the face of the destruction of the planet, but for our own fullness of life. If not we will continue to suffer anxiety, alienation and despair. As Bloom says, we will continue to suffer the effects of secondary trauma, living in a violent world disconnected from Earth and Spirit. 'Our individualistic self-preoccupied and disconnected point of reference has brought us to a biological, personal, social, economic, political and spiritual end' (Bloom,1997: 255).

SECURITY OR VULNERABILITY?

Having, in these two chapters, examined the underlying and more fundamental causes and consequences of growing vulnerability and identified how it finds expression in violence (to ourselves, to others and to nature), it is now time to return to an issue discussed briefly in Chapter 1: the relationship between the concept of vulnerability and that of security. As outlined in Box 7.3, the concept of security has since the end of the Cold War been adapted from discourse on military defence and applied to a range of threats to human livelihood, both environmental and social. As the Commission on Human Security put it in its report *Human Security Now*:

> Today's global flow of goods, services, finance, people and images spotlight the many interlinkages in the security of all people. We share a planet, a biosphere, a technological arsenal, a social fabric. The security of one person, one community, one nation rests on the decisions of many others – sometimes fortuitously, sometimes precariously. ... Thus people throughout the world, in developing and developed countries alike, live under varied conditions of insecurity. (Commission on Human Security, 2003: 2)

Used in this way, the concept of human security seems virtually interchangeable with that of vulnerability. Why then promote the concept of vulnerability if that of human security is already better established? A brief answer to this question was given in Chapter 1 where it was mentioned that the concept of human security suffers from analytical imprecision and from ambiguities as to what exactly it means which can result in prescriptions very much at odds with what it seeks to achieve. Though human security and vulnerability are closely related, the differences between them have important implications which require attention.

An important starting point for examining the differences between the two concepts is to note their origins. Human security derived from debates about the changing threats to security associated with the end of the Cold War, shifting from military threats to those

BOX 7.3   HUMAN SECURITY: RAMBO WARRIOR OR MOTHER AND CHILD?

During the Cold War security was almost exclusively seen as a military issue relating to the need to protect states from military threats from other states or from armed groups within states. The principal way of doing this was to invest in armaments and to maintain effective military forces. In Bill McSweeney's image, this could be called a 'Rambo warrior' conception of security. McSweeney, however, introduces an entirely different image, that of the Mother and Child, which 'is hardly an icon to grace the walls of the Rand Corporation or the Pentagon', he writes. The difference between these two images, he elaborates, is the difference between security as a commodity and security as a relationship or, one might add, the difference between state security and human security (McSweeney, 1999: 13–16).

As military threats seemed to recede following the end of the Cold War, the concept of human security, with its focus on a wider range of threats such as environmental destruction or social breakdown, emerged. Though the need for such a wider conception had been previously mentioned (for example in the 1980 Brandt Report), the concept itself was introduced by the United Nations Development Programme in its 1994 *Human Development Report*. This defined the concept as follows:

> Human security can be said to have two aspects. It means, first, safety from such chronic threats as hunger, disease and repression. And second, it means protection from sudden and hurtful disruptions in the patterns of daily life – whether in homes, in jobs or in communities. Such threats can exist at all levels of national income and development. (UNDP, 1994: 23)

For the UNDP, this required moving from an objective of territorial security to a much greater stress on people's security, and from the means of achieving security through armaments to achieving it through sustainable human development. The focus therefore turns inwards, based on the view that a state is secure when its people can live secure lives.

While the concept of 'human security' has generated much debate among academics, with realists strongly resisting any dilution of traditional threats to state security and insisting on the need for capable military forces to deter them, no consensus has emerged about either the validity of the concept or what it might mean. However, while these debates rage, the concept has become influential in the world of practical politics. A number of states, notably Canada and Japan, have made the concept central to the security doctrines they have elaborated to respond to the challenges of a post-Cold War world. Japan played a major role in the establishment of the Commission on Human Security which had the active support of the UN Secretary General Kofi Annan and issued its report *Human Security Now* in 2003. Canada and Norway formed a Human Security Network which plans to publish a regular *Human Security Report* to complement the UNDP's *Human Development Report*. Among the other states which form part of the network are Austria, Chile, Greece, Ireland, Jordan, Mali, the Netherlands, Slovenia, Switzerland and Thailand, with South Africa as an observer. Finally, within the European Union international development NGOs have campaigned for human security to be a central dimension of the Union's security policy.

deriving from social and environmental causes. Vulnerability, in contrast, has emerged from the empirical analyses done by various intergovernmental organisations of the impact on human well-being of processes associated with globalisation. The identification by these analyses of growing threats and the erosion of coping mechanisms gives the concept of vulnerability an analytical precision – it makes clear what it is about threats and eroding coping mechanisms that result in vulnerability. While such analyses do not elaborate on what such vulnerability might mean (this has been the task of these two chapters), they show how it is resulting from the processes they describe. Turning to the concept of human security, one also finds it is used tellingly in a descriptive fashion to identify threats (and, of course, the threats identified by both concepts are very similar). However, it is much less clear what the analytical connection is between these threats and human security. For what it promises is not just to identify the impact on people of such threats but to relate them to a more positive condition called security. What might constitute such security is left very vague.

This lack of clarity is obvious from examining the range of definitions of human security that are encountered in the literature. Some influential ones define it simply as a means without making clear what the end is. For example, Alkire's definition states that 'the objective of human security is to safeguard the vital core of all human lives from critical pervasive threats, in a way that is consistent with long-term human fulfilment' (Alkire, n.d.: 2). The definition offered by the Commission on Human Security – 'to protect the vital core of all human lives in ways that enhance human freedoms and human fulfilment' – echoes this. Clearly 'human fulfilment' is the end here but how does this relate to human security: Are they equivalent? If so, why use the term human security? If not, what is the relationship between both? By contrast, Thomas is more explicit in her definition when she writes that 'human security describes a condition of existence in which basic material needs are met, and in which human dignity, including meaningful participation in the life of the community can be realised' (Thomas, 2002: 115). The difficulty with this is that it is equivalent to a definition of successful development. So are we to take it that security equals development; that they are simply interchangeable terms? If so, why use the term 'human security' at all? If one ranges more widely in the literature, one encounters an even greater variety of meanings. In their survey, Hampson and Hay identify three distinct conceptions of human security: a natural rights/rule of law conception anchored in the fundamental liberal assumption of basic individual rights to 'life, liberty, and the pursuit of happiness'; a humanitarian conception informing international efforts to deepen and strengthen international law; and a developmental conception, relating to the social and environmental threats treated here (Hampson and Hay, 2002). All in all, then, it is not surprising that the concept of human security has been criticised for being 'vague, incoherent, or merely impossible' (Alkire, n.d.: 6). In this situation, the danger is that different analysts assign the term meanings that suit their normative preferences. If so, it evacuates it of any useful analytical precision.

The significance of this lack of clarity is identified when examining policy prescriptions that flow from the use of the term 'human security'. Two issues arise, the first relating to agency and the second to means. Agency here refers to whoever or whatever is to counteract the threats identified. On this issue, human security analysts take a broad view. For example, the *Human Security Now* report identifies protection strategies and empowerment strategies to achieve the objective of 'reducing and – where possible – removing the insecurities that plague human lives' (Commission on Human Security, 2003: 8). These are two-fold: protection strategies by states, international agencies, NGOs and the private sector to 'shield people from menaces' and empowerment strategies to enable people to develop their resilience to different conditions. 'Both are required in nearly all situations of human insecurity, though their form and balance will vary tremendously' (2003: 10). This echoes the emphasis of vulnerability analysis on threats and coping mechanisms: any response needs to protect against the former and strengthen the latter. Yet, while the concept of vulnerability *necessarily* involves both approaches, this is not true of the concept of human security. Deriving from its origins in discourse on state security, it could be consistent with state action to safeguard its own citizens from outside threats (for example, unilateral US actions withdrawing from the Kyoto treaty on climate change or subsidising its cotton producers). Hough draws attention to the fact that some scholars who widen the range of security threats to include non-military issues still maintain a state-centrism even if in a subtler form (Hough, 2004: 5). Indeed, pushed even further, human security is not inconsistent with the actions of the 'national security states' of South America in the 1970s and 1980s, which targeted minority sectors of their populations as a threat but thereby fostered a strong sense of security and even active support among other sectors of the population (not all of them middle or upper class). It can be concluded therefore that there is nothing in the concept of human security that precludes it being used by states in ways that are harmful to some people, whether some of its own citizens or citizens in other states. In such examples, human security can be used to justify violence against those seen as a threat.

A second issue relates to means. Again deriving from its origins in state security doctrine, human security can be entirely consistent with a methodological individualism. In other words, if the threat is seen as coming from the Other (in the doctrine of military security this meant other states, but in terms of human security it could mean threats from other people such as immigrants, the poor and gays), the solution adopted is to protect oneself against that Other. The result is gated communities, armed guards and alarm systems. While this is far from what proponents of human security advocate, it is entirely consistent with one understanding of human security, namely that one secures oneself *against* those whom one sees as a threat. For the concept of security is consistent with a very atomised society divided into the secure and the insecure; when this point is reached a sort of vicious circle sets in whereby the secure resort to ever more elaborate efforts and investments to secure themselves against others. This reflects the notion of security as a commodity, something we can possess, even buy, for ourselves. As long as security can mean a condition we attain to protect ourselves against others, then it is an unreliable basis for theorising individual and, even more so, social well-being. For, as McSweeney puts it: 'Security is a slippery term indeed, rooted in a fundamental human emotion which takes on different forms and emphases as it expresses itself at different levels of community' (McSweeney, 1999: 199).

Yet McSweeney's work opens the possibility of understanding security as a relational concept, rooted in the needs of individuals who satisfy material needs through belonging to a wider collective that therefore provides them with the basis for a secure identity. It is in this sense that the concept of human security could have real promise. But this conception of security points in very different directions to the ways it has been used in security studies and in international relations. By contrast, the concept of vulnerability gives far more unambiguous expression to such a relational understanding of the roots of social order, an expression that is more consistent with the insights of contemporary psychology and psychotherapy on the relationship of the individual to society (see Box 7.4), and with the insights of Karl Polanyi on the need to embed the market in society, as outlined in Chapter 6. By definition, vulnerability and a relational conception of security both theorise the roots of social order and human well-being as resting in a sense of belonging to society in a way that satisfies both material and psychological needs and offers security to the individual as part of the collectivity (and, indeed, of the biosphere). But, unlike security which can allow very individualist understandings, vulnerability is an unambiguously collective concept since it gives priority to actions, whether by policy makers or by civil society groups, that strengthen social solidarities and satisfy the material needs of the collectivity not just those of individuals. The Millennium Development Goals are one such action at a global level, yet the inadequate financial contributions of the richest states to their realisation shows the limits of the commitment to such an understanding of what is required for a more secure world.

BOX 7.4   VULNERABILITY: BETWEEN LIFE AND DEATH

Existential psychology sees death as the human person's ultimate and innate vulnerability, creating 'ontological anxiety', meaninglessness and despair. Essentially alone, the only authentic source of meaning for the individual is the meaning created from her or his conviction, action and choice. Within religious traditions on the other hand, our basic vulnerability is the seed of enlightenment already present within us. 'This capacity to be vulnerable – to the raw edges in our own experience – is what allows us to truly connect with ourselves, with others and with life itself' (Welwood, 2000: 162).

We may continue to deny our connectedness to society and the earth and continue to exploit precious resources; but as we destroy the earth we also destroy ourselves: 'What humans do to their outer world, they do to their own interior world. As the natural world recedes in its diversity and abundance, so the human finds itself impoverished in its economic resources, in its imaginative powers, its human sensitivities, and in significant aspects of its intellectual intuitions' (Swimme and Berry, 1992: 242). Or we can shift to new levels of social consciousness and empowerment reconnecting with the larger web of life. 'By recognising our capacity to suffer with our world, we dawn to newer dimensions of being. In those dimensions there is still pain, but also a lot more. There is wonder, even joy, as we come home to our mutual belonging and there is a new kind of power' (Macy, 1995: 253).

In one very important sense, therefore, vulnerability points beyond all conceptions of security, thereby showing they are not interchangeable terms. For vulnerability opens us up to our need for others and for a connectedness with nature, but it also opens us up to our ultimate mortality. Thus, in one sense, vulnerability is the most essential feature of the human condition. If we are insecure we may aspire to security but if we are vulnerable, we can never aspire to invulnerability. This is not an insubstantial difference since it reinforces our common fate as human beings, no matter how divided the human race may be. Therefore, instead of seeking security against one another, vulnerability leads us, through our common actions, to seek both to lessen our vulnerabilities but also to support one another in living with the essential vulnerability of the human condition, thereby curbing our tendency to inflict violence on ourselves, one another and the natural world. A more widespread acknowledgement of vulnerability in policy discourse and social science theorising has the potential to focus attention on what unites us as human beings as distinct from promoting actions through which we seek to gain advantage over one another. In these ways, it better reflects the insights of the latest scientific understanding of the structure of our world (see Box 8.1).

CONCLUSIONS

These two chapters have invested the term 'vulnerability' with a deeper meaning and a theoretical coherence, identifying both threats to well-being but also clearly pointing to the need to strengthen networks of belonging if we are to achieve well-being. Through subjecting the claim that 'there is no such thing as society' to critical interrogation and showing how it is dangerously eroding social solidarities, through drawing on the insights of psychology and psychotherapy to understand the human person's need for connectedness, and through examining the ambiguities of the concept of human security, this chapter has strongly validated the core insights of Polanyi on the social nature of the human person and the damage, indeed violence, done when the bonds of secure belonging to society and to the wider natural world are eroded. In conclusion, it can be said that both chapters point to the need for a more ambitious agenda of social analysis and change if the challenges posed by increasing vulnerability and violence are to be adequately addressed. As Polanyi put it: 'To overcome such doctrines, which constrict our minds and souls and greatly enhance the difficulty of the life-saving adjustment, may require no less than a reform of our consciousness' (1968: 61). In turning to examine remedies to today's neoliberal globalisation in the book's final part, the discussion will be guided by the insights of these two chapters.

Part IV

Remedies

8
'So What Should We Do?'

[M]any progressive forces are often characterized, wrongly, as 'anti-globalization'. Indeed what most of these forces seem to want is a form of social justice and a more humane, better regulated and more democratically responsive form of globalization, not its elimination.
(Gill, 2003: 156)

The question reportedly asked by a frustrated student at the opening of the 2005 World Social Forum in Porto Alegre is one that echoes insistently around lecture halls, meeting rooms, and public protests at the beginning of the new millennium: 'So what should we do?' (Loewenberg, 2005). Motivating this question very often is the desire for, as this chapter's epigraph puts it, 'a more humane, better regulated and more democratically responsive form of globalization'. It is an appropriate question with which to open the final part of this book, which examines remedies. For remedying, in the sense of rectifying or making good, is a concern of all sides in the globalisation debate. Obviously critics of neoliberal globalisation seek to remedy what they see as its many defects, already outlined at some length in this book. Different approaches to doing this will constitute an important topic of this two-chapter part. But it must not be forgotten that those who firmly support today's form of globalisation as the best hope for global economic growth and development, as well as for the alleviation of poverty around the world, also recognise that many defects need to be remedied. Foremost among these is the failure to liberalise markets more completely in different parts of the world and in different sectors of the economy (such as, for example, agriculture). But, increasingly, many proponents of real existing globalisation are also facing the challenge of ensuring its benefits reach the poor everywhere. For this reason, the agenda of meetings of the G-8 countries throughout 2005, was rather surprisingly dominated by the challenge of poverty alleviation. Remedies are therefore integral to all discussions of globalisation.

The subject of vulnerability provides a particular focus to this discussion of remedies. What concerns us are remedies that help address the sources of growing vulnerability and violence as identified in this book, both the increase in threats to human well-being and the erosion of coping mechanisms, as they manifest themselves in the life experience of people around the world and in the various spheres of life – the financial and the economic, the social and the political, the cultural and the environmental. Finding remedies for these cumulative vulnerabilities is therefore the objective of these two chapters. Furthermore, the two chapters of Part III, on society and the market, and on the individual and society, offer pointers towards what needs to be addressed if these vulnerabilities are to be remedied. Drawing on the work of Karl Polanyi, Chapter 6 analysed the destructive impact on society of disembedding the market so that society was made to serve the economy rather than the other way around. Polanyi's identification of the treatment of land, labour and money as commodities offers further insights into the sources of growing vulnerability in today's world and their destructive impact. Chapter 7 mirrored some of these themes of disembedding and commodification in its treatment of how individual freedom has come to take precedence over social solidarities with the result that there is a growing disjuncture between our individual and our collective destinies. Therefore, any remedies to combat increasing vulnerability and violence need to be able effectively to offer some prospect for achieving a more equitable and sustainable balance between individual freedom and social solidarity. These core insights will guide the discussion throughout the remaining chapters.

The division between Chapters 8 and 9 is as follows. This chapter looks at *what* needs to be done, namely the sorts of remedies that are necessary if the vulnerabilities and violence identified in this book are to be effectively addressed. The next chapter will look at *who* are advancing remedies and *how* they are seeking to realise them. It could be said therefore that this chapter treats proposals for change while the next chapter treats the politics of change. Inevitably the two are intimately connected but the distinction between them allows a separate treatment of, on the one hand, what needs to be done and, on the other, how likely it is that it might actually be done given the present politics of global change. The present chapter advances its argument in three sections. The first section following this introduction examines how change happens, offering a theoretical overview of an issue that is often treated as if it were self-evident, an overview that helps elucidate the empirical sections that follow in both chapters. Next comes a section that examines the principal remedies currently being proposed, what some call 'ideologies of globalisation' (see Mittelman, 2004, Chapter 5). Three remedies or agendas are identified and treated separately: the maintenance agenda, the reformist agenda and the radical agenda. Having outlined each of these, the chapter's third section discusses how adequate each is to address the concerns of this book, using in particular the insights of the two chapters of Part III to interrogate them. The concluding section offers a tentative answer to the question posed in the chapter's title.

HOW DOES SOCIAL CHANGE HAPPEN?

Understanding how social change happens is a far more complex task than is often recognised, either in the social sciences or in practical politics. For, as theorists like Cox (1996; 2002) and Gill (in Bakker and Gill, 2003) remind us, social sciences such as politics or economics have tended to look at change within fixed assumptions about the nature of the political and economic system. As a consequence, this leads them to limit the range of options that are considered and to see change as something incremental, evolutionary and broadly progressive. However, by focusing on incremental change within the existing power structures, rather than on the potential for changing those power structures themselves, 'this mode of reasoning dictates that, with respect to essentials, the future will always be like the past' (Cox, 1996: 92). The consequence of such an approach to analysing social change is that the existing power structures remain unchallenged and the hegemonic order is maintained.

Raising these issues about how social change is understood is by no means a distraction from the task of achieving real change but rather the first step on this road. For, as Gill puts it, 'knowledge is also a process of social struggle ... between hegemonic and counter-hegemonic perspectives and principles' (Gill, 2003: 38). Therefore the starting point for social change is the development of a critical understanding, a new self-awareness that results in 'a more complex and coherent understanding of the social world' and of the possibilities for change that can thereby be identified (Gill, 2003: 31). As Gramsci emphasised, a necessary condition for social change is critical consciousness. However, in any historical epoch, this critical consciousness is inevitably bounded by the dominant prevailing epistemologies or frameworks of knowledge. In earlier centuries, these were based on religious understandings of the world but for the past 200 years or so our social understandings have been heavily marked, indeed bounded, by the dominance of a scientific world view based on Newtonian physics and Cartesian philosophy. While we are often unaware of how knowledge frameworks orient our thinking, we need to remind ourselves that so-called fundamental and seemingly incontrovertible 'truths' – such as the existence of an 'objective' reality divorced from the human subject and operating according to its own 'laws' which can be identified through rigorous, value-free, methods of inquiry seeking to uncover fundamental causes – rest on a particular physics and philosophy. For decades, some social scientists have sought to distinguish their activities from those of natural scientists, arguing that there is no 'objective' social reality to be known through rigorous methods of value-free inquiry, but that we are social subjects who actively create our own history. For example, this is expressed in Gramsci's rich concept of praxis which rests on a rejection of any absolute distinction between 'subjective' and 'objective' and instead combines theory and practice in a mutually enriching relationship. Yet, despite the promotion of critical views of the dominant epistemology by some social scientists (particularly within a Marxist tradition), the influence of this epistemology is very evident in the strongly deterministic theories of social change that have become deeply embedded in the social sciences (notably modernisation theory) and in attempts to replicate the 'objective', value-free methods of inquiry of the natural sciences (notably in economics, but also in much political science and more widely throughout the social sciences). As Box 8.1 shows, however, the very basis of this epistemology is now demolished due to the findings of quantum mechanics. It appears the critical social scientists were right all along! We human beings are indeed active participants in the creation of our own reality and there is no basis in the physical world for predicting the outcomes of these creative acts. Therefore the more complex and coherent understanding of the social world opened up by the new physics provides the basis for a new epistemology that leads us to conceive of the nature and potential of social change in very new ways. As a result, social change suddenly becomes an adventure of possibilities.

This, of course, does not mean that everything is possible. We face what Gill calls the 'intransigence of social reality' (Gill, 2003: 21), namely that social reality is structured in ways that perpetuate how things are and that strongly resist fundamental reorientation. But the lessons of quantum mechanics remind us that the nature of

BOX 8.1   THE NEW PHYSICS: WESTERN PHYSICISTS MEET EASTERN MYSTICS

The social sciences have for long been drawn to the idea of emulating the natural sciences. Indeed Giddens identified as part of the 'orthodox consensus' of the social sciences in the post-war period the notion that they could be modelled on the natural sciences (Giddens, 1996: 65–7). The result was an attempt to create a value-free social science, through which the detached observer would generate 'facts' about social reality using methods as rigorous as possible to maintain 'objectivity'. The reality to be observed was accepted as a given and the scientist's task was to probe detailed elements so as to establish a more firm knowledge of how society operated, with a particular focus on distinguishing causes and effects. While such an understanding of social science has been on retreat for decades, it has maintained a dominance in economics, arguably the most influential of the social sciences. In this way, it has had a major impact on the way most people view the social world around them.

Yet, while social scientists were seeking to emulate a model of what they regarded as objective science, a series of remarkable breakthroughs in the natural sciences were leading to a paradigm shift in our scientific understanding of the physical universe, a move 'from the metaphor of the machine to the metaphor of the living organism' (Korten: 1999: 9) which has revolutionary implications for how we understand the social world also. At the heart of this revolution are the findings of the new physics of quantum mechanics which tells us that there is no such thing as objectivity, that we as observers are not detached from but are part of what we observe. Furthermore, quantum mechanics tells us that in observing reality we are also changing it. As Wheeler, a Princeton physicist, put it: 'May the universe in some strange sense be "brought into being" by the participation of those who participate? … The vital act is the act of participation. "Participator" is the incontrovertible new concept given by quantum mechanics' (quoted in Zukav, 1979: 54). Far from the universe being determined by 'laws' as understood by Newtonian physics (and as transferred to the economic realm by neoclassical economics), quantum mechanics tells us that we have minimal knowledge of future phenomena and that we are limited to knowing only probabilities, with the result that we are more involved in creating the future than we realised. Finally, since quantum mechanics has no way of predicting individual events, it concerns itself with group behaviour, abandoning the laws that govern individual events and dealing only with the statistical probabilities that govern collections of events.

These stunning breakthroughs also have implications for social scientists. Instead of being detached observers whose role is limited to finding out about the objective laws that govern the way the world operates, we now find ourselves to be participants in a living world involved in endless acts of unpredictable creation. In this sense, our agency is more important than the given structure. Our attention is drawn not to the detailed fragments of reality but to the bigger picture of the whole global reality, 'to understand the processes of change in which both parts and whole are involved' (Cox, 1996: 87). As Berry puts it, we are being awakened again to the universe not 'as a collection of objects [but] rather … as a communion of

▶

subjects' (Berry, 1999: 16). If Newtonian physics led to social scientific approaches that fostered a plundering and exploitative relationship with one another and the environment, the new physics holds the promise of fostering a more participative and creative relationship. The changes required go to the heart of how we conceive of knowledge for, in Zukav's words, 'the languages of Eastern mystics and Western physicists are becoming very similar' (Zukav, 1979: 54).

social reality is not predetermined by forces beyond collective human action; rather, social reality is intransigent or resistant to change because of power relations, not because it is eternally decreed that things must be as they are. To undertake social change, therefore, requires us to focus on power. As Cox puts it: 'Really existing social power relations is the fundamental object of enquiry' (Cox, 2002: 79). It is these power relations that maintain the hegemony of the present order, such that possibilities for changing that order can only be identified through an analysis of how these power relations operate in any particular situation. Focusing on power relations helps identify contradictions within them and the spaces for change that these open up. For example, Mittelman argues that

globalization has opened spaces, expanding the boundaries associated with political life. Of course, one cannot predict the future from a set of structural tendencies. But one can gauge the balance of constraints and possibilities. History is fundamentally propelled by human will, albeit subject to evolving global forces; it is an open-ended process. If globalization was made by humankind, then it can be unmade or remade by political agency. (Mittelman, 2004: 89)

To undertake such a revealing analysis of power relations, we need a guiding method, such as that offered by Cox's theory of historical structures.

For Cox, social change happens within limits which he calls 'frameworks for action'. Such frameworks, which are never eternal or frozen, take the form of historical structures in any particular epoch and provide 'a picture of a particular configuration of forces' which does not determine actions in any mechanical way but does impose pressures and constraints on actions (Cox, 1996: 97–8). 'Individuals and groups may move with the pressures or resist and oppose them, but they cannot ignore them' (Cox, 1996: 98). Three categories of forces interact in any historical structure:

material capabilities (technological and organisational capabilities, industries and armaments, and the wealth that directs these), ideas (the intersubjective meanings that constitute the 'common sense' of any particular historical period as well as the different images of social order that compete for dominance, such as ideas of justice and the common good), and institutions (reflecting power relations, they are a means of stabilising and perpetuating a particular order). One can have stable social structures that achieve high levels of legitimacy due to a successful 'fit' between material capabilities (how adequate the wealth and resources produced are to the needs of society), ideas (that accept this order as legitimate and just) and institutions (that underpin through their actions and operation the structure's legitimacy) and that therefore do not require a lot of active management (for example, through applying repressive force). Such a successful social structure is another way of describing what is referred to as an hegemonic order, namely one that achieves stability not through force but through the free consent of the ruled.

It is important to remember that the basis for the stability of an historical structure is not primarily state power but the 'fit' between different forms of power, namely economic and financial power, 'ideas' or cultural power and the power of institutions. This is what distinguishes Cox's view from more mainstream analyses of power that give priority to political power over other forms. To illustrate what it means, Cox takes the global dominance of Britain in the nineteenth century as an instance, arguing that it rested not just on its military power (the Royal Navy) but also on the norms of liberal economics (free trade, the gold standard and the free movement of capital and people) and on institutions such as the City which could act 'as administrator and regulator according to these universal rules' (Cox, 1996: 103). This broke down with the decline of British economic and political power in the early twentieth century to be replaced by the global dominance of the United States in the post-Second World War era. Again this was based not only on its military power and alliances (NATO) but also on the economic strength of US corporations, on the dominance of managed or embedded liberalism (see Box 6.2), and on the domestic institutions of the 'New Deal' or welfare state and the multilateral Bretton Woods institutions, both of which helped support this managed liberalism. The usefulness of this understanding is illustrated by present-day debates about the changing nature of US hegemony. In discussing these, Gill reminds us that 'the issue is not so much the decline of American hegemony;

rather the question is how far and in what ways hegemony is being reconstituted, in a historical process that involves continuity and discontinuity, limits and contradictions' (Gill, 2003: 69). It is through identifying the limits and contradictions that the spaces for change can also be identified.

But how is this done? Who or what is opening up these spaces for change? These are important questions since analysing historical structures is not simply an intellectual exercise but a necessary part of a wider process of influencing social change. To begin to answer them Cox introduces the concept of social forces, which help to explain the origins, growth and demise of historical structures. In any particular historical period, then, one can analyse what is happening in terms of the social forces generated by the productive system and how these are changing, the forms of state that emerge out of the social struggles generated by these social forces, and finally the world orders, namely the particular configurations of forces that successfully define the nature of the global order at that time. So, for example, the dominance of Britain in the nineteenth century was based on the ascendancy of manufacturing capitalism and of the social power of the new bourgeoisie, but the emergence of a strong working class due to the productive forces of manufacturing capitalism and the self-organisation of workers in the core capitalist countries in the late nineteenth and early twentieth centuries challenged the dominance of the bourgeoisie as a social force and the hegemony of economic liberalism. This emergent class eventually succeeded in forging a social compact, through the agency of national states, that ushered in a new 'welfare-nationalist form of state' (Cox, 1996: 106) and an international order based on it. Applying this framework of analysis to the present period of globalised capitalism raises the need to identify the emerging social forces and how they may be challenging today's dominant historical structure. This is how spaces for change and 'the emergence of rival structures expressing alternative possibilities of development' (Cox, 1996: 100) can be identified, offering the possibility of finally replacing the dominant historical structure. This framework, based on social forces and how they challenge or constitute an historical structure, will be used in the following sections to analyse the present era.

'IDEOLOGIES' OF GLOBALISATION

While much analysis of today's world order deals with the strengths and weaknesses of the economic, political, social and cultural dimensions of globalisation, the discussion here takes as its subject an examination of the principal competing agendas or sets of proposals about our globalised world. The word 'ideology' is used loosely for these agendas to indicate that they at least aspire to constituting a coherent set of ideas about how the economic, political and social system should be organised. The word also indicates 'a way of looking at the world that justifies or undermines an existing order', so that its use draws attention to the fact that these different agendas are more than simply alternative sets of ideas but reflect different positions 'on the hierarchies of power and privilege'. This is well illustrated by the fact that, as Mittelman puts it, for those who hold wealth and power, globalisation is seen as an ideology of freedom whereas for those lower down today's global power hierarchies it is experienced as an ideology of domination (Mittelman, 2004: 47). The agendas outlined here therefore reflect different social forces and their positions on the power hierarchies of contemporary global social structures. Three such agendas are outlined: the maintenance agenda of those who seek to maintain and deepen neoliberal globalisation; the reformist agenda of those who propose a series of far-reaching reforms to make globalisation more equitable and sustainable; and the radical agenda of those who seek an alternative form of globalisation. In outlining these agendas, the focus is on the core logic informing them; inevitably there are many differences of emphasis and even substance *within* each of these positions that will be lost in the outline offered here. Furthermore, this outline may obscure the fact that not all agendas are easily grouped into one of these three positions as some may overlap (for example, some of those who seek to maintain neoliberal globalisation may share points proposed by reformists). Despite this, the outline to follow offers a clear map of the main contending perspectives on today's globalisation. Drawing on the analysis of historical structures in the previous section, each agenda is analysed to identify the forms of historical structure (the 'fit' between material capabilities, ideas and institutions) underlying it, the fundamental logic informing it, and the social forces promoting it. In the process, it will be seen how hegemony is being reconstituted or challenged, and how alternative historical structures may be emerging.

i) Maintenance

The maintenance agenda constitutes the hegemonic core of today's neoliberal globalisation. It reflects the global order promoted by those social forces that benefit from the liberalisation of financial and economic flows and seeks to establish and strengthen a global institutional superstructure that underpins and guarantees as far as possible this liberalised order. It has emerged over the past 30 years as technological advances opened up new opportunities for the intensification of profit-making at a level beyond the nation state, since the regulation of economic activities by states acted as an impediment for those social groups seeking to avail themselves of these opportunities (financial speculators, transnational entrepreneurs, globalising bureaucrats and politicians). The objective of the maintenance agenda therefore is to harness this increased economic dynamic to achieve higher levels of economic growth around the world through facilitating greater flows of capital, trade and services and integrating into these flows countries that have previously isolated themselves. It is therefore based upon the material capabilities of what is sometimes referred to as the post-Fordist or 'knowledge' economy. From the 1970s onwards this agenda has been promoted by key political leaders such as Reagan and Thatcher, by the leading international financial institutions (the World Bank and the IMF), by the Organisation for Economic Cooperation and Development (OECD) and, since its establishment in 1995, by the World Trade Organisation (WTO). These have provided the ideas driving the emergence of this historical structure of neoliberal globalisation, offering detailed policy prescriptions to governments around the world which enable them to revise their own policy regimes and state institutions so that they facilitate more and more the extension and deepening of this economically liberalised order. While the institutions promoting this order at an international level provide one level of its institutional ordering, more important and fundamental is the restructuring of states around the world, so that their financial, industrial, agricultural, welfare, educational and development policies and strategies are all based on promoting and facilitating the requirements of private free-market actors. In this way, therefore, in a remarkably short space of time a 'fit' has been established throughout the world between the material capabilities of the new economy based on globalised flows of capital, trade and services, the 'common sense' idea that private corporations provide the only rational and beneficial way to order today's economy, and public institutions at international and national levels that stabilise and perpetuate this order.

In labelling this an agenda for maintenance, it needs to be borne in mind that before it emerged to dominance in the early

1990s, with the collapse of communism and the liberalisation of economies around the world, it saw itself as a radical agenda for change. Reaching dominance does not mean that it ceases actively to reinforce and strengthen the historical structure it promotes, at times in ways that are not evident to many people (see Box 8.2 on accountancy norms). Indeed, as the so-called 'anti-globalisation' movement emerged in the late 1990s to challenge the claims that economic liberalisation would result in social benefits for the poor, thereby undermining the legitimacy of the maintenance agenda, those promoting that agenda have begun to devote more attention to 'winning a different war, the fight against poverty', as the former World Bank president James Wolfensohn put it (quoted in Thomas, 2002: 113). This at times results in rhetoric that appears similar to that of proponents of the reformist and the radical agenda (see Box 8.3). However, what distinguishes the maintenance agenda is that it promotes the free market as the fundamental foundation of today's historical structure and the key dynamic that informs how it operates. This is its core logic and it serves the interests of the speculators, the business entrepreneurs, the globalising bureaucrats and politicians and the intellectual elites who actively promote it. These are the social forces which have shaped and very actively maintain today's historical structure.

ii) Reformist

The reformist agenda is the clearest alternative being advanced to counter the dominance of the maintenance agenda. It reflects concerns at growing global inequality and insecurity being articulated by senior-level officials at the United Nations (including the Secretary General, Kofi Annan), officials and politicians within nation states, leaders of some states, and sectors of civil society throughout the world (expressed through NGOs and social movements). It promotes a series of reforms centred on the need for public policies and institutions to extend and deepen democracy globally and to direct market processes so that they respond more effectively to social needs, especially those of the most vulnerable. In doing this, it offers itself as an alternative both to the maintenance agenda of neoliberal globalisation and to the radical agenda of the so-called 'anti-globalisation' movement, 'a comprehensive yet practical programme of political, social and economic reform – a new global covenant for our global age' (Held, 2004: xv). As David Held is a leading exponent of this reformist agenda, his formulation of it is drawn on here.

BOX 8.2   USHERING IN 'THE AGE OF THE FUND MANAGER'

From 1 January 2005, all companies in the European Union listed on the stock exchange, some 700 companies in all, began using new accounting standards called the International Accounting Standards (IAS). Yet this apparently technical and innocuous shift has 'meant a major shift in governance, towards the private and transnational level', with the result that 'certain social constituencies have been advantaged and others disadvantaged' (Nölke and Perry, 2004: 15, 16). Among the former are shareholders, fund managers and financial analysts while the latter comprises company managers, workers and pensioners. The shift has further extended market values throughout society and further transferred risk from employers to workers. Despite this, it has gone virtually unnoticed in society, and trade unions have raised no objections.

This is because the move has been advocated by the accountancy profession and justified by the need for greater economic efficiency. The EU bases its decisions in the matter on the advice of the private sector European Financial Advisory Group (EFRAG), an umbrella network of organisations representing European employers, banks, accountants, insurers, stock exchanges and financial analysts. In making the move, the EU has taken control over setting accounting standards from national, public sector bodies, and given it to the International Accounting Standards Board (IASB), a private body very actively supported by the Big Four accountancy firms and incorporated in the US state of Delaware. As Nölke and Perry put it: 'In hardly any other case has so wide-ranging authority been delegated to a private body' (2004: 16).

The consequences flow from the power shifts which the move involves, shifts not analysed by the free-market economics which justifies it. For, in changing the ways balance sheets are drawn up and presented, the new accounting standards reduce the discretion of managers and give more power to shareholders (mostly large fund managers and the financial analysts who advise them). Nölke and Perry conclude that 'we may thus be living in the age of the fund manager' (2004: 10). As a result it involves a shift away from the stable management of firms with a focus on their long-term well-being (as embodied in the Rhenish model of stakeholder capitalism) to the 'pressures of "short-termism" that plague American and British companies – pressure from shareholders to maximize dividends by concentrating on quarterly results and short-range return on investment variables' (Sally, quoted in Nölke and Perry, 2004: 12). One example is the fact that employers are citing accounting standards to justify replacing defined-benefit pensions with defined-contribution ones, amounting to a redistribution of income away from labour and a transfer of the burden of risk to workers. The new accounting standards 'could thus herald a new era of intensified economic restructuring [and] could be a decisive factor in bringing about new divisions of income in society' (Nölke and Perry, 2004: 15).

Held bases his notion of a global compact on the national compacts of social democratic governance – between rulers and the ruled, and between capital, labour and the state. He offers comprehensive reform proposals for both dimensions. To strengthen global governance he proposes 'creating an enlightened multilateralism, built on the principles of extending open markets, strong coordinated governance, and providing protection against social vulnerabilities wherever possible' (Held, 2004: 103). This would include: a reformed UN General Assembly to consider major global problems and involving a stakeholder process of consensus among states, intergovernmental organisations, NGOs, citizen groups and social movements; regional parliaments and governance structures (modelled, for example, on the European Union); making intergovernmental organisations and international financial institutions more transparent and accountable; establishing new global organisations where necessary as, for example, to deal with environmental and social problems; enhancing the transparency and accountability of the organisations of national and transnational civil society; the use of general referenda at regional or global levels on key issues of public importance; and the development of law enforcement and coercive capabilities including peacekeeping and peacemaking (2004: 107–13). Complementing these institutional reforms, he proposes a 'multilevel citizenship', namely one 'based not on exclusive membership of a territorial community, but on general rules and principles which can be entrenched and drawn on in diverse settings' (2004: 114).

Equally important would be the compact governing markets. Here the objective is, through robust and accountable political institutions, 'to help mediate and manage the economic forces of globalization' so as to 'shape an economic system that was both free and fair' (2004: 58). His proposals towards this end include the following: a more balanced liberalisation of trade so that developing countries could benefit; meeting the UN target of 0.7 per cent of GNP in overseas aid; new revenues and redistributive mechanisms through a range of regional and global taxes (on consumption of energy, on carbon emissions, on the extraction of resources, on financial turnover in foreign exchange markets) and funds to meet global needs; the enhancing of countries' capacity to regulate financial markets; and 'a world financial authority to monitor and supervise global financial markets and capital flows' (2004: 68). Held recommends that the UN's Global Compact (a voluntary code of conduct for companies) be extended and deepened 'into a set of codified and mandatory rules' on such issues as health, child labour, trade union activity, environmental protection, stakeholder consultation and corporate governance', what he calls 'a Global Compact with teeth' (2004: 155). The rationale for such reforms, he clarifies, is 'not to control and regulate markets for their own sake, but to provide the basis for a free, fair and just world economy, and to ensure that the values of efficient and effective global economic processes are compatible with the agenda of social democratic values' (2004: 69–70). This reformist agenda provides some elements for an alternative historical structure. While the ideas that inform it and its institutional makeup are clearly outlined, its main weakness lies in the fact that it rests on the same material capabilities as the neoliberal historical structure except that it appeals to a more enlightened sense of public interest among those social forces that are promoting and benefiting from the liberalisation of markets and the privatisation of economic activity. The closest Held gets to addressing this issue is when he identifies 'a coalition of political groupings [that] could develop to push the agenda of global social democracy further', among them European countries with strong liberal and social democratic traditions; liberal groups in the US which support multilateralism; developing countries; NGOs, transnational social movements; and 'those economic forces that desire a more stable and managed global economy' (2004: 166). While the core logic of strong public institutions clearly distinguishes the reformist agenda from the market-based logic of the maintenance agenda, the failure to specify the material capabilities that might give rise to social forces adequate to promote and sustain such strong public institutions (as the organised working class forged the national compacts of social democratic governance) remains a major weakness of the reformist agenda.

iii) Radical

The main weakness of the reformist agenda has emerged as the main strength of the radical agenda given the growing evidence since the late 1990s of the coming together of a transnational social movement mobilised around a platform of challenging the hegemony of neoliberal globalisation (see Box 9.2). Widely labelled the 'anti-globalisation' movement by the media, this fails to capture the extent to which the movement is both a product of globalisation and seeks, not its reversal, but its transformation. The French-language term '*alter-mondialisation*' is therefore a much more accurate label since it expresses the movement's goal as an alternative form of globalisation, and an English-language version, 'alter-globalisation', is now beginning to be used (see Mittelman, 2004: the title of Chapter 8). Mittelman identifies a broad constellation of social forces, generally the victims of globalisation, which support this agenda, including many elements of civil society, trade unions, sectors of the political left and some intellectuals. A second major feature of this alternative, distinguishing it from the reformist agenda, is its lack of a clearly defined programme of structural change leading reformers like Scholte to dismiss it as offering only 'fairly vague and insufficiently convincing visions of alternative futures' (Scholte, 2000: 288). Yet the differences between the radical and the reformist agendas are ones of substance (see Box 8.3 on poverty). Indeed, the very breadth and vitality of the movement, with its many constituent members espousing between them a virtually limitless range of causes and issues, can serve to obscure some core values that unite and motivate the radical agenda, informing vigorous debates about how to translate such values into practical programmes of action.

The mass gatherings of this movement in the World Social Forum every January provide a focus point for identifying the alternative historical structure promoted by the radical agenda. More than a programme of action or reforms, this is a radically democratising movement which, through its practice, embodies an alternative exercise of power. Mittelman captures this well when he writes that it 'affirms the importance of engaging yet localizing the global, and of bottom-up processes' so that it 'entails a greater diffusion of power' (Mittelman, 2004: 94). Furthermore, in the importance it attaches to inclusive values of multiculturalism, respect for diversity and opposition to the homogenising and environmentally destructive practice of consumerism, the movement lives out alternative values of equality and respect both in how people relate to one another across differences of culture, gender, ethnicity, religion and sexual orientation, as well as in how the human species relates to all other species and to the biosphere itself. In these ways, therefore, the alter-globalisation movement subverts the economic, market-oriented and consumerist values that dominate hegemonic globalisation. However, this does not mean that it neglects the economic, as it emphasises the importance of small-scale, cooperative production and the values of local self-sufficiency. While huge differences exist within the movement (for example between socialist, environmental, anarchist, feminist, indigenous and multiculturalist alternatives), its unity lies less 'in a shared vision of an outcome than in a shared commitment to a process [which] is best reflected in the widely asserted commitment to the reinvention of democracy' (Ponniah and Fisher, 2003: 13).

BOX 8.3   PUTTING POVERTY ON THE GLOBAL AGENDA

Since its founding in 2001 in Porto Alegre, Brazil, the annual World Social Forum has provided a platform for critics and social activists to challenge the pro-corporate agenda of the World Economic Forum held in Davos, Switzerland. Since its first meeting in 1970, Davos has grown to become the leading meeting place for business and political leaders from all over the world to discuss a wide agenda of global issues. Meeting simultaneously during the final days of January every year, Porto Alegre and Davos have come to symbolise both sides of the globalisation debate (while Davos attracts both maintainers and reformers, Porto Alegre attracts mostly radicals).

Perhaps few events illustrate so well the impact of the so-called 'anti-globalisation movement' on global agendas as the key events that took place at both venues on 27 January 2005. Brazil's President Lula visited the World Social Forum to launch the Global Call to Action against Poverty (GCAP) through which hundreds of social movements worldwide seek to put pressure on governments to take serious action to eliminate world poverty. Meanwhile at Davos the same day, the British Prime Minister, Tony Blair, issued a call for the world's richest countries to make a 'quantum leap forward' to address poverty in Africa, including the doubling of aid, completing debt relief, tackling protectionism by developed countries, fighting corruption and resolving conflicts. Flanked by former US President Bill Clinton, the presidents of Nigeria and South Africa, Microsoft's Bill Gates and the Irish rock singer, Bono, Blair promised to use the British government's influence to advance this ambitious agenda.

So, have the differences been bridged between both sides of the debate, as some commentators claimed? Is there agreement on how to tackle poverty that spans the proponents and the critics of globalisation? While few at Porto Alegre would disagree that elements of Blair's agenda could benefit the poor, there are fundamental differences. Blair emphasises free trade whereas the emphasis in Porto Alegre is on 'fair trade', requiring not just liberalisation but structural reforms that will provide greater opportunities for less developed countries and the poor within them. The GCAP calls on countries to meet the UN target of 0.7 per cent of GNP on aid, whereas Blair seeks a doubling of G-7 aid to Africa. More fundamentally, the GCAP seeks measures to protect public services from liberalisation and privatisation as well as securing the right of the poor to food and to essential drugs. At heart, as Bono made clear in his comments at Davos, the Blair agenda is perfectly consistent with the interests of global corporations; Bono said: 'If we're honest, brands are in trouble. ... There's a commercial agenda here too.' In Porto Alegre, however, Lula urged the poor to unite to further their interests: 'We need to build another force so we can change the world's economic and social geography.' Behind the similarities in rhetoric lurk fundamental differences towards today's global power structures.

This process gives rise to vigorous debates on what concrete changes the movement espouses in the nature of today's political economy. The survey of debates conducted by Fisher and Ponniah at the 2002 World Social Forum in Porto Alegre stands as one expression of the key differences and convergences that exist within the alter-globalisation movement. They identify the following five debates:

- Revolution versus reform: the most familiar manifestation is the difference between whether to abolish the IMF, the WTO and the World Bank or to reform them through the engagement of civil society.
- Environment versus economy: the tension here relates to the environmental demand for a reduction of economic growth and the labour demand for more growth and jobs.
- Human rights or protectionism: on this issue Northern demands for human rights to be included within international trade agreements clash with Southern concerns that this involves a hidden protectionism directed against them.
- The universality of values: this relates to the debate between those who seek to uphold universal values (on human rights, for example) against those who see this as a veil for the extension of Western values.
- Local, national or global: the differences here relate to the levels to which priority is given, whether it should be on the self-sufficiency of local communities producing goods for their own consumption (a localisation agenda), on the responsibility of the state to ensure food and livelihood security for its people, or on global actions such as the Tobin tax on cross-border financial transactions, on a world parliament and on global referenda (Ponniah and Fisher, 2003: 8–10).

Despite these differences, what unites the movement is a common critique of corporate globalisation with its market-liberalising logic, imposed by elites on communities throughout the world with devastating consequences for both social solidarity and provision and for ecological sustainability. Or, as Mittelman found in his survey of attitudes among participants in globalisation protests, there was 'general accord on the need for democratic accountability, redistribution of wealth and opportunities, and respect for local culture in shaping alterglobalization' (Mittelman, 2004: 73).

More than does the reformist agenda, the radical agenda 'contains the elements of a counter-hegemonic alliance of forces on the world scale' (Cox, 2002: 103–4), being promoted by social forces reacting against their marginalisation by the material capabilities that neoliberal globalisation favours, articulating an ideology and values that run directly counter to those of hegemonic globalisation and, in the movement's activities, embodying the seeds of alternative institutions to constitute new power relations. In this regard, criticisms of the movement's vagueness and lack of programmatic clarity miss the point that, much more so than the reformist agenda, the emergence of the alter-globalisation movement has put the proponents of neoliberal globalisation on the defensive and opened new spaces for mobilising the powerless. Indeed, for Michael Hardt and Antonio Negri, its emergence may well mark 'the end of the historical cycle of social democracy and the beginning of the democracy of the multitude' (Hardt and Negri, 2003: xix).

ADDRESSING VULNERABILITY AND VIOLENCE

Assessing these 'ideologies' or agendas of globalisation depends on what objectives are being sought. For example, someone whose main purpose is to increase economic efficiency and growth will tend to be very dismissive of the radical agenda and, depending on their views of the relative importance of the market or of political and social institutions, will opt for the maintenance agenda or the reformist agenda as being best able to achieve their objectives. Given the concern of this book with vulnerability and violence, the three agendas will be assessed here in terms of how likely they are to address these, both reducing the extent of risk faced by individuals and societies and strengthening their mechanisms to cope. But assessing which agenda offers the greatest likelihood of reducing vulnerability and violence requires summarising what has already been learnt about their causes. Chapters 4 and 5 identified a fundamental shift in relations between governing elites and their citizens as states increasingly give priority to the requirements of private market forces (particularly transnational corporations) and impose competitive disciplines on society. The impacts of this fundamental power shift from state to market, and from public to private authority, constituted the most common and pervasive cause of the many forms of increased risk surveyed in Chapter 2 (financial, economic, social, political, environmental and personal) and of the weakening of coping mechanisms surveyed in Chapter 3 (physical, human, social and environmental assets). As Chapter 5 highlighted, in identifying consumerism as the culture of neoliberal globalisation, this shift in power relations is generalising and deepening market values throughout society and, as Chapter 7 pointed out, resulting in a heightened individualism and the erosion of social networks of belonging. The significance of these shifts was underlined in Chapter 6 which, drawing on the work of Karl Polanyi, identified them as a new instance of the 'utopian experiment' to make society subservient to the self-regulating market which treats labour, land and capital as commodities to be bought and sold (a 'market society'). ECLAC's summary of the social situation in Latin America expresses well the dynamics being generated worldwide by the fundamental power shift from state to market: 'Without the traditional social networks and bonds, and with a State whose protective role has been downgraded, people are becoming isolated in their dealings with the market, so that they are less protected and consequently more vulnerable' (ECLAC, 2000: 51).

Addressing vulnerability and violence, therefore, requires a strengthening of public authority over the market and the generation of renewed forms of political and social rationality to challenge the current dominance of economic rationality with its narrow conceptions of human motivation and its economic determinism, as identified by Karl Polanyi (see Chapter 6). The re-establishment of strong forms of public authority can be effected at the level of the national state, as was the principal method during the era of national development (whether capitalist or socialist) or through new forms of public authority that could be constituted at levels other than that of the national state, for example through forms of local public authorities (perhaps involving participative forms of democracy) or through transnational public authorities of various kinds (the UN system is the closest we get to this at the moment, but more robust and publicly accountable forms could be created). The particular institutional form this public authority might take is not as important as the principle that it embody the power and will to restrain market forces and ensure they serve goals that are established through public debate and deliberation. In doing this, such a public authority would regulate market forces; hedge the use and exchange of land, labour and capital with restrictions that ensure they cannot be treated as commodities ('decommodification'); redistribute wealth and resources away from the wealthy and towards the poor both within national societies and at a global level; and create mechanisms that protect people and society from threats. One essential contribution towards the protection of society would be the reconstitution of strong social networks of belonging such as the family, trade unions, neighbourhood associations, production and distribution cooperatives, and civil society organisations. As Salsano put it, outlining a Polanyian approach towards reversing the dominance of the market: 'we have to work out forms of organization (at the level of enterprise) and of institutions (at the state level) that will let us subordinate the economy to society once again, while guaranteeing the greatest possible degree of personal liberty' (Salsano, 1990: 144).

Which of the three agendas outlined in the previous section can most effectively undertake these tasks? Due to the key role which the free market plays in the maintenance agenda, it offers the least prospect of addressing vulnerability and violence. Indeed, the success of this agenda is a principal reason for the growth in both. The reformist agenda does offer proposals that go some way in seeking to embed the market in society and thereby to reduce vulnerability and violence, particularly through establishing strong public authorities at state and transnational level, through mechanisms of taxation and redistribution of resources, and through new forms of democratic accountability at global level. All of these, if realised, could go quite some way towards curbing threats and strengthening coping mechanisms. However, there are two principal problems with the reformist agenda that cast doubts on its ability to address some of the dynamic causes of vulnerability and on whether it is realisable. The first is a certain ambiguity at the heart of the agenda relating to the role of markets. As outlined by Held, his 'global compact' seems to want both to regulate and restrain markets but also to liberalise them. As a result, it is doubtful whether it could adequately address such major manifestations of 'market society' as consumerism, the power of transnational corporations, or the potential contradiction identified by Cox between two components of the global economy – the fragile condition of global finance threatening the stability of global production (Cox, 2002: 82). To this extent, the reformist agenda does not seem to go far enough in addressing the sources of vulnerability and violence deeply structured into the present global order. Secondly, the reformist agenda seems quite naive about power in that it presumes that those social forces which benefit from the present form of neoliberal globalisation will easily agree to the reforms proposed. As Scholte warns: 'Global social democracy cannot be imposed from above. Neoliberals have usually pursued their agenda with top-down politics, an approach that has generally proved untenable. Reformers must not repeat this mistake' (Scholte, 2000: 312). Yet, in focusing on the political and paying less attention to economic and social forms of power (and the ways the 'fit' between these three forms of power constitute an historical structure), the reformist agenda continues to remain a largely elitist project.

Because it uses social and cultural forms of power, as well as political ones, the radical agenda does recognise more fully and adequately the range of transformations needed to address vulnerability and violence. In doing so, it has fostered a movement that is very publicly challenging the maintenance agenda and, while sharing with the reformist agenda many ideas on the concrete reforms needed to the present political and economic system, goes well beyond it in fostering cultural and social challenges to consumerism and transnational corporations and in recognising the links between present-day forms of production and consumption on the one hand and environmental destruction on the other. It therefore argues in theory, and lives out in practice, the need for a fundamental shift of power from markets to democratic and accountable public authorities. In these ways, much more so than does the reformist agenda, it embodies elements of an emerging historical structure capable of mobilising emerging social forces, identifying spaces for change and actively using these to advance its agenda, thereby opening up alternative possibilities for development. Of course, its critics dismiss it as unrealistic and vague, proposing transformations that are not feasible in the real world. Such criticisms, however, lack any appreciation of how longer-term historical change happens. Similar criticisms were made against those who 200 years ago proposed the abolition of monarchies and landowning elites, criticised societies of inherited privilege and inequalities, promoted democratic systems based on one-person one-vote, and dreamed of establishing gender and racial equality in law. History is therefore on the side of those who allow themselves to see the root causes of their contemporary malaise and promote transformations they deem adequate to overcome these. Such transformations do not happen overnight but the efforts to achieve them sow firm seeds that put down deep roots and eventually flourish and bloom. There is much evidence, to be examined in the next chapter, that we are today on the cusp of such an historical moment.

CONCLUSIONS: 'SO WHAT SHOULD WE DO?'

As already mentioned in Chapter 6, Karl Polanyi recognised that beyond the immediate attempts to embed the market in society lay an even greater challenge, that of adapting human living to the demands of technology or, as he put it, of 'how to organise human life in a machine society' in which 'science itself is haunted by insanity'. He added that no one knows whether such an adaptation is possible or whether humankind 'must perish in the attempt' (1968: 59, 60). Polanyi regarded late nineteenth and early twentieth-century market society as one very inadequate response to that challenge. But it could also be said that the embedded liberalism of the post-Second World War era, in embedding the market in ways that did not resolve the fundamental challenge identified by Polanyi, failed also to provide an adequate response, simply postponing the fundamental issue. If so, we are now facing it in a heightened form, acutely aware of the threat to human life itself from environmental destruction and social breakdown as the opportunities provided by the latest technological innovations have been given free rein to expand market power and make human and social well-being ever more beholden to the market. These are the ultimate sources of the vulnerabilities and violence we face in today's society. In answering the question 'What should we do?', therefore, we need to be aware that this is not a time for tinkering (modest reforms here and there) but a time that calls for more bold and fundamental transformations inspired by a new consciousness of possibilities and new values recognising our *common* vulnerabilities and interdependence (on one another and on the biosphere). So what we should do first of all is to firmly ground ourselves in the conviction that we are living and working not to sustain the present order but to transform it. The most important way any of us can do this is to live every aspect of our lives out of values of radical truthfulness, equality, generosity and sharing, and respect for one another and for all of nature, as outlined in Chapter 7. To this extent, the personal is political, since any challenge to the hegemony of the ideas and the values of the dominant order begins with our own efforts to embody different ideas and values in the ways we live.

If we do live out of a new consciousness of the urgent need for radical social change, then it will help us identify opportunities for bringing this about in our neighbourhoods, our work, our leisure, our political engagement. Obviously, such opportunities differ from person to person but the fundamental test of whether any of us are sowing the seeds of social transformation is that we challenge aspects of today's dominant order and lay the foundations of a new social order. Following our use of the concept of historical structure, these actions can change people's ideas (through teaching, writing, journalism, drama, ritual), change our material capabilities (though cooperative forms of production and distribution, through service provision such as local support networks or eco-tourism), and change our institutions (through developing new forms of education, health care, political forums, lobby groups, spiritual practices). There is no one who is not faced with numerous opportunities for involvement in such activities in their daily lives. While, to some, this may not seem spectacular enough, immediate enough, nor adequate to the challenges we face, it is extending and firmly rooting the emergence of a new historical structure. For, to slightly adapt a key point made by Cox, a new historical structure does not derive 'from some abstract model of a social system or mode of production, but from ... the historical situation to which it relates' (Cox, 1996: 100). Today's historical situation and the evidence it shows of emerging forms of radical social change adequate to address the challenges of vulnerability and violence is the subject of the next chapter.

9
Contesting Globalisation

[G]lobalization is animated by not only a surge in global flows but also fundamental power relations involving both maintenance of the dominant order and impulses for resistance to it. As with the Zapatistas, local grievances are combined with discontents over globalizing processes, be they structural adjustment programmes, privatization, deregulation, or liberalization. The globalization protests are linked to prior popular protests over policies that are perceived as harming the interests of the poor and dispossessed. ...

Inasmuch as contemporary globalization unsettles old solidarities based on nation and state, today's protests are about the construction of new collective identities that increasingly transcend territorial units.
(Mittelman, 2004: 59)

In his book which has the same title as this chapter, André C. Drainville warns about imposing modes of thinking that have their origins in nineteenth-century social science or political struggles to the realities of globalisation since the latter 'challenges all existing conceptualizations'. As examples, he cites the distinction between what is radical and what is reformist or between what is imposed from above and what comes from below. He argues that 'these distinctions have in fact more to do with ideological presuppositions than with a serious analysis of the limits and possibilities of global social relations'. Instead, he proposes that 'we need to enquire into the making of global subjects rather than take them for granted' and, to do that, 'we need to stay with global practices long enough to see what they might carry that is significant and, perhaps, transformative' (Drainville, 2004: 7–9). In surveying the 'ideologies' or agendas of globalisation, and in asserting that these reflect the positions of different social forces on today's power hierarchies, the previous chapter has resorted to the modes of thinking about which Drainville warns. It is difficult to avoid this as one needs to impose some interpretative framework to make sense of differing analyses of globalisation and of the remedies being proposed for it. The previous chapter outlined the principal proposals for change; yet Drainville's warning reminds us that at a time of fundamental change such as the present (change in our conceptual categories and frameworks as much as in the social structures and forces we seek to analyse), this needs to be complemented by a more careful empirical analysis of the potential of *actual* social actors to transform globalisation in the ways outlined towards the end of that chapter. Only in doing this can the real prospects for reducing vulnerability and violence be identified. This is the task of the current chapter.

The chapter has four sections. Guided by the emphasis of some analysts of globalisation on the importance of localisation (see Chapter 5), the first section looks at practices of resistance as they manifest themselves at a local level and examines the extent to which they constitute a counterpower. The following section takes civil society as its subject, analysing whether the emergence of a transnational or global civil society holds the promise of transforming globalisation. The third section examines global governance, namely the means by which rules for governing the economy and society are being made in today's globalised context, asking what prospects this holds for addressing vulnerability and violence. The final section concludes both the chapter and also the book. In doing so, it draws conclusions about whether it is likely that the heightened vulnerability and violence resulting from the processes we label neoliberal or corporate globalisation can be reversed, through reducing threats and strengthening coping mechanisms. The concluding section also revisits the book's central conceptual claim, that the concept of vulnerability offers the ability to capture the distinctive impact on human and social livelihoods of today's form of globalisation.

TRANSFORMATIVE RESISTANCES

The epigraph to this chapter identifies the 'impulses for resistance' that constitute an essential part of the power relations of globalisation. It also suggests that local grievances lie at the heart of what motivates popular protests. Yet the extensive focus of attention on the many protests against globalisation often fails to reach down to the local level to identify how discontent is manifesting itself, and what these manifestations might tell us about the social forces resisting today's neoliberal globalisation. As Sassen has written, 'it is in the concrete spaces of locality that we can observe and detect this assemblying global subject' (Sassen, 2004: xii). These local resistances may be subtle or latent and can be limited, for example, to consumer choices (including the move to alternative forms of health care) and to expressions of popular discontent in TV dramas, plays, songs and films. If so limited, they remain personal and largely private or passive and may never join with more public expressions such as consumer boycotts or protest actions. Yet, more indicative of what has been called 'micro-resistance' is the myriad of alternatives emerging at local level, from changing forms of livelihood to cooperative services and production, from neighbourhood democracy to public transport initiatives, from non-profit access to technology to providing alternative forms of health care. The significance of such initiatives is that they 'can generate a slow molecular accumulation of dissidence and withdrawal from recognized social practices' and provide the basis for the emergence of 'a coordinated force with a strategy of confronting society' (Cox, 2002: 123).

What may be contentious in this account is the labelling of what are recognised everyday practices as resistance to globalisation. Obviously such practices may not constitute resistance and can be entirely compatible with full acceptance of neoliberal globalisation. But they can also be expressions of the erosion of the hegemony of the dominant order as people grow more critical of it and withdraw their full consent from it in 'countless diverse acts and beliefs that send forth ripples of doubt and questions concerning the viability and sustainability of neoliberal globalization' (Mittelman, 2004: 76). Indeed, in many cases the ripples of doubt may not translate into explicit questions about neoliberal globalisation and may remain simply instinctive reactions against aspects of today's economic, political and social order that either impact in a direct way on people's own lives and livelihoods (such as anti-social working hours, poor pay, health care that is poor in quality or difficult to access, or concerns about pollution of the food chain) or that anger people who observe them impacting on the lives of others, especially the most vulnerable (low-quality public services, socio-natural disasters, opulent overconsumption side by side with meagre underconsumption, political corruption or the perception of it). These ripples of doubt may never translate into a critique of globalisation but they can result in the withdrawal of consent from the prevailing order and help provide passive and, at times, active support for attempts to undermine or change that order. As this happens, it is creating the conditions for the emergence of new social subjects committed to changing the dominant order. For, as Mittelman reminds us, resistance is not merely a negation: 'Resistance is more than opposition, evasions, challenges, or reactions. ... Resistance involves new ideas, organizations and institutions, daily practices, and a plurality of dispersed, local, and personal points of counterpower' (Mittelman, 2004: 61). What we need to examine, therefore, is the extent to which local practices constitute a counterpower to neoliberal globalisation.

In his book *The Post-Corporate World*, David C. Korten identifies numerous examples of local initiatives that 'are driven more by a simple desire to create viable living spaces in the midst of a troubled world than by grand visions of planetary change' (Korten, 1999: 241). In Seattle, a taxi driver and a part-time poet, at a cost of $2,000, together led a successful campaign that forced the city council to extend the city's monorail system. The Mothers of East Los Angeles (MELASI), a local group made up mostly of Hispanic American women, first resisted the siting of hazardous and disruptive projects in their neighbourhood and then went on to implement a variety of constructive projects including litter clean up, a community youth garden, a tobacco prevention programme and a water conservation programme. MELASI became an active member of an international network of similar local communities. In Portland, Oregon, a campaign by community groups in working-class neighbourhoods successfully opposed plans for a motorway and helped reverse urban decay, resulting in a light rail system and a free bus service that has brought new life back to the city centre. Korten quotes an estimate that 1,500 communities around the world have issued local currencies to facilitate local production and distribution. He describes several producer networks including the Vermont Family Forests, a network of small, independent owners of forest lots in the US state of Vermont; the Anand Milk Producers' Union in India, a union of small milk-producer cooperatives, and Appropriate Technology International (ATI), which aids small-scale producers in countries of Asia, Africa and Central America. These sorts of initiatives, he argues, are creating 'a post-corporate world' in which economic, political and social power is more widely shared and returned to the local level.

While Korten's focus is firmly on the local and he does not see these initiatives as micro-resistances to neoliberal globalisation, the examples of such resistances as given by Mittelman show that both are dealing with similar kinds of local activities. Examining Japan, a country that has not witnessed major macro-resistances against globalisation despite its present economic crisis, Mittelman found substantial, diverse and varied forms of micro-resistance to it, from defending the right of child prostitutes (such prostitution is linked to the transnational sex industry), through consumer networks linking to producer networks in developing countries in order to ensure the benefits of trade reach small producers, to resistance by Japanese consumers and small farmers to liberalising the market for rice, seeing it as a threat not only to their livelihood but to their health, identity and spiritual heritage. As Mittelman concludes, much of the resistance to globalisation may not be high drama as in the Battle of Seattle, but simply 'the scenes enacted in ways of life, many of them more improvised than rehearsed' (Mittelman, 2004: 86). So widespread have such initiatives become that it is difficult any longer to describe them as 'alternatives' since, as Box 9.1 indicates, they are increasingly entering the mainstream as they reflect the values of ever-growing sectors of the population in the countries surveyed.

In themselves, micro-resistances constitute no more than the creation of spaces in which people can live by values contrary to those of the dominant order. As one Eastern European dissident, Václav Benda, described this practice under communism, the aim 'is not to replace the power with another kind, but rather under this power – or beside it – to create a structure that represents other laws and in which the voice of the ruling power is heard only as an insignificant echo from a world that is organised in an entirely different way' (quoted in Kaldor, 2003: 56). This well describes the attitudes of many people involved in the sorts of alternatives just described. Many of these don't consider themselves as being involved in politics; rather, many are reacting against politics and consider what they do to be a sort of 'anti-politics'. But, as is clear from the consequences for the totalitarian regimes of Eastern Europe or the authoritarian dictatorships of Latin America in the 1980s, social activities created the conditions for eroding the power of such regimes so that they eventually collapsed. In other words, far from being anti-political, civil society has emerged as a new kind of political actor, transforming power not through a frontal challenge at elite level but from below and from within, as it were. This is the way in which micro-resistances create the conditions which can constitute a counterpower. As Gill has put it: 'Resistance can be active or passive, localized or global, negative or creative. Transformative resistance involves not only negation but also creation and the personal and the political' (Gill, 2003: xi).

What is happening therefore, may be likened to the experience of resistance in colonised countries or those ruled by dictatorships in which the values, consciousness and institutions of a more

BOX 9.1   ARE ALTERNATIVES NOW THE MAINSTREAM?

People who practice non-conventional forms of health care, engage in personal growth and spiritual development, or are active in environmental movements, international development or feminist groups are often labelled 'alternative' and their lifestyle and values are seen as being different from those of the majority of society. Yet growing evidence is emerging of what Inglehart calls 'deep-rooted changes in world views [that] seem to be reshaping economic, political and social life in societies around the world' (Inglehart, 2000: 215). Drawing on World Values Surveys that have measured public values and beliefs on all six continents since the early 1980s, representing almost 75 per cent of the world's population, Inglehart finds an accelerating shift from materialist to post-materialist values particularly in the most developed countries. The materialists he calls those 'who gave top priority to economic and physical security' while the post-materialists 'gave top priority to belonging and self-expression' (2000: 222). Those with post-modern values are less deferential to authority and are tolerant of difference; they reject rigid sexual norms in favour of wider latitude for individual self-gratification, and they give expression to their political views not through mainstream politics but through new social movements. Though less interested in conventional religion, their concern for the purpose and meaning of life leads Inglehart to conclude that 'we are not witnessing a decline in spiritual concerns but rather a redirection of them' (2000: 224). Perhaps most tellingly, he writes: 'Postmodern values give priority to environmental protection and cultural issues, even when these goals conflict with maximizing economic growth' (2000: 223).

In the United States also, seen by many as the heartland of consumer capitalism, evidence is emerging of a similar shift. Korten quotes evidence showing that those who reject the country's mainstream materialist values are now in a majority. This divides the US population into three groups:

- Modernists: those who embrace dominant materialist values.
- Heartlanders: those who favour more conservative values.
- Cultural creatives: those who reject dominant media and business values and the intolerance of the Religious Right.

National surveys find that 88 million people belong to the first group (47 per cent of the population), 56 million to the second group (29 per cent) and 44 million to the last group (24 per cent). Furthermore, the latter group are growing rapidly, from virtual invisibility in the 1970s. A core group of them, the 'core Cultural creatives', who 'are engaged with the world, tend to be leading-edge thinkers and creators, and are deeply aware of modernism's failings', comprise 20 million adults or 10 per cent of the population. By contrast, there are 33 million 'solid Modernists' which leads Korten to conclude: 'If not for its stranglehold on our dominant institutions, modernism would be little more than a minority faith' (Korten, 1999: 217). While this evidence does not mean that the majority favour the radical change of social institutions in a progressive direction, it does show that most are dissatisfied with the mainstream and are searching for alternatives.

independent society were gradually created within the dominated society so that, as Jordan put it of apartheid in South Africa, it 'had been transformed from within by the individual actions of millions of citizens' before its formal structures were finally abolished (Jordan, 2004: 81). Recalling the years of dissident activity under communism when all that was possible was truthful interaction at a personal level, one leading Polish political activist, Jacek Kuro, described these 'simplest human actions' as 'a time bomb ticking away under totalitarianism' (quoted in Kaldor, 2003: 53). A similar dynamic is associated with the cultural nationalism that, during colonial times, created the seeds of a new society within the old one through an active civil society promoting alternative projects of economic, social and political organisation leading to a redefinition by civil society of who constituted the 'imagined community' of the nation (see Kirby, 2002b: 21–37 on the Irish case). This points therefore to the fact that micro-resistances are not a new form of refashioning society; what is new is that they are not limited to particular nation states but are fashioning new networks of global solidarity.

If micro-resistances can therefore constitute a counterpower, it is however not always clear that this favours an alternative, more cosmopolitan and egalitarian globalised world. Jordan reminds us that many marginalised communities breed 'cultures of dissent, deviance and lawlessness, based on various ethnic solidarities and criminal loyalties'. Alienated from public authorities, such communities 'have sometimes been based on racist, xenophobic, sexist or homophobic ideas, and used bullying, shaming, excluding and punitive methods'. Indeed, he sees these cultures of dissent, apparent in some British cities, as ways in which 'the world's losers and outsiders' react to globalisation – 'jurisdictions of faith and patriarchy, mobilizations for Holy War, suicide bomb squads, terrorist cells, and so on' (Jordan, 2004: 194–7). Jordan is certainly correct in highlighting the other side of micro-resistances, namely that they are not always of a benign and progressive variety. Indeed, the consolidation of a conservative, inward-looking, intolerant and sometimes belligerent politics among swathes of the US voting public, as evidenced in that country's 2004 presidential election, confirms that as modernism wanes the extremes of tolerance and intolerance both grow.

The evidence therefore points in many countries to an erosion at local level of the hegemony of the dominant system and its values. What is being witnessed is a polarisation of attitudes and values, with some sectors turning back to forms of self-protection against threats which are identified as coming from outsiders (whether from immigrants or others within the national community, or from other countries), what Mittelman calls a 'resurgent nationalism' (2004: 85), while other sectors of the population are drawn to creating new networks of transnational solidarity. Both can be seen as responses to a growing sense of vulnerability, but the first response misinterprets the source of the threat and adopts a security response (self-protection against others, as outlined towards the end of Chapter 7), while the second response more correctly diagnoses the threat and responds by finding ways of lessening it and strengthening common coping mechanisms. It is this second response that constitutes 'transformative resistance'. Yet, whether today's micro-resistances against neoliberal globalisation are constituting new social subjects with the potential to transform globalisation, and what kind these might be, requires more careful analysis, which is the purpose of the next section.

CAN GLOBAL CIVIL SOCIETY TRANSFORM GLOBALISATION?

The end of the Cold War and the spreading of liberal democracy and free-market economics around the world also led to the concept of 'civil society' being enthusiastically adopted by academics, policy makers and political leaders. In Kaldor's view, this was because it 'seemed to offer a discourse within which to frame parallel concerns about the ability to control the circumstances in which individuals live, about substantive empowerment of citizens' (Kaldor, 2003: 4). As such, it combined the personal with the political as it both built upon the promise of fundamental political changes in places such as Eastern Europe, Latin America and South Africa but also embodied the concerns of social movements such as the environmental, feminist and peace movements with their emphasis upon value and lifestyle changes as much as upon political change (or as a means to political change). In the new circumstances of a more globalised and interconnected world, it also offered the example of creating transnational civil society networks alongside the transnational activities of states and of corporations. For the civil society movements of the 1980s, though often focused on change within national societies, had also forged strong links with similar groups in other countries or, as in the case of the huge peace protests against the siting of US cruise missiles in Western Europe, actually created a transnational movement. It can be concluded therefore that what distinguishes the term 'civil society' from the sorts of micro-resistances outlined in the previous section is that it refers to a social actor. Organised and mobilised in social movements, non-governmental organisations, transnational advocacy networks and nationalist or fundamentalist groups, the emergence of a global civil society offers the means either of contesting neoliberal globalisation or of deepening and extending it. This section firstly surveys the emergence of a global civil society before going on to examine its transformative potential.

Williams offers three ways of determining the emergence of a global civil society: is there 'a dense network of regular and wide-ranging interactions among groups and organizations operating across national borders'; are there 'issues that are intrinsically transnational or global in character'; and are transnational groups pursuing transnational or global goals and objectives (Williams, 2005: 350–1)? After all, such campaigns as the abolition of slavery in the nineteenth century or the establishment of the International Red Cross in 1864 remind us that transnational civil society activity is nothing new. However, what distinguishes today's global order is the wide range of non-governmental organisations that operate transnationally, the many transnational advocacy networks on international development, ecological issues, women's rights, human rights and peace issues that exist, and the emergence of global social movements, especially the alter-globalisation movement (see Box 9.2). As their character suggests, these civil society actors do not limit themselves to issues that concern one nation state alone but, in dealing with issues such as HIV/AIDS, international debt, human rights violations, immigration and global warming, their agendas are truly global. Finally, in working and campaigning on these issues, such global social actors are pursuing global goals. The extent and spread of such global civil society activity is well documented in the annual Global Civil Society Yearbook (Anheier et al., 2005). The 2004–05 edition gives a total of 282,851 international NGOs (INGOs) in the world in 2003, which have members in at least three countries and formal structures for the election of governing officers from several member countries. This figure had grown from 188,381 in 1993. Though the majority is still in the developed world, the highest growth took place in Eastern Europe and Central Asia. The Yearbook also lists the number of INGOs by purpose: it found that economic development and infrastructure constitute the largest group, followed by research and, some distance behind, purposes such as law, policy and advocacy; social development; culture and

recreation; education; religion; health and politics. Th
wide range of issues that concerns global civil society.
INGO meetings, and about employment, volunteering ar
of the sector, as well as analyses of global civil society
movements and pioneers all testify to the existence of a gr⌐ ͺ and
diverse global civil society.

There is extensive evidence that global civil society, in engaging
with key economic and political powers in this globalised world
order, has become a significant social actor. For example, campaigns
against Nestlé for its infant milk formula, against Nike for its labour
conditions, against toy makers in China and other developing
countries for their labour conditions, against pharmaceutical
corporations for their control of HIV/AIDS drugs and their refusal to
allow developing countries like South Africa and Brazil to manufacture
cheaper generic drugs, against Monsanto for genetic engineering, and
against Shell for its activities in Nigeria have all gained a high level
of international media coverage and elicited changes in the practices
of the corporations involved (through critics claim such changes
are often more cosmetic than substantial). Activities by global civil
society organisations such as the Fair Trade Network, which seeks
outlets for a range of consumer goods grown or manufactured by poor
people in developing countries so as to ensure that more of the gains
go directly to the producers, also indirectly challenge the power of
global corporations. Other campaigns have targeted transnational or
intergovernmental organisations. One well-known example was the
success of a campaign by international NGOs in 1997 and 1998 against
the OECD negotiations of a Multilateral Agreement on Investment
(MAI) which eventually led to the negotiations being terminated
without agreement (Naím, 2000). Another example is the Jubilee
2000 campaign for the cancellation of poor countries' debt which
has highlighted the issue and helped put it on the agenda of the G-
7 group of industrialised countries. In the early 1990s, negotiation
of the North American Free Trade Agreement (NAFTA) between the
US, Canada and Mexico was the occasion for extensive transnational
mobilisation by civil society groups across the three countries against
the agreement that succeeded in having labour and environmental
clauses inserted by the incoming Clinton administration. Of course,
these campaigns are only the visible tip of the iceberg of a constant level
of engagement, discussions, monitoring, advocacy and campaigns by
global civil society organisations directed at (and at times against)
global corporations and intergovernmental organisations. As early

as 1982, the World Bank set up an NGO–World Bank committee to institutionalise the dialogue between both sides and this dialogue has been extended in numerous ways throughout the 1990s. The IMF and the WTO have also institutionalised links with civil society organisations. Such forms of engagement have resulted in pressuring these major global bodies to be more transparent and accountable (see Williams, 2005: 357–67).

Yet, for all its activism, global civil society's achievements have been modest at best. It may have helped modify some of the harder edges of neoliberal globalisation, slightly lessening the extent of vulnerability faced by some groups (for example, some workers in sectors of global manufacturing targeted by campaigners) and strengthening in a modest way some coping mechanisms (such as environmental regulations). Overall, however, it has done little to curb the extension of market values into almost every domain of our social lives. This may not be due to any failure on the part of global civil society but rather due to the fact that large sectors of it may either uphold and promote neoliberal globalisation (for example, business lobbies, professional associations and philanthropic foundations) or else cooperate with states and intergovernmental organisations in projects and programmes that are in no way inconsistent with neoliberal globalisation (after all many civil society organisations are subcontracted by states to provide services). As Tarrow reminds us, social movements that seek more radical changes 'are hard to construct, [and] are difficult to maintain' (Tarrow, 2001: 2). The term 'civil society' at a global level therefore covers a wide range of groups with very divergent and conflicting aims and inherits the ambiguity associated with the term as it emerged in national contexts over hundreds of years. Three quite distinct meanings of the term can be traced and expressions of each identified in today's global civil society:

- Civil society as an agent of the state: seventeenth- and eighteenth-century thinkers like Locke, Smith and Hegel saw civil society as helping constitute the state and the state as the guarantor of civil society. This cooperative view of state–civil society relations, working together as they sought to civilise 'uncivil' society, finds expression today in what Kaldor calls 'tamed' NGOs – professionalised, and institutionalised by the state as compliant implementers of state programmes or providers of state services (Kaldor, 2003: 13, 86–95).

- Civil society as contesting and transforming established power: derived from thinkers like de Tocqueville and, in our times, Habermas, this views civil society as providing a check on state and market power, holding them to account. Indeed Marx and Gramsci saw the form that the state took and the interests it served as being constituted through the struggles of civil society (class struggle between workers and capitalists or the struggle of different social groups for hegemony). This tradition has for long found expression in the role of trade unions and is embodied today in the contestatory activities of many civil society movements.

- Civil society as a realm of contests over identity: this views civil society as a sphere in which social and cultural differences find expression and that can give rise to distinctly 'uncivil' movements like terrorist groups or the ultra-right.

As Kaldor reminds us, the term 'civil society' has been ambiguous enough to allow such diverse groups as neoliberals, post-Marxists and Islamicists all to adopt it with enthusiasm (Kaldor, 2003: 2). Global civil society therefore spans the spectrum of positions from the maintenance agenda to the radical agenda outlined in Chapter 8 and it can be seen as a handmaiden of the state (a view congenial to the neoliberals), as a force to challenge and help change dominant power (a view held by some reformers and many radicals) or as a terrain of anti-social activity (a space occupied by terrorist and other groups motivated by revenge). Instead of seeing these different forms of civil society as alternatives (for example, Kaldor presents them as succeeding one another as new social movements emerged in the 1970s and 1980s, NGOs and transnational civic networks in the late 1980s and 1990s, nationalist and fundamentalist movements in the 1990s and the anti-capitalist movement in the late 1990s and 2000s (see Kaldor, 2003: Table 4.1, pp. 80–1)), it would be more accurate to see them as competing against one another and therefore to see global civil society as a terrain of struggle. What unites the different forms of actors competing on this terrain is that they are non-hierarchical, decentralised and often local groups that network with one another across state boundaries. Indeed Waterman argues that the international labour movement is now taking on these same characteristics (Waterman, 2001: 71–3). However, what divides them is that they can take on very different expressions: from the alter-globalisation movement to street gangs (on the latter, see Papachristos, 2005). Neither do civil society groups always emerge as spontaneous expressions of local aspirations or grievances. Drainville asks provocatively: 'What if what comes "from below" is also being structured, or over-determined, or manufactured, "from above"'? (Drainville, 2004: 9). This reminds us that states and intergovernmental organisations are adept at co-opting and controlling civil society organisations, often fragmenting and atomising them in the process so that they implement the agendas of donors rather than promoting structural changes to benefit those being marginalised by globalisation. This finds expression in what is sometimes called the 'NGOisation' of civil society (Kaldor, 2003: 92) as social groups and movements are pressurised to structure themselves in response to the funding opportunities and demands of governments and other donor agencies, a process in which those involved are not always willing participants (in other words, they are privately critical of what survival forces them to do). Civil society can also be structured from above through strong cultural and religious influences such as Christian fundamentalism in the United States and parts of Latin America and Africa, through Islamicist groups in Africa and Asia and among immigrant populations in Europe, or through ethnic group identification that can be especially strong in cases of state disintegration such as former Yugoslavia, Rwanda and Somalia. The civil society groups that emerge from such influences often contest neoliberal globalisation in ways that are very destructive. Yet, despite all these pressures, global civil society also includes groups that contest state and market power in ways that strengthen social solidarities and express citizens' disquiet. It is from such groups that the promise of global civil society to transform neoliberal globalisation derives, as shown in the sudden emergence of a global movement challenging the values and practices of today's dominant form of globalisation (Box 9.2).

Central to the transformative potential of this global movement is its 'new impetus to build organisations of civil society as a force for achieving and deepening democracy or rebuilding it in a radically new context' (Wainwright, 2005: 97). This derives from a more egalitarian relationship between civil society organisations and movements in the North and the South 'based more on a sense of a common struggle and a common search for democratic and economically just alternatives' (Wainwright, 2005: 100). Two examples

BOX 9.2   A NEW GLOBAL MOVEMENT IS BORN

What is most striking about the so-called 'anti-globalisation' movement is its swift emergence and its enormous capacity to mobilise at a global level. It can be dated back to the 1998 defeat of the OECD negotiations on a Multilateral Agreement on Investment (MAI) by a network of social activists, particularly in France, the United States and Canada. However it first public manifestation came in June 1999 when 50,000 people formed a human chain around the G-7 summit in Cologne seeking a cancellation of debts to the poorest countries. Yet the movement's coming of age is dated to the gathering of 40,000 people for the WTO ministerial summit in Seattle in November 1999 when a mixture of determined street protests and internal divisions led to the meeting's collapse. More high-profile protests followed outside the World Bank and IMF meetings in Washington in April and in Prague in September and outside the EU summit in Nice in December 2000.

January 2001 saw the founding of the World Social Forum in Porto Alegre with 15,000 participants. Major protests followed outside the Summit of the Americas in Quebec City in April, and the EU summit in Gothenburg in June 2001. But the movement got its baptism of fire at the G-8 summit in Genoa in July 2001 when 200,000 gathered to protest and police violence led to the death of a young protester. In January 2002, 50,000 people turned up to the second World Social Forum while 300,000 protested in March outside the EU summit in Barcelona. In November of that year, the first European Social Forum was held in Florence with 60,000 in attendance while the third World Social Forum in January 2003 brought 100,000 to Porto Alegre. A year later, the World Social Forum was held in Bombay and attracted 120,000 people. When it returned to Porto Alegre in January 2005, 150,000 people came to take part.

And so the growth continued, indicating that the movement's critique of free-market liberalisation and the commodification of social services and wider public spaces has struck a deep cord amid large sectors of society, especially the young. As *Le Monde* put it, in the four years between the WTO ministerial meetings in Seattle and Cancun (December 1999–September 2003), the 'anti-globalisation' movement has become the 'alter-globalisation' movement and 'has unleashed a debate on globalisation which – buoyed by strong sympathy from public opinion – has played a major role in a very noticeable change in the dominant discourse on the benefits of liberalisation' (*Le Monde*, 2004).

illustrate how this potential is finding expression. The first relates to the Zapatistas who, as mentioned in the epigraph to this chapter, stand as an emblem of the emerging alter-globalisation movement. For Olesen, the Zapatistas have given rise to a new form of globalised solidarity based on mutuality rather than the sorts of dependent relationships between North and South that characterised earlier periods. This new form of solidarity has helped turn their local struggles into global ones, showing how all local grievances can be seen as illustrations of the larger power and resource inequalities of our neoliberal globalised world. Based on this, they 'propose a radicalisation of liberal democracy that includes questions of socioeconomic inequalities and narrows the distance between people and decision-making structures' (Olesen, 2004: 262). But the power of this proposal derives from the fact that it is not asking people around the world just to support the Zapatistas' struggle for democratisation in Mexico but is proposing that everyone engages in this struggle in their own locales through the agency of civil society. In undertaking these struggles, there is no 'defined point of arrival' other than the transformation of neoliberal globalisation (Olesen, 2004: 261). In this way, therefore, the Zapatistas have helped foster 'a new conception of solidarity that involves a reconfiguration of the relationship between the local, the national and the global' (Olesen, 2004: 256). Examining the World Social Forum, Wainwright similarly finds it spearheading new forms of global democracy. She identifies four ways in which this is happening: firstly, through strengthening the transformative power of civil society, extending its reach and stimulating wider strategic thinking; secondly, through calling governments to account and highlighting the undemocratic nature of so much international treaty and rule-making; thirdly, through producing a new relationship between civil society organisations and political parties as the latter begin to recognise civil society's autonomous sources of power and understand themselves as just one actor among others in the process of radical transformation; and fourthly, through experimentation with new forms of consultation and programme development in a participatory way. In these ways, therefore, the WSF is an incubator or a laboratory, finding new ways of resolving age-old dilemmas about achieving effective common action with a diversity of actors, creating a framework for debate while serving the needs of activists, and developing strategy and visions rooted in the experience of those seeking to create new sources of power (Wainwright, 2005: 109–16).

Through these expressions, global civil society can be seen as embodying today the spontaneous 'double movement' by society against the destructive inroads of the market identified by Karl Polanyi in his work (2001: 156) and as used by contemporary theorists of the role of civil society in neoliberal globalisation (see Murphy, 2003). Yet Murphy and his co-authors find themselves agnostic about the prospects for such a double movement to re-embed the global market in society, conscious as they are of the limited opportunities open to civil society under different political systems and of the capacity by opponents to divide civil society (Murphy, 2003: 205–11). Similarly, Olesen emphasises the fragility of the emerging new form of global solidarity he identifies. Yet, against this, the immense mobilising capacity of the alter-globalisation movement indicates that it is giving expression to widely held political convictions and values, rooted in micro-resistances. These can be repressed, but not extinguished as long as the conditions of neoliberal globalisation remain fundamentally unchanged. Furthermore, as threats to livelihood increase from the destruction of the biosphere, from polarising social structures and from the erosion of democratic systems (see Cox, 2002: 82–8), so are the alternative values expressed in the alter-globalisation movement likely to attract more adherents. If, as argued here, global civil society is a terrain of struggle, the indications are that the struggles over the future of globalisation will intensify. It is far too early to see what the likely outcome may be; indeed, it is probably far more accurate to identify the struggle between neoliberal globalisation and alter-globalisation as the great political struggle that will dominate much of the twenty-first century and beyond, just as the struggle for the democratisation of national societies which emerged at the end of the eighteenth century dominated the following century and beyond. The most that can be affirmed is that global civil society is showing itself to be the incubator of an alternative way forward, thereby emerging as a new social subject opening spaces for transformative resistance. In this, it embodies another conviction of Karl Polanyi's as expressed by Rotstein: 'Premature, passive, or complacent resignation is not what is called for. It is instead a commitment to and a probing for the limits, which remain unknown. Those limits can be discovered only in the course of grasping for the new possibilities' (Rotstein, 1990: 109).

GLOBAL POWERPLAYS

Polanyi's double movement reminds us that while civil society might have supplied the pressure, it was political action channelled through states that implemented new governance structures to re-embed the market in society (Murphy, 2002: 169). Addressing vulnerability and violence in this globalised age will therefore require new forms of global governance; the purpose of this section is to examine the forms these are taking and their potential for reducing vulnerability. In beginning, it is important to emphasise the continuities with the subject of the previous section, since global civil society is itself one important constitutive element of today's complex and emerging global governance. As Wilkinson emphasises, global governance means far more than intergovernmental organisations like the United Nations or the Bretton Woods Institutions or regional organisations like the European Union or Mercosur. It combines an array of actors, both public and private, that are combining in very different ways to manage a growing range of political, economic and social affairs, facilitated by the possibilities of communication and networking provided by new information and communications technologies (see Chapter 5). Among the actors involved are transnational organisations like those just mentioned and the states that constitute them, but also such informal groupings as the Group of 7 leading industrialised countries and the World Economic Forum that meets at Davos every January, private groups like the International Chamber of Commerce or credit-rating agencies like Moody's Investors Service and Standard & Poor's Ratings Group, global accountancy and law firms, NGOs like the Worldwide Fund for Nature and Oxfam, and many other social groups such as churches, social movements and terrorist organisations.

In this way, global governance can be thought of as the various patterns in which global, regional, national and local actors combine to govern particular areas. Global governance, then, is not defined simply by the emergence of new actors or nodes of authority; instead it comprises a growing complexity in the way in which its actors interact and interrelate. (Wilkinson, 2002: 2)

Unlike previous forms of governance, mostly focused on the nation state, emerging forms of governance at global level are not characterised by hierarchical control. Instead, as Rosenau writes, 'governance is the process whereby an organization or society steers itself, and the dynamics of communication and control are central to that process' (Rosenau, 2005: 46). This steering takes place through establishing a system of rule over a particular aspect of public affairs, but this system of rule is as likely to be established by a private as by a public body or group. As a result, 'global governance is the sum of myriad – literally millions of – control mechanisms driven by different histories, goals, structures, and processes ... but there are no characteristics or attributes common to all mechanisms' (Rosenau, 2005: 48). For this reason, Rosenau likens the present state of global governance to 'a new form of anarchy' involving both the absence of a higher form of authority and 'such an extensive disaggregation of authority as to allow for much greater flexibility, innovation, and experimentation in the development and application of new control mechanisms' (2005: 48). The effect is to undermine the capacities for governance located at the state level (though efforts continue to be made at this level, see Box 9.3 on South American states) since the effectiveness of any arrangements worked out at the level of the state 'is likely to be undermined by the proliferation of emergent control mechanisms both within and outside their jurisdictions' (2005: 50). Rosenau concludes by pointing to the ambiguity of this situation: 'Global governance, it seems reasonable to anticipate, is likely to consist of proliferating mechanisms that fluctuate between bare survival and increasing institutionalization, between considerable chaos and widening degrees of order' (2005: 51). The task here is to examine what prospects this holds for addressing vulnerability and violence.

Some general comments about the nature of the rules being made to govern the global economy and society are warranted before examining how effective they are in addressing the sorts of vulnerabilities and violence described in Chapter 2. Many analysts point to the uneven nature of their development: Wilkinson comments that in economic governance rules are highly developed, but in areas like health, environment and human rights they are underdeveloped and in other areas they are barely existent or wholly absent (Wilkinson, 2002: 3). Harriss-White writes that:

> procedures with 'teeth' are confined to the functions most important to capital (the management of global communication and common standards), while the settlement of disputes, the representation of the interests of labour, the stabilization of markets and the regulation and management of adverse environmental externalities are poorly addressed. (Harriss-White, 2002: 8)

A marked imbalance in global governance has also been noted between accommodating the needs of global capital and much weaker representation of the needs of citizens, especially those in the developing world (Thomas, 2002: 117–22). Indeed, as Falk puts it: 'It seems evident that a coalition of global market forces and geopolitical actors is resistant to all efforts to give coherent political form to the strivings of global civil society' (Falk, 2005: 117). This therefore reflects the logic of the structures of contemporary global governance and the rules it generates – prioritising the needs of the market over those of society. It makes it an unlikely source for the

BOX 9.3   ARE SOUTH AMERICAN STATES CREATING AN ALTERNATIVE?

The inauguration of left-wing leader Tabaré Vazquez as Uruguay's president in March 2005 confirmed the decisive leftward shift of most leading South American states. Attending were Presidents Chávez of Venezuela, da Silva of Brazil, Kirchner of Argentina and Lagos of Chile. President Castro of Cuba was only prevented from attending by his doctors' advice. Each employing a discourse critical of the impact of globalisation on their countries' poor, these new leaders signal the widespread discontent throughout the sub-continent at the failures of economic liberalisation. Can they use state power to reduce the vulnerability of their citizens?

Commentators note that behind the facade of unity lurk many differences. Some of these presidents (especially Lula in Brazil, but also Lagos and Vazquez) represent parties with strong socialist policies and traditions. Chávez and Kirchner, on the other hand, are more populist and nationalist in background and party affiliation (Kirchner is a Peronist). Chávez employs a highly populist discourse denouncing neoliberal globalisation as 'a sickness' (quoted in Kirby, 2003: 190), while Lagos and Vazquez are much more moderate and measured in their discourse. Lula is willing to attend the World Social Forum at Porto Alegre but from there flies to the World Economic Forum at Davos.

Yet important common approaches can be identified amid these differences. Each of these leaders seeks to use state power to address the huge social deficits they inherited, breaking to some extent with the prevailing neoliberal orthodoxy in doing so. Four common features can be identified:

- stable macroeconomic management as a condition for economic growth (Chávez's rhetoric often masks this dimension of his policies);
- strengthening state capacity and efficiency through ceasing and even reversing the privatisation of state companies (Kirchner has created a state-run airline and energy holding company while Vazquez has led attempts to stop the privatisation of energy and is committed to keeping water in public ownership) and through decisive actions to root out corruption;
- developing innovative schemes of social investment (Lula's Zero Hunger campaign is probably the best known) some of which include high levels of democratic participation;
- strengthening regional integration (particularly through Mercosur) as a means to counter US dominance and reap greater benefits for South America (Lula and Kirchner are agreed on the need for social transfers from the better off to the poorer countries in Mercosur, as happens in the EU).

This is far from a socialist revolution. It has been described as 'economic credibility with social sensibility' (Paranagua, 2004) or, by EU foreign policy chief Javier Solana as 'a new model for the democratic and responsible left' (Colitt, 2003). Whether it is sufficient to reverse the growing vulnerability of most South Americans, only time will tell.

kinds of actions required to address vulnerability (as outlined in the penultimate section of Chapter 8), namely restraining market forces to ensure they serve goals that are established through public debate and deliberation. This would require the decommodification of land, labour and capital, robust redistributive measures at global level and mechanisms to protect people and societies from threats. Is it likely that today's global governance institutions and rules can achieve such goals?

Since the financial system was identified in Chapter 2 as a major source of the vulnerabilities associated with globalisation, and as Polanyi identified the commodification of capital as one of the pillars of market society, the changing governance of the global financial system is a good place to begin to give an answer to this important question. Germain reminds us that the 'unpredictable financial turbulence' of the 1990s has sparked 'the most radical overhaul of the structure of global financial governance since 1945' (Germain, 2002: 31). He argues that this has generated a consensus on the reforms required which he sums up as the 'three Ss': strengthening transparency, strengthening support and strengthening regulation (2002: 20). Standards for data dissemination and transparency have been improved and implemented by the IMF and specialised international bodies; a new credit facility has been established by the IMF to provide funds for countries that might run into crisis; and a new regulatory body (the Financial Stability Forum or FSF) has been set up to bring together key national and international regulators 'to eliminate the perceived regulatory gap that enables financial contagion to spread' (Germain, 2002: 20). Yet, while Germain stresses the importance of the involvement of key developing countries (or emerging markets as they are called) in these initiatives, he acknowledges that 'the pendulum may still be well within a neoliberal arc', though he hopes that the involvement of a wider range of actors will shift the focal point 'from a US-centred structure of governance' (2002: 27). Nothing identified by Germain however contradicts the key nature of global financial governance as described by Pauly: 'Globalizing financial markets remain at base a political experiment at an early stage' whose architects (the US and its key allies) 'have demonstrated little serious interest in advancing any alternative experiment'. He concludes: 'Ever more open financial markets might not ultimately succeed in generating a more stable, more prosperous, and fairer world order. But no other plan was on offer in the early twenty-first century' (Pauly, 2005: 201). Changes in the international financial system therefore hold few prospects for fundamentally curbing the vulnerability associated with a more liberalised system.

Polanyi's emphasis on the damage wrought by the commodification of land reminds us of the importance of the regulation of environmental activities, an issue that became an important subject of international diplomacy at the first UN conference on the environment held in Stockholm in 1972, and continued in the major UN conferences in Rio de Janeiro in 1992 (the 'Earth summit') and in Johannesburg in 2002. As a result, governance conventions have proliferated for a wide range of environmental concerns, including the atmosphere (such as the Kyoto Protocol on climate change finally ratified in 2005 or the Montreal Protocol on Substances that Deplete the Ozone Layer that successfully terminated the manufacture of ozone-depleting CFCs), hazardous substances, the marine environment, nature conservation, nuclear safety and freshwater resources. Each of these lays down rules for participating states, sets up implementation and monitoring mechanisms and establishes decision-making bodies (for a full list of conventions, see Stokke and Thommessen, 2003). Furthermore, over 30 specialist UN agencies and programmes are now involved in governance of aspects of the environment. However, as Elliott writes, this 'congested institutional terrain still provides more of an appearance than a reality of comprehensive global governance' and it has come 'to legitimise a neoliberal ecopolitics, characterised by a rehabilitation of the state, liberal-individual notions of justice, and a technocratic emphasis on managerialism, standard setting and rules-based behaviour' (Elliott, 2002: 58). Paradoxically, despite so much diplomatic activity, it appears that efforts to improve the environment are largely failing and that practices of unsustainable development continue to degrade the environment in ways that heighten threats to human livelihoods. This leads some to conclude that regimes and conventions may be distracting attention from the fundamental changes in production and consumption required to address the scale of the problems adequately (Dauvergne, 2005: 386–7). It can therefore be concluded that 'environmental multilateralism does little to acknowledge or address the *structural* causes (and consequences) of environmental degradation' (Elliott, 2002: 71; emphasis in original).

We finally examine social regulation, echoing Polanyi's third form of commodification, that of labour (by which he meant human beings). Deacon sees a global social policy regime emerging which includes three elements: transnational redistribution, supranational regulation, and global or supranational provision or empowerment. 'All three types of supranational activity already take place but they are often confined within one regional economic trading bloc such as the European Union. Elements of all three, however, are to be found at a global level' (Deacon, 1999: 214). As examples of each of the three forms, he suggests: economic assistance from the West to the East (aid from North to South would probably be a better example); WTO actions to prevent 'social dumping' by multinational capital; and citizenship entitlements for stateless persons operated by the UN High Commission for Refugees. However, while Deacon's schema points to the *potential* for robust global social governance, the practice is still dominated by the goal of 'global economic integration via the free market' (Thomas, 2002: 124). As a result, in examining the institutions of global governance, Yeates finds 'that the range of welfare alternatives backed by these institutions is currently confined to variants of liberalism, and there is a marked absence of any international institution advancing a social democratic or redistributive agenda' (Yeates, 2001: 29). Indeed, in studying the Comprehensive Development Framework (CDF) announced by the World Bank in 1999 and presented as a way in which developing countries could take ownership over their own economic and social policies, Cammack draws attention to the fact that it masks a deeper process of the surveillance of developing countries, giving the Bank 'increasing scope for an unprecedented level of intervention in the domestic affairs of states' (Cammack, 2002: 45). Referring to the Poverty Reduction Strategy Papers (PRSPs) being implemented in some highly indebted countries, he writes that this process

> is structured and employed to ensure direct IMF intervention in dictating the broad framework of macroeconomic policy, while the World Bank takes the lead in ensuring that social and structural policies are systematically subordinated to it, and will induce the institutional and behavioural changes that will lock it in place. (Cammack, 2002: 45)

The World Bank is thereby creating 'an institutional framework within which global capitalist accumulation can be sustained, while simultaneously seeking to legitimate the project through policies of controlled participation and pro-poor propaganda' (Cammack, 2004:190). Therefore, as Thomas concludes: 'In an increasingly co-ordinated fashion, key global governance institutions and the interests they represent, are overseeing a process of increased economic, political and social stratification. They are complicit in this outcome' (Thomas, 2002: 129). On balance, therefore, it can be concluded that elements of redistribution, regulation and social protection as identified by Deacon all remain very weak in the face of pressures for market liberalisation and direct intervention by the World Bank and the IMF to ensure compliance by countries with such pressures.

Co-opting civil society so as to lend legitimacy to existing patterns of global governance reminds us that if the terrain of global civil society itself is one of struggle, then so too is that of global governance 'in which struggles over wealth, power, and knowledge are taking place' (Murphy, 2005: 98). However, while possibilities may exist for the emergence of a new historical structure as outlined in Chapter 8, what concerns us here is the actual practice of the institutions of global governance and the rules being implemented to govern global economic and social activities. Despite examples that seem to offer some promise of reducing vulnerabilities, it is difficult to fault Murphy's conclusion of the principal thrust behind today's global governance:

> Global governance is likely to remain inefficient, incapable of shifting resources from the world's wealthy to the world's poor, pro-market, and relatively insensitive to the concerns of labour and the rural poor, despite the progressive role that it recently may have played in promoting liberal democracy and the empowering of women. (Murphy, 2005: 90)

For these reasons, it offers little hope of reversing the vulnerabilities and violence associated with globalisation in any decisive way.

PROSPECTS: WHAT FUTURE LIES AHEAD?

The introduction to this chapter referred to Drainville's advice 'to stay with global practices long enough to see what they might carry that is significant and, perhaps, transformative' (Drainville, 2004: 7–9). In examining how globalisation is being contested, therefore, this chapter has focused on three different levels of activity where significantly new developments can be identified – the local, the domain of civil society, and rule-making arenas of global governance. Attention throughout has been devoted to the extent to which what is happening at these levels may be transforming globalisation, particularly in terms of reducing vulnerabilities and violence. At local level, manifold micro-resistances were identified that seem to be eroding the hegemony of neoliberal or corporate globalisation, but these can find expression in forms that weaken social solidarities as much as strengthen them. Global civil society was found to be a terrain of struggle between different understandings and orientations, though potential for transforming neoliberal globalisation was identified in more progressive sectors which constitute an incubator of an alternative politics of transformation. Turning to global governance, the chapter was less sanguine as it concluded that, in practice, the main effect of global rule-making so far has been to deepen and extend neoliberal globalisation and the vulnerabilities and violence associated with it.

In discussing the prospects for transforming globalisation, the concept of 'social contract' is a useful one. It harks back to the national social contracts which were the central means by which the market was re-embedded in society through compromises between capital and labour after the Second World War. But the concept is also central to Kaldor's view of global civil society, which she defines as 'the medium through which one or many social contracts between individuals, both women and men, and the political and economic centres of power are negotiated and reproduced'. For her, this is not an abstract and hypothetical idea but a concrete reality, an 'agreed institutional outcome' through which the power of both political institutions and large corporations can be counterbalanced (Kaldor, 2003: 44–5). She also makes clear that she expects this to happen not at the level of the national state but at a global level (2003: 146). Forging a new global social contract between economic and political power on the one hand and citizens on the other therefore conceptualises the task that requires undertaking. It can also serve to summarise the principal themes running through this book. For it highlights that the vulnerabilities and violence associated with today's neoliberal globalisation (as described in Chapters 2 and 3) are linked to the unravelling of the national social contracts of the post-Second World War period (Chapter 4) and to the fragmentation of the cultural identities that reinforced and legitimated them (Chapter 5). The impact of these changes, it was argued in Chapter 6, echoes that of the destructive impact on society of the imposition of the self-governing market (as analysed in the work of Karl Polanyi) which destroyed earlier forms of social contract embedding the market in society. The concept of a social contract also implies effective mechanisms of redistribution and reciprocity (or mutual obligation) identified by Polanyi as essential features of a just society, and forges a new relationship between the individual and society, thereby countering the extreme individualism identified in Chapter 7 as a feature of vulnerability. An example is the proposal by the UN Economic Commission for Latin America and the Caribbean that goods and services required for a basic level of well-being should be subject to regulation, be supplied by public authorities, and claims to them should be enforceable (Ocampo and Martin, 2003: 175–6). Indeed, the UN Global Compact is one very weak initial step in this direction, depending on the good will of the private sector to uphold human and labour rights and to protect the environment, and to support public policies on these issues.

The central concept this book has introduced is vulnerability, defined as an increase in threats to well-being and an erosion of coping mechanisms. It was argued in Chapter 1 that vulnerability is a more adequate concept than those more commonly used (poverty/ inequality, risk and insecurity) to capture the distinctive impact of globalisation on livelihoods and well-being. Only vulnerability gives an unambiguous answer to the question raised: is globalisation the cause of, or the solution to, the absence of well-being so widely documented? In other words, is globalisation the cause or the cure? As argued in this book, today's globalisation, identified as neoliberal corporate globalisation, is fuelling vulnerability and violence even in situations where it results in increased incomes and material provision. Examining the nature of vulnerability has pointed to a deeper destruction being wrought as market forces increase threats and erode coping mechanisms around the world. Introducing the need for a social contract as a response to this situation also highlights the utility of vulnerability since there is nothing inherent in the concepts of poverty/inequality, risk or insecurity that would point to the need for a social contract if they are to be successfully reduced. After all, proponents of globalisation believe that poverty can be resolved through a deepening of global flows (World Bank, 2002); those who theorise risk see it as an essential feature of modernity; and strengthening security points to securing oneself against others who are seen as threats (Chapter 7). In none of these cases is a social contract required. Alone of these concepts, vulnerability points decisively and unambiguously to the need to strengthen our networks of solidarity and mutual obligation and would therefore require some form of robust social contract. As UN General Secretary

Kofi Annan put it, in his report *In Larger Freedom*: common threats require collective responses (United Nations, 2005).

In concluding this final part on Remedies, it must be admitted that the evidence indicates that achieving a global social contract will be a long and hard-fought struggle. Yet, as argued in Chapter 8, stepping back from the flux of present events and viewing them as a transition from one historical structure to another can offer a new and more hopeful perspective on the deeper shifts taking place. As the epigraph which opened this chapter reminds us, as old solidarities are being eroded new collective identities and solidarities are being forged. This is certainly a strong feature of the alter-globalisation movement. There are, of course, no inevitable outcomes of this struggle, and the erosion of civil liberties, extensive surveillance of the population and military responses to threat – all central features of reactions to the 'new terrorism' – may well mute struggles for a new social contract. Despite this, as vulnerabilities and violence increase, such struggles are unlikely to disappear. The struggle against growing vulnerability and violence, to counteract threats and strengthen coping mechanisms, looks set to dominate the new century.

Bibliography

A.T. Kearney/Foreign Policy (2001) 'Measuring Globalization', in *Foreign Policy*, January/February, pp. 56–65.

—— (2002) 'Globalization's Last Hurrah?', in *Foreign Policy*, January/February, pp. 38–51.

—— (2003) 'Measuring Globalization: Who's Up, Who's Down?', in *Foreign Policy*, January/February, pp. 60–72.

—— (2004) 'Measuring Globalization: Economic Reversals, Forward Momentum', in *Foreign Policy*, March/April, pp. 54–69.

—— (2005) 'Measuring Globalization', in *Foreign Policy*, May/June, pp. 52–60.

Adam, Barbara and van Loon, Joost (2000) 'Introduction: Repositioning Risk: the Challenge for Social Theory', in Barbara Adam, Ulrich Beck and Joost van Loon, eds, *The Risk Society and Beyond: Critical Issues for Social Theory* (London: Sage Publications), pp. 1–31.

ADB (2003) 'Strategy on Mobility and HIV Vulnerability Reduction in the Greater Mekong Subregion 2002–2004', downloaded from <http://www.adb.org/Documents/Guidelines/Preventing_AIDS/default.asp>, March 2004.

Alger, Dean (1998) *Megamedia: How Giant Corporations Dominate Mass Media, Distort Competition, and Endanger Democracy* (Lanham, MD: Rowman & Littlefield).

Alkire, Sabina (n.d.) 'A Conceptual Framework for Human Security', Working Paper 2, Centre for Research on Inequality, Human Security and Ethnicity, CRISE, Queen Elizabeth House, University of Oxford.

Altvater, Elmar (1993) *The Future of the Market* (London: Verso).

Amnesty International (2004) *It's In Our Hands: Stop Violence against Women* (London: Amnesty International Publications).

Anheier, Helmut, Glasius, Marlies and Kaldor, Mary, eds (2005) *Global Civil Society 2004/5* (London: Sage Publications).

Aoyama, Yuko, and Castells, Manuel (2002) 'An Empirical Assessment of the Informational Society: Employment and Occupational Structures of G-7 Countries, 1920–2000', in *International Labour Review*, Vol. 141, Nos 1–2, pp. 123–59.

Bagdikian, Ben H. (1997) *The Media Monopoly* (Boston: Beacon Press, fifth edition).

—— (2000) *The Media Monopoly* (Boston: Beacon Press, sixth edition).

Bakker, Isabella and Gill, Stephen, eds (2003) *Power, Production and Social Reproduction* (Basingstoke: Palgrave Macmillan).

Baudrillard, Jean (1998) *The Consumer Society: Myths and Structures* (London: Sage Publications).

Bauman, Zygmunt (1998) *Globalization: The Human Consequences* (Cambridge: Polity Press).

Bebbington, Anthony (2004) 'Livelihood Transitions, Place Transformations: Grounding Globalization and Modernity', in Robert N. Gwynne and Cristóbal Kay, eds, *Latin America Transformed: Globalization and Modernity* (London: Arnold, second edition), pp. 173–92.

Beck, Ulrich (1992) *Risk Society* (London: Sage Publications).

—— (2000a) 'Risk Society Revisited: Theory, Politics and Research Programmes', in Barbara Adam, Ulrich Beck and Joost van Loon, eds, *The Risk Society and Beyond: Critical Issues for Social Theory* (London: Sage Publications), pp. 211–29.

—— (2000b) *What Is Globalization?* (Cambridge: Polity Press).

—— (2001) 'Living Your Own Life in a Runaway World: Individualisation, Globalisation and Politics', in Will Hutton and Anthony Giddens, eds, *On the Edge: Living with Global Capitalism* (London: Vintage), pp. 164–74.

Beinfield, Harriet and Korngold, Efrem (1991) *Between Heaven and Earth: A Guide to Chinese Medicine* (New York: Ballantine Wellspring).

Berardo, Felix M. and Shehan, Constance L. (2004) 'Family Problems in Global Perspective', in George Ritzer, ed., *Handbook of Social Problems: A Comparative International Perspective* (Thousand Oaks, CA: Sage Publications), pp. 246–60.

Berry, Thomas (1999) *The Great Work* (New York: Bell Tower).

Beynon, John (2002) *Masculinities and Culture* (Buckingham: Open University Press).

Blaikie, Piers, Cannon, Terry, Davis, Ian and Wisner, Ben (1994) *At Risk: Natural Hazards, People's Vulnerability, and Disasters* (London: Routledge).

Blom, Raimo, Melin, Harri and Pyöriä, Pasi (2002) 'Social Contradictions in Informational Capitalism: The Case of Finnish Wage Earners and Their Labor Market Situation', in *The Information Society*, Vol. 18, pp. 333–43.

Bloom, Sandra (1997) *Creating Sanctuary* (New York: Routledge).

—— (1998) *Bearing Witness* (New York: Haworth Press).

Blyth, Mark (2002) *Great Transformations: Economic Ideas and Institutional Change in the Twentieth Century* (Cambridge: Cambridge University Press).

Boli, John, Elliott, Michael A., and Bieri, Franziska (2004) 'Globalization', in George Ritzer, ed., *Handbook of Social Problems: A Comparative International Perspective* (Thousand Oaks, CA: Sage Publications), pp. 389–415.

Boseley, Sarah (2004) 'The Allergy Epidemic: By 2015 Half of Us may be Carrying One of These', *Guardian*, 10 February.

Bourdieu, Pierre (1990) *In Other Words: Essays Towards a Reflexive Sociology* (Stanford CA: Stanford University Press).

Bowles, Samuel and Gintis, Herbert (1993) 'The Revenge of *Homo Economicus*: Contested Exchange and the Revival of Political Economy', in the *Journal of Economic Perspectives*, Vol. 7, No. 1, pp. 83–102.

Brennan, Martin (1969) 'Language, Personality and the Nation', in Brian Ó Cuív, ed., *A View of the Irish Language* (Dublin: The Stationery Office), pp. 70–80.

Briguglio, Pascal Lino (2003) 'Some Conceptual and Methodological Considerations Relating to the Construction of an Index of Social Vulnerability with Special Reference to Small Island Developing States', in ECLAC, *Towards a Social Vulnerability Index in the Caribbean* (Port of Spain: ECLAC), pp. 39–62.

Cammack, Paul (2002) 'The Mother of all Governments: The World Bank's Matrix for Global Governance', in Rorden Wilkinson and Steve Hughes, eds, *Global Governance: Critical Perspectives* (London: Routledge), pp. 36–53.

—— (2004) 'What the World Bank Means by Poverty Reduction, and Why it Matters', in *New Political Economy*, Vol. 9, No. 2, pp. 189–211.

Cane, Patricia (2000) *Trauma Healing and Transformation* (Watsonville: Capacitar Inc).

Caramel, Laurence (2004) 'Incontournables altermondialistes' in *Le Monde Dossiers & Documents*, September, p. 1.

Carmody, Pádraig (2002) 'The Liberalization of Underdevelopment or the Criminalization of the State? Contrasting Explanations of Africa's Politico-Economic Crisis under Globalization', in B. Ikubolajeh Logan, ed., *Globalization, the Third World State and Poverty-Alleviation in the Twenty-First Century* (Aldershot: Ashgate), pp. 47–62.

Carrier, James G., ed., (1997) *Meanings of the Market* (Oxford: Berg).

Castells, Manuel (1996) *The Rise of the Network Society* (Oxford: Blackwell).

—— (1997) *The Power of Identity* (Oxford: Blackwell).

—— (2001) 'Information Technology and Global Capitalism', in Will Hutton and Anthony Giddens, eds, *On the Edge: Living with Global Capitalism*, (London: Vintage), pp. 52–74.

Cerny, Philip G. (1999) 'Globalising the Political and Politicising the Global: Concluding Reflections on International Political Economy as a Vocation', in *New Political Economy*, Vol. 4, No. 1, pp. 147–62.

—— (2000) 'Structuring the Political Arena: Public Goods, States and Governance in a Globalizing World', in Ronen Palan, ed., *Global Political Economy: Contemporary theories* (London: Routledge), pp. 21–35.

Chant, Sylvia (2004) 'Urban Livelihoods, Employment and Gender', in Robert N. Gwynne and Cristóbal Kay, eds, *Latin America Transformed: Globalization and Modernity* (London: Arnold, second edition), pp. 210–31.

Clare, Anthony (2000) *On Men: Masculinity in Crisis* (London: Chatto & Windus).

Cockerham, William C. (2004) 'Health as a Social Problem', in George Ritzer, ed., *Handbook of Social Problems: A Comparative International Perspective* (Thousand Oaks, CA: Sage Publications), pp. 281–97.

Colitt, Raymond (2003) 'Politician with the Human Touch', *Financial Times*, 23 January, p. 8.

Commission on Human Security (2003) *Human Security Now: Protecting and Empowering People* (New York: UN Publications).

Conn, Sarah (1995) 'When the Earth Hurts, Who Responds?', in Theodore Roszak, Mary E. Gomes and Allen D. Kahner, eds, *Ecopsychology* (San Francisco: Sierra Club Books), pp. 156–71.

—— (1998) 'Living in the Earth: Ecopsychology, Health and Psychotherapy', in *The Humanistic Psychotherapist*, Vol. 26, Nos 1–3, pp. 179–98.

Cortright, Brant (1997) *Psychotherapy and Spirit* (Albany, New York: SUNY Press).

Cox, Robert W. (1996) 'Social Forces, States, and World Orders: beyond international relations theory' [1981], in Robert W. Cox with Timothy J. Sinclair: *Approaches to World Order* (Cambridge: Cambridge University Press), pp. 85–123.

—— (2002) *The Political Economy of a Plural World: Critical Reflections on Power, Morals and Civilization* (London: Routledge).

Crystal, David (2000): *Language Death* (Cambridge: Cambridge University Press).

Dauvergne, Peter (2005) 'Globalization and the Environment', in John Ravenhill ed., *Global Political Economy* (Oxford: Oxford University Press), pp. 370–95.

Deacon, Bob (1999) 'Social Policy in a Global Context', in Andrew Hurrell and Ngaire Woods, eds, *Inequality, Globalization, and World Politics* (Oxford: Oxford University Press), pp. 211–47.

Dicken, Peter (2003) *Global Shift: Reshaping the Global Economic Map in the 21st Century* (London: Sage Publications, fourth edition).

Drainville, André C. (2004) *Contesting Globalization: Space and Place in the World Economy* (London: Routledge).

Drori, Gili S. (2004) 'The Internet as a Global Social Problem', in George Ritzer, ed., *Handbook of Social Problems: A Comparative International Perspective* (Thousand Oaks, CA: Sage Publications), pp. 433–50.

Eagleton, Terry (2000) *The Idea of Culture* (Oxford: Blackwell).

ECLAC (2000) *Social Panorama of Latin America 1999–2000* (Santiago: ECLAC).

—— (2001) *Panorama Social de América Latina 2000–01* (Santiago: ECLAC).

—— (2002a) *Globalization and Development* (Santiago: ECLAC).

—— (2002b) *Social Panorama of Latin America, 2001–2002* (Santiago: ECLAC).

—— (2003) 'Towards a Social Vulnerability Index in the Caribbean', in ECLAC, *Towards a Social Vulnerability Index in the Caribbean* (Port of Spain: ECLAC), pp. 6–38.

Elliott, Lorraine (2002) 'Global Environmental Governance', in Rorden Wilkinson and Steve Hughes, eds, *Global Governance: Critical Perspectives* (London: Routledge), pp. 57–74.

Elliott, Richard (2004) 'Making Up People: Consumption as a Symbolic Vocabulary for the Construction of Identity', in Karin M. Ekström and Helene Brembeck, eds, *Elusive Consumption* (Oxford: Berg), pp. 129–43.

ESCAP (2003) 'Economic Vulnerability', UN Economic and Social Commission for Asia and the Pacific.

Esping-Anderson, Gosta (2002) 'The Sustainability of Welfare States: Reshaping Social Protection', in Barbara Harriss-White, ed., *Globalization and Insecurity: Political, Economic and Physical Challenges* (Basingstoke: Palgrave), pp. 218–32.

Falk, Richard (1996) 'An Enquiry into the Political Economy of World Order', in *New Political Economy*, Vol. 1, No. 1, pp. 13–26.

—— (2005) 'Humane Governance for the World: Reviving the Quest', in Rorden Wilkinson, ed., *The Global Governance Reader* (London: Routledge), pp. 105–19.

Ferguson, Niall (2001) *The Cash Nexus: Money and Power in the Modern World 1700–2000* (London: Allen Lane).

Fisher, Andy (2002) *Radical Ecopsychology* (New York: Suny Press).

FitzGerald, Valpy (2002) 'The Security of International Finance', in Barbara Harriss-White, ed., *Globalization and Insecurity: Political, Economic and Physical Challenges* (Basingstoke: Palgrave), pp. 149–72.

Foreign Policy (2004) 'The Davos Report', a report on the 2004 World Economic Forum published as a supplement to *Foreign Policy*, March–April.

Friedman, Jonathan (1994) *Cultural Identity and Global Process* (London: Sage Publications).

Friedman, Thomas (2000) *The Lexus and the Olive Tree* (London: HarperCollins).

Galbraith, James K., Jiaqing, Lu, and Darty, William A., Jr, (1999) 'Measuring the Evolution of Inequality in the Global Economy', UTIP Working Paper No. 7, Austin, TX: University of Texas at Austin.

Garrett, Geoffrey (2000) 'Shrinking States? Globalization and National Autonomy', in Ngaire Woods, ed., *The Political Economy of Globalization* (Basingstoke: Palgrave), pp. 107–46.

George, Vic and Wilding, Paul (2002) *Globalization and Human Welfare* (Basingstoke: Palgrave).

Germain, Randall D. (2002) 'Reforming the International Financial Architecture: the New Political Agenda', in Rorden Wilkinson and Steve Hughes, eds, *Global Governance: Critical Perspectives* (London: Routledge), pp. 17–35.

Giddens, Anthony (1996) *In Defence of Sociology: Essays, Interpretations and Rejoinders* (Cambridge: Polity Press).

—— (1999) *Runaway World: How Globalisation is Reshaping our Lives* (London: Profile Books).

Gill, Stephen (2003) *Power and Resistance in the New World Order* (Basingstoke: Palgrave Macmillan).

Gini, Al (2000) 'The Work, Spend and Debt Syndrome', in *Business and Society Review*, Vol. 104, No. 3, pp. 243–59.

Glendenning, Chellis (1994) *My Name is Chellis and I'm in Recovery from Western Civilization* (Boston: Shambala).

Goodman, Douglas J. (2004) 'Consumption as a Social Problem', in George Ritzer, ed., *Handbook of Social Problems: A Comparative International Perspective* (Thousand Oaks, CA: Sage Publications), pp. 226–45.

Guichard, Éric (2003) 'Does the "Digital Divide" Exist?', in Paul van Seters, Bas de Gaay Fortman and Arie de Ruijter, eds, *Globalization and Its New Divides: Malcontents, Recipes, and Reform* (Amsterdam: Dutch University Press), pp. 69–77.

Gwynne, Robert N. and Kay, Cristóbal (2004) 'The Alternatives to Neoliberalism', in Robert N. Gwynne and Cristóbal Kay, eds, *Latin America Transformed: Globalization and Modernity* (London: Arnold, second edition), pp. 253–67.

Hall, Stuart (1992) 'The Question of Cultural Identity', in Stuart Hall, David Held and Tony McGrew, eds, *Modernity and its Futures* (Cambridge: Polity Press), pp. 273–316.

Hall-Matthews, David (2003) 'Does Globalisation Make Famines More or Less Likely?', paper given at a conference entitled 'Implications of Globalisation: Present Imperfect, Future Tense?', University College Chester, November.

Hamilton, Clive (2003) 'Overconsumption in Britain: A Culture of Middle-Class Complaint?', Discussion Paper Number 57, Canberra: The Australia Institute.

Hampson, Fen Osler and Hay, John B. (2002) 'Human Security: A Review of the Scholarly Literature', in *The Human Security Bulletin*, Vol. 1, No. 2, pp. 1–36.

Hardt, Michael and Negri, Antonio (2003) 'Foreword', in William F. Fisher and Thomas Ponniah, eds, *Another World is Possible: Popular Alternatives to Globalization at the World Social Forum* (London: Zed Books), pp. xvi–xix.

Harriss-White, Barbara, ed. (2002) *Globalization and Insecurity: Political, Economic and Physical Challenges* (Basingstoke: Palgrave).

Hay, Colin (2003) 'What's Globalisation Got To Do With It?', downloaded from <www.bham.ac.uk/POLIS/department/staff/publications/hay_inaugural.htm>, April 2004.

Hay, Colin and Marsh, David (2000) 'Introduction: Demystifying Globalization', in Colin Hay and David Marsh, eds, *Demystifying Globalization* (Basingstoke: Macmillan), pp. 1–17.

Held, David (2004) *Global Covenant: The Social Democratic Alternative to the Washington Consensus* (Cambridge: Polity Press).

Held, David and McGrew, Anthony (2002) *Globalization/Anti-Globalization* (Cambridge: Polity Press).

Held, David and McGrew, Anthony, eds (2000) *The Global Transformations Reader* (Cambridge: Polity Press).

Held, David, McGrew, Anthony, Goldblatt, David, and Perraton, Jonathan (1999) *Global Transformations: Politics, Economics and Culture* (Cambridge: Polity Press).

Herman, Judith (1992) *Trauma and Recovery* (New York: Basic Books).

Hertz, Noreena (2001) *The Silent Takeover: Global Capitalism and the Death of Democracy* (London: William Heinemann).

—— (2003) 'Interview with Noreena Hertz', in *DevISSues*, Vol. 5, No. 1, pp. 14–15.

Hillebrand, Ernst (2003) 'South–South competition: Asia versus Latin America?', Berlin: Friedrich-Ebert-Stiftung, Dialogue on Globalization, downloaded from <http://fes.globalization.de/pubDriver/clients/fesDog/attachments/031201_01_Chil.pdf>, February 2004.

Hillman, James (1995) 'A Psyche the Size of the Earth', in Theodore Roszak, Mary E. Gomes and Allen D. Kahner, eds, *Ecopsychology* (San Francisco: Sierra Club Books), pp. xvii–xviii.

Hirst, Paul and Thompson, Grahame (1996) *Globalization in Question* (Cambridge: Polity Press).

Hirst, Paul and Thompson, Grahame (1999) *Globalization in Question* (Cambridge: Polity Press, second edition).

Hough, Peter (2004) 'Who's Securing Whom? The Need for International Relations to Embrace Human Security', paper given to the BISA annual conference, Warwick University, December 2004.

Huntington, Samuel P. (2004) 'The Hispanic Challenge', in *Foreign Policy*, March/April, pp. 30–45.

IDEA (2004) 'Voter Turnout from 1945 to Date', downloaded from <www.idea.int>, March 2004.

Ignazi, Piero (2003) 'The Development of the Extreme Right at the end of the Century', in Peter H. Herkl and Leonard Weinberg, eds, *Right-Wing Extremism in the Twenty-First Century* (London: Frank Cass), pp. 143–59.

ILO (1997) *World Employment Report 1996–97*, (Geneva: ILO), downloaded from <http://www.ilo.org/public/english/bureau/inf/pkits/wlr97.htm>, April 2004.

—— (2002) *Global Employment Agenda* (Geneva: ILO).

IMF (2003) 'Vulnerability Indicators: A Factsheet', downloaded from <http://www.imf.org/external/np/exr/facts/vul.htm>, November 2003.

—— (2004) *World Economic Outlook 2004* (Washington DC: IMF).

Inglehart, Ronald (2000) 'Globalization and Postmodern Values', in *The Washington Quarterly*, Vol. 23, No. 1, pp. 215–28.

IPCC (2001) 'Climate Change 2001: Impacts, Adaptation , and Vulnerability', a Report of Working Group II of the Intergovernmental Panel on Climate Change.

Jackson, Richard and Howe, Neil (2003) *The 2003 Aging Vulnerability Index*, (Washington DC: Center for Strategic and International Studies).

Jessop, Bob (1994) 'The Transition to post-Fordism and the Schumpeterian Workfare State', in Roger Burrows and Brian Loader, eds, *Towards a Post-Fordist Welfare State?* (London: Routledge), pp. 13–37.

Jordan, Bill (2004) *Sex, Money and Power: The Transformation of Collective Life* (Cambridge: Polity Press).

Kaldor, Mary (2001) *New and Old Wars: Organized Violence in a Global Era* (Cambridge: Polity Press, second edition).

—— (2003) *Global Civil Society: An Answer to War* (Cambridge: Polity Press).

Kanbur, Ravi and Squire Lyn (1999) 'The Evolution of Thinking about Poverty: Exploring the Interactions', mimeo, World Bank, September.

Keay, Douglas (1987) 'Aids, Education and the Year 2000', *Woman's Own*, 23 September 1987. Downloaded from <www.margaretthatcher.org/speeches/displaydocument.asp?docid=106689>, February 2005.

Kellner, Douglas (2004) 'The Media and Social Problems', in George Ritzer, ed., *Handbook of Social Problems: A Comparative International Perspective* (Thousand Oaks, CA: Sage Publications), pp. 209–25.

Keohane, Robert O. and Nye, Joseph S. (2001) *Power and Interdependence* (New York: Longman, third edition [first edition: 1977]).

Kim, Chigon and Gottdiener, Mark (2004) 'Urban Problems in Global Perspective', in George Ritzer, ed., *Handbook of Social Problems: A Comparative International Perspective* (Thousand Oaks, CA: Sage Publications), pp. 172–92.

Kirby, Peadar (2002a) *The Celtic Tiger in Distress: Growth with Inequality in Ireland* (Basingstoke: Palgrave).

—— (2002b) 'Contested Pedigrees of the Celtic Tiger', in Peadar Kirby, Luke Gibbons and Michael Cronin, eds, *Reinventing Ireland: Culture, Society and the Global Economy* (London: Pluto Press), pp. 21–37.

—— (2003) *Introduction to Latin America: Twenty-First Century Challenges* (London: Sage Publications).

—— (2004) 'The Irish State and the Celtic Tiger: A "Flexible Developmental State" or a Competition State?' in Graham Harrison, ed., *Global Encounters* (Basingstoke: Palgrave), pp. 74–94.

Kjeldgaard, Dannie (2002) 'Youth Identities and Consumer Culture: Navigating Local Landscapes of Global Symbols', in *Advances in Consumer Research*, Vol. 29, pp. 387–92.

Klein, Naomi (2000) *No Logo* (London: Flamingo).

Korten, David C. (1999) *The Post-Corporate World: Life after Capitalism* (West Hartford, CT: Kumarian Press).

Krizsán, Andrea and Zentai, Violetta, eds (2003) *Reshaping Globalization: Multilateral Dialogues and New Policy Initiatives* (Budapest: Central European University Press).

Kvist, Jon and Meier Jaeger, Mads (2003) 'Pressures on Post-industrial Societies: Better is More or Less State Welfare?', 4th International Research Conference on Social Security, Antwerp, 5–7 May.

Laïdi, Zaki (1998) *A World Without Meaning: The Crisis of Meaning in International Politics* (London: Routledge).

Lichtenstein, Bronwen (2004) 'AIDS as a Social Problem', in George Ritzer, ed., *Handbook of Social Problems: A Comparative International Perspective* (Thousand Oaks, CA: Sage Publications), pp. 316–34.

Lie, John (1997) 'Sociology of Markets', in *Annual Review of Sociology*, Vol. 23, pp. 341–60.

Loewenberg, Samuel (2005) 'Where Energy and Mushy Thinking Collide', *Irish Times*, 31 January.

Macy, Joanna (1995) 'Working through Environmental Despair', in Theodore Roszak, Mary E. Gomes and Allen D. Kahner, eds, *Ecopsychology* (San Francisco: Sierra Club Books), pp. 240–62.

Marcuse, Herbert (1986) *One-Dimensional Man* (London: Ark Paperbacks).

Marlowe, Lara (2004) 'From the Ghetto to Guantanamo Bay', *Irish Times*, Weekend Review, 7 February, p. 3.

Martin, Gus (2004) 'Sea Change: The Modern Terrorist Environment in Perspective', in George Ritzer, ed., *Handbook of Social Problems: A Comparative International Perspective* (Thousand Oaks, CA: Sage Publications), pp. 355–67.

Mayhew, Anne, Neale, Walter C. and Tandy, David W. (1985) 'Markets in the Ancient Near East: A Challenge to Silver's Argument and Use of Evidence', in the *Journal of Economic History*, Vol. 45, No. 1, pp. 127–34.

McCloskey, James (2001) *Voices Silenced* (Dublin: Cois Life).

McDonagh, Sean (2003) *Dying for Water* (Dublin: Veritas).

McDowell, Linda (2000) 'The Trouble with Men? Young People, Gender Transformations and the Crisis of Masculinity', in the *International Journal of Urban and Regional Research*, Vol. 24, No. 1, pp. 201–9.

McGrew, Tony (2001) 'Feature Review', in *New Political Economy*, Vol. 6, No. 2, pp. 293–301.

McSweeney, Bill (1999) *Security, Identity and Interests: A Sociology of International Relations* (Cambridge: Cambridge University Press).

Merkl, Peter H. (2003) 'Stronger than Ever', in Peter H. Herkl and Leonard Weinberg, eds, *Right-Wing Extremism in the Twenty-First Century* (London: Frank Cass), pp. 23–45.

Mishra, Ramesh (1999) *Globalization and the Welfare State* (Cheltenham: Edward Elgar).

Mittelman, James H. (2004) *Whither Globalization? The Vortex of Knowledge and Ideology* (London: Routledge).

Moser, Caroline O. N. (1998) 'Reassessing Urban Poverty Reduction Strategies: The Asset Vulnerability Framework', in *World Development*, Vol. 26, No. 1, pp. 1–19.

Moulian, Tomás (1997) *Chile Actual: Anatomía de un mito* (Santiago: ARCIS, LOM).

—— (1998) *El consume me consume* (Santiago: LOM).

Munich Re Group (2004) *Annual Review: Natural Catastrophes 2003* (Munch: Münchener Rück).

Murphy, Craig N. (2002) 'The Historical Processes of Establishing Institutions of Global Governance and the Nature of the Global Polity', in Morten Ougaard and Richard Higgott, eds, *Towards a Global Polity* (London: Routledge) pp. 169–88.

—— ed. (2003) *Egalitarian Politics in the Age of Globalization* (Basingstoke: Palgrave Macmillan).

—— (2005) 'Global Governance: Poorly Done and Poorly Understood', in Rorden Wilkinson, ed., *The Global Governance Reader* (London: Routledge), pp. 90–104.

Naím, Moisés (2000) 'Lori's War', in *Foreign Policy*, spring, pp. 29–55.

Narayan, Deepa (2000) *Can Anyone Hear Us?* (New York: Oxford University Press for the World Bank).

NESC (2003) *An Investment in Quality: Services, Inclusion and Enterprise* (Dublin: NESC).

Nölke, Andreas and Perry, James (2004) 'International Accounting Standards and Transnational Private Authority', paper given at the BISA annual conference, December.

Nussbaum, Martha (2004) 'Religious Intolerance', in *Foreign Policy*, September/October, pp. 44–5.

O'Brien, Robert and Williams, Marc (2004) *Global Political Economy: Evolution and Dynamics* (Basingstoke: Palgrave Macmillan).

O'Connell Davidson, Julia (2004) 'Modern-Day Folk Devils and the Problem of Children's Presence in the Global Sex Trade', in George Ritzer, ed., *Handbook of Social Problems: A Comparative International Perspective* (Thousand Oaks, CA: Sage Publications), pp. 542–60.

Ocampo, José Antonio and Martin, Juan, eds (2003) *Globalization and Development: A Latin American and Caribbean Perspective* (Stanford, CA: Stanford University Press).

Olesen, Thomas (2004) 'Globalising the Zapatistas: From Third World Solidarity to Global Solidarity?' in *Third World Quarterly*, Vol. 25, No. 1, pp. 255–67.

Ostler, Nicholas (2003) 'A Loss for Words', in *Foreign Policy*, November/December, pp. 30–1.

Papachristos, Andrew V. (2005) 'Gang World', in *Foreign Policy*, March/April, pp. 48–55.

Paranagua, Paulo A. (2004) 'La gauche sud-américaine que évite l'autoritarisme', in *Le Monde*, 14 February.

Pauly, Louis W. (2005) 'The Political Economy of International Financial Crises', in John Ravenhill, ed., *Global Political Economy* (Oxford: Oxford University Press), pp. 176–203.

Pearson, Harry W. (1977) 'Editor's Introduction', in Karl Polanyi: *The Livelihood of Man* (New York: Academic Press), pp. xxv–xxxvi.

Pierson, Christopher (2004) *The Modern State* (London: Routledge, second edition).

PNUD (2002) *Desarrollo humano en Chile: Nosotros los chilenos: un desafío cultural* (Santiago: PNUD).

Polanyi, Karl (1968) *Primitive, Archaic and Modern Economies: Essays of Karl Polanyi*, George Dalton, ed. (New York: Anchor Books).

—— (1977) *The Livelihood of Man* (New York: Academic Press).

—— (2001) *The Great Transformation* (Boston: Beacon Books [first edition: 1944]).

Ponniah, Thomas and Fisher, William F. (2003) 'Introduction: The World Social Forum and the Reinvention of Democracy', in William F. Fisher and Thomas Ponniah, eds, *Another World is Possible: Popular Alternatives to Globalization at the World Social Forum* (London: Zed Books), pp. 1–20.

Pronk, Jan (2003) 'Security and Sustainability', in Paul van Seters, Bas de Gaay Fortman and Arie de Ruijter, eds, *Globalization and Its New Divides: Malcontents, Recipes, and Reform* (Amsterdam: Dutch University Press), pp. 25–34.

Putnam, Robert D. (1995) 'Tuning In, Tuning Out: The Strange Disappearance of Social Capital in America', in *PS: Political Science and Politics*, December 1995, pp. 664–83.

—— (2000) *Bowling Alone: The Collapse and Revival of American Community* (New York: Simon & Schuster).

—— (2001): 'Robert Putnam on Community', downloaded from <http://www. abc.net.au/rn/talks/lm/stories/s422145.htm>, April 2004.

Radcliffe, Sarah A. (1999) 'Civil Society, Social Difference and Politics: Issues of Identity and Representation', in Robert N. Gwynne and Cristóbal Kay, eds, *Latin America Transformed: Globalization and Modernity* (London: Arnold, first edition), pp. 203–23.

Radford, Tim (2004) 'The Decline of Species...', *Guardian*, 19 March, p. 1.

Raheem, Aminah (1987) *Soul Return: Integrating Body, Psyche & Spirit* (Lower Lake, CA: Aslan Publishing).

Rakodi, Carole (1999) 'A Capital Assets Framework for Analysing Household Livelihood Strategies: Implications for Policy', in *Development Policy Review*, Vol. 17, pp. 315–42.

Rapley, John (2004) *Globalization and Inequality: Neoliberalism's Downward Spiral* (Boulder, CO: Lynne Rienner).

Ravallion, Martin (2003) 'The Debate on Globalization, Poverty and Inequality: Why Measurement Matters', in *International Affairs*, Vol. 79, No. 4, pp. 739–53.

Rheingold, Howard (2000) *Tools for Thought: The History and Future of Mind-Expanding Technology* (Cambridge, MA: MIT Press).

Ritzer, George (2004) 'Social Problems: A Comparative International Perspective', in George Ritzer, ed., *Handbook of Social Problems: A Comparative International Perspective* (Thousand Oaks, CA: Sage Publications), pp. 3–13.

Rogers, Paul (2000) *Losing Control: Global Security in the Twenty-first Century* (London: Pluto Press).

Roseberry, William (1997) 'Afterword', in James G. Carrier, ed., *Meanings of the Market* (Oxford: Berg), pp. 251–60.

Rosenau, James N. (2005) 'Governance in the Twenty-First Century', in Rorden Wilkinson, ed., *The Global Governance Reader* (London: Routledge), pp. 45–67.

Rotstein, Abraham (1990) 'The Reality of Society: Karl Polanyi's Philosophical Perspective', in Kari Polanyi-Levitt, ed., *The Life and Work of Karl Polanyi* (Montreal: Black Rose Books), pp. 98–110.

Ruggeri Laderchi, Caterina, Saith, Ruhi and Stewart, Frances (2003) 'Does it Matter That We Don't Agree on the Definition of Poverty? A Comparison of Four Approaches', Working Paper No. 107, Queen Elizabeth House, University of Oxford.

Ruggie, John Gerard (1982) 'International Regimes, Transactions, and Change: Embedded Liberalism in the Postwar Economic Order', in *International Organization*, Vol. 36, No. 2, pp. 379–415.

—— (2003) 'Taking Embedded Liberalism Global: The Corporate Connection', in David Held and Mathias Koenig-Archibugi, eds, *Taming Globalization: Frontiers of Governance* (Cambridge: Polity Press), pp. 93–129.

Salsano, Alfred (1990) '*The Great Transformation* in the Oeuvre of Karl Polanyi', in Kari Polanyi-Levitt, ed., *The Life and Work of Karl Polanyi* (Montreal: Black Rose Books), pp. 139–44.

Scharpf, Fritz W. (2000): 'The Viability of Advanced Welfare States in the International Economy: Vulnerabilities and Options', in *Journal of European Public Policy*, Vol. 7, No. 2, June, pp. 190–228.

Schirato, Tony and Webb, Jen (2003) *Understanding Globalization* (London: Sage Publications).

Schmidt, Johannes Dragsbaek and Hersh, Jacques, eds (2000) *Globalization and Social Change* (London: Routledge).

Scholte, Jan Aart (2000) *Globalization: A Critical Introduction* (Basingstoke: Palgrave).

—— (2002a) 'Civil Society and the Governance of Global Finance', in Jan Aart Scholte and Albrecht Schnabel, eds, *Civil Society and Global Finance* (London: Routledge), pp. 11–32.

—— (2002b) 'Civil Society and Governance in the Global Polity', in Martin Ougaard and Richard Higgott, eds *Towards a Global Polity* (London: Routledge), pp. 145–65.

Scholte, Jan Aart and Schnabel, Albrecht, eds (2002) *Civil Society and Global Finance* (London: Routledge).

Sen, Amartya (1999) *Development as Freedom* (Oxford: Oxford University Press).

Sennett, Richard (2001) 'Street and Office: Two Sources of Identity', in Will Hutton and Anthony Giddens, eds, *On the Edge: Living with Global Capitalism* (London: Vintage), pp. 175–90.

Silver, Morris (1983) 'Karl Polanyi and Markets in the Ancient Near East: The Challenge of the Evidence', in the *Journal of Economic History*, Vol. 43, No. 4, pp. 795–829.

—— (1985) 'Karl Polanyi and Markets in the Ancient Near East: Reply', in the *Journal of Economic History*, Vol. 45, No. 1, pp. 135–7.

Sklair, Leslie (1993) 'Consumerism Drives the Global Mass Media System', in *Media Development*, No. 2, pp. 30–5.

—— (1999) 'Competing Conceptions of Globalization', in Johannes Dragsbaek Schmidt, ed., *Globalization, Regionalization and Social Change: Theoretical and Methodological Perspectives*, Development Research Series Occasional Papers No. 1, Research Center on Development and International Relations, Aalborg University, pp. 2–23.

—— (2002) *Globalization: Capitalism and its Alternatives* (Oxford: Oxford University Press, third edition).

Spangler, David (1993) 'Imagination, Gaia and the Sacredness of the Earth', in Fritz Hull, ed., *Earth and Spirit* (New York: Continuum Publishing Company), pp. 70–82.

Steger, Manfred B. (2003) *Globalization: A Very Short Introduction* (Oxford: Oxford University Press).

Stevens, Anthony (1996) *Private Myths* (Cambridge, MA: Harvard University Press).

Stiglitz, Joseph (2003) *The Roaring Nineties: Seeds of Destruction* (London: Allen Lane).

Stokke, Olav Schram and Thommessen, Øystein B., eds (2003) *Yearbook of International Co-operation on Environment and Development 2003/2004* (London: Earthscan).

Strange, Susan (1998) *Mad Money* (Manchester: Manchester University Press).

Sweeney, Paul (2003) 'Globalisation: Ireland in a Global Context', in Maura Adshead and Michelle Millar, eds, *Public Administration and Public Policy in Ireland: Theory and Methods* (London: Routledge), pp. 201–18.

Swimme, Brian and Berry, Thomas (1992) *The Universe Story* (San Francisco: Harper).

Tarrow, Sidney (2001) 'Transnational Politics: Contention and Institutions in International Politics', in *Annual Review of Political Science*, Vol. 4, pp. 1–20.

The Nation (2001) 'The Big Ten', downloaded from <www.thenation.com/special/bigten.html>, June 2004.

Thomas, Caroline (2002) 'Global Governance and Human Security', in Rorden Wilkinson and Steve Hughes, eds, *Global Governance: Critical Perspectives* (London: Routledge), pp. 113–31.

Thompson, John B. (1995) *The Media and Modernity: A Social Theory of the Media* (Cambridge: Polity Press).

Tomlinson, John (2003) 'Globalization and Cultural Identity', in Anthony McGrew and David Held, eds, *The Global Transformations Reader* (Cambridge: Polity, second edition), pp. 269–77.

Touraine, Alain (2000) *Can We Live Together?: Equality and Difference* (Cambridge: Polity Press).

Tsakalotos, Euclid (2004) 'Homo Economicus, Political Economy and Socialism', in *Science & Society*, Vol. 68, No. 2, pp. 137–60.

Tulloch, John (2004) 'Risk', in George Ritzer, ed., *Handbook of Social Problems: A Comparative International Perspective* (Thousand Oaks, CA: Sage Publications), pp. 451–64.

Turner, Stephen (1991) 'Rationality Today', in *Sociological Theory*, Vol. 9, No. 2, pp. 191–4.

Twaddle, Andrew (2004) 'How Medical Care Systems Become Social Problems', in George Ritzer, ed., *Handbook of Social Problems: A Comparative International Perspective* (Thousand Oaks, CA: Sage Publications), pp. 298–315.

UNDP (1994) *Human Development Report 1994* (New York: Oxford University Press).

—— (1997) *Human Development Report 1997* (New York: Oxford University Press).

—— (1999) *Human Development Report 1999* (New York: Oxford University Press).

—— (2001) *Human Development Report 2001* (New York: Oxford University Press).

—— (2002) *Human Development Report 2002: Deepening Democracy in a Fragmented World* (New York: Oxford University Press).

—— (2003a) *Human Development Report 2003* (New York: Oxford University Press).

—— (2003b) 'Disaster Reduction and Climate Change Adaptation', downloaded from <http://www.under.org/erd/disred/climate.htm>.

UNEP (2002) *Change and Challenge* (United Nations Environmental Programme).

—— *Global Environment Outlook 3*, downloaded from <www.unep.org/GEO/geo3/>, March 2004.

UNHCR (2003) 'Refugees by Numbers 2003', downloaded from <www.unhcr.ch>, March 2004.

United Nations (1999) *Global Report on Crime and Justice* (New York: Oxford University Press).

—— (2003) *Report on the World Social Situation: Social Vulnerability: Sources and Challenges* (New York: United Nations Department of Economic and Social Affairs).

United Nations (2005) *In Larger Freedom: Towards Development, Security and Human Rights for All* (New York: UN Publications).

Vargas Llosa, Mario (2001) 'The Culture of Liberty', in *Foreign Policy*, January/February, pp. 66–71.

Volcker, Paul A. (2001) 'The Sea of Global Finance', in Will Hutton and Anthony Giddens, eds, *On the Edge: Living with Global Capitalism* (London: Vintage), pp. 75–85.

Wade, Robert Hunter (2003a) 'The Disturbing Rise in Poverty and Inequality: Is it All a "Big Lie"?', in David Held and Mathias Koenig-Archibugi, eds, *Taming Globalization: Frontiers of Governance* (Cambridge: Polity Press), pp. 18–46.

—— (2003b) 'Poverty and Income Distribution: What is the Evidence', in Ann Pettifor, ed., *Real World Economic Outlook: The Legacy of Globalization: Debt and Deflation* (Basingstoke: Palgrave Macmillan), pp. 138–51.

Wainwright, Hilary (2005) 'Civil Society, Democracy and Power: Global Connections', in Helmut Anheier, Marlies Glasius and Mary Kaldor, eds, *Global Civil Society 2004/5* (London: Sage Publications), pp. 94–119.

Waterman, Peter (2001) *Globalization, Social Movements and the New Internationalisms* (London: Continuum).

Waters, Malcolm (1995) *Globalization* (London: Routledge).

Webster, Frank and Erickson, Mark (2004) 'Technology and Social Problems', in George Ritzer, ed., *Handbook of Social Problems: A Comparative International Perspective* (Thousand Oaks, CA: Sage Publications), pp. 416–32.

Weimann, Gabriel (2000) *Communicating Unreality: Modern Media and the Reconstruction of Reality* (London: Sage Publications).

Weiss, Linda (1998) *The Myth of the Powerless State* (Cambridge: Polity Press).

Welwood, John (2000) *Towards a Psychology of Awakening* (Boston, MA: Shambala).

Wilkinson, Rorden (2002) 'Global Governance: A Preliminary Interrogation', in Rorden Wilkinson and Steve Hughes, eds, *Global Governance: Critical Perspectives* (London: Routledge), pp. 1–13.

Williams, Marc (2005) 'Globalization and Civil Society', in John Ravenhill ed., *Global Political Economy* (Oxford: Oxford University Press), pp. 344–69.

Winter, Deborah Du Nann (1996) *Ecological Psychology: Healing the Split between Planet and Self* (New York: HarperCollins).

World Bank (2000) *World Development Report 2000–01: Attacking Poverty* (New York: Oxford University Press).

—— *Globalization, Growth, and Poverty: Building an Inclusive World Economy* (New York: Oxford University Press with the World Bank).

Yeates, Nicola (2001) *Globalization and Social Policy* (London: Sage Publications).

Zukav, Gary (1979) *The Dancing Wu Li Masters: An Overview of the New Physics*, (London: Rider).

Index

Compiled by Sue Carlton

9/11 attacks 10, 43–4, 45
accounting standards 183, 184
addiction 161–2
Afghanistan 7, 43
Africa 51, 71, 91
Aging Vulnerability Index 9–10
Aizenstat, Stephen 159
Alger, Dean 112
Alkire, Sabina 165
allergies 61
alliance capitalism 88
Altvater, Elmar 132
Amnesty International 42
Anand Milk Producers' Union,
    India 199
Anderson, Elizabeth 155
Angola 43
Annan, Kofi 12, 164, 183, 221
anti-globalisation movement 1, 2,
    66, 173, 183, 186–90, 196
    and alter-globalisation 186,
        189–90, 209, 211
    differences within 187–9
    emergence of 208, 209
AOL/Time Warner 113
Aoyama, Yuko 97
Appropriate Technology
    International (ATI) 199
Arab states 39, 40
Argentina 71, 214
Aristotle 152
Asia
    desertification 71
    East Asian Tigers 36
    and education 62
    financial crisis 7
    and social risk 40
Asian Development Bank (ADB) 9
assets 13, 18, 25, 55–72
    environmental 18, 25, 55–6,
        69–72
    human 13, 18, 25, 55, 60–4, 94
    physical 13, 18, 25, 55, 56–60
    social 13, 18, 25, 55, 64–9, 94

AT&T 113
Aum Shinrikyo cult 46
Australia 58, 59
Austria 45, 163

Bagdikian, Ben 112
Bakker, Isabella 21
Bangkok 43
Bangladesh 15, 16
Barings Bank 34
Barnardos 51
Baudrillard, Jean 116
Bauman, Zygmunt 110, 115, 116
Beck, Ulrich 19, 20, 32, 50, 52
Beinfield, Harriet 156, 157
Belgium 45
Benda, Václav 200
Bentham, Jeremy 155
Berlinguer, Enrico 63
Berry, Thomas 157, 162, 168, 177–8
Bertelsmann 113
Beynon, John 124
bin Laden, Osama 47
biodiversity 48, 49, 69, 71
Blaikie, Piers 54
Blair, Tony 112, 154, 188
Blom, Raimo 97
Bloom, Sandra 158, 161–3
Blyth, Mark 141
Bombay 43
Bono 188
Bosnia 42, 43, 123
Bourdieu, Pierre 11
Bowles, Samuel 155
Brazil 7, 15, 16, 36, 71, 214
Brennan, Martin 107
Briguglio, Pascal Lino 17
Britain 43, 45, 58–9, 59
British Telecom 59
Brunei Darussalam 7
Burundi 43
Bush, George W. 57, 112

Cable & Wireless 59

Cairo 43
Cambodia 7, 70
Cammack, Paul 217
Canada 63, 70, 163
cancer 61, 62
capabilities 55, 60, 143, 147
capital, commodification of 174,
    191, 215
Caribbean 40, 62, 107
Carrier, James G. 133
Castells, Manuel 34–5, 64–5, 86, 97,
    110, 120, 121, 122
Castro, Fidel 214
Cerny, Philip 24, 81, 92–4
Chant, Sylvia 147
Chávez, Hugo 214
Chiapas 123
children, and vulnerability 51
Chile 36, 71, 118, 163, 214
China 15–16, 37, 41, 63, 70
Chinese triads 39
Chirac, Jacques 45
chlorofluorocarbons (CFCs) 48, 49,
    216
citizenship 120–1, 217
    multilevel 185
civil society
    achievements of 206
    as agent of state 206
    as check on state power 207
    and contests over identity 207
    and democracy 208–10
    different forms of 206–8
    and global governance 212, 218
    links with institutions 206
    and new social contract 219
    range of issues 204–5
    significant campaigns 205
    and social movements 66–7,
        203–4
    structured from above 208
    and transformation of
        globalisation 187, 189, 197,
        200, 203–11, 219
    transnational networks 203–4
Clare, Anthony 124
class structure 96–8
climate change 19, 48–9, 71, 151
Clinton, Bill 188
Cockerham, William C. 62

Cold War, end of 163–5, 203
Colombia 51
Commission on Human Security
    163, 164, 165, 166
Commonwealth Vulnerability
    Index 7
communist states
    and dissident activity 202
    and reciprocity 90
Comprehensive Development
    Framework (CDF) 217
Conn, Sarah 157, 159
consumerism 114–19, 125, 151,
    159, 190, 192, 201
    and credit 118
    and developing countries 118–19
    and environment 157
    infrastructure of 117
    and symbolic meanings 115–16
    and transnational advertising
        industry 115–16
    and values 116–17
    and young people 119
Contras, Nicaragua 46
Cortright, Brant 160
Costa Rica 37
Cote d'Ivoire 43
Council of All Beings 160
Cox, Robert W. 24, 98, 99, 175, 177,
    178–80, 192, 195, 198
credit 57–9, 118
crime 12
    organised crime 38–9
Crockett, Andrew 33
Cuba 214
culture 101–26
    and consumerism 114–19, 125
    globalisation of 78, 103–8
    homogenisation-hybridity debate
        102–3, 104–5, 108, 125
    and identity 119–24
    and languages 106–7
    meaning of concept 102, 105
    and media mediation 108–14
Cyprus 17
Czech Republic 44
Czechoslovakia 123

Danish People's Party 45
Darity, William A. Jr. 37

Deacon, Bob 216–17
deforestation 69
Democratic Republic of the Congo
    43, 51
Denmark 45
desertification 71
deterritorialisation 79
developing countries
    and consumerism 118–19
    and economic growth 90–1
Dewinter, Filip 45
diamonds, illegal trade in 39
Dicken, Peter 37, 38, 89
digital divide 86
disability 62
Disney 113
Djakarta 43
Dominican Republic 37
Drainville, André C. 196–7, 208,
    218

Eagleton, Terry 101, 102–3, 105
Early Warning System (EWS) 8
Earth, as living soul 160
East Timor 10, 123
economic liberalisation 14, 15–16,
    181–2, 183
Economic Vulnerability Index (EVI)
    7
Economist, The 60
economy
    conceptions of activities 137–9
    economic risks 35–9
    see also global economy
education 60–1, 62–4
Egypt 70
elections, voter turnout 44
Elliott, Richard 115, 119, 216
embedded liberalism 141, 194
employment 37–8
    job insecurity 50
    wage inequality 37
empowerment 55, 143–4, 166
enfranchisement 55
entitlement 55
environment
    assets 18, 25, 55–6, 69–72
    collective mourning for 160
    and economic growth 189
    and global governance 216

impact of consumerism 151,
    157–8
people's relationship to 24,
    157–8, 158–63, 194
and regulation 216
risks from 47–9, 54
and vulnerability 4, 8–9, 11
Ethiopia 123
Euphrates River 70
European Financial Advisory Group
    (EFRAG) 184
European Union, and human
    security 164
European Union summit, and anti-
    globalisation protests 209
exchange 146
exclusion 24, 98, 99

fair trade 188, 205
Falk, Richard 213
family networks 64–5, 68
famines 83
female genital mutilation 42
fibre optics 85
Financial Stability Forum (FSF) 215
financial system
    crises 7, 34
    and global governance 215–16
    risks 33–5
Finland 97
Fisher, Andy 160–2
Fisher, W.F. 187, 188–9
Fitzgerald, Valpy 34
foreign direct investment (FDI) 36
Foreign Policy magazine 15–16, 52,
    77–8
Fortuyn, Pim 45
Fox 113
France 10, 43, 45, 66
freedom 147, 154
Freedom Party, Austria 45
Friedman, Jonathan 121
Friedman, Thomas 36

G-7 209, 212
G-8 1, 173, 209
Galbraith, James K. 37
Gates, Bill 188
General Electric 113
George, Vic 37

Germain, Randall D. 215
Germany 43, 45
Giddens, Anthony 19–20, 31, 177
Gill, Stephen 21, 173, 175, 176,
    179–80, 200
Gintis, Herbert 155
Glendinning, Chellis 158
Global Call to Action against
    Poverty (GCAP) 188
Global Civil Society Yearbook 204–5
global compact 184–5, 192
    see also United Nations, Global
    Compact
global economy
    and competitiveness 35–7, 39, 92
    concentration of ownership 35–7
    employment 37–8
    and organised crime 38–9
global governance 197, 211–18
    actors 212
    and environmental rules 216
    and financial system 215–16
    as new form of anarchy 212–13
    prioritising needs of market 213–
    15
    and rules 213, 215
    social regulation 216–18
Global Report on Crime and Justice
    (UN) 12
globalisation
    concept of 77–8, 79–84
    and culture 78, 101–26
    definitions of 79–82
    as field of battle 1–3
    and health threats 63
    and identity 110–11, 121–4
    ideologies of 180–90
    and insecurity 13, 20–1, 27, 183
    local resistances to 104, 105, 189,
    197–203, 219
    maintenance agenda 181–3, 192,
    196
    micro-resistances 198, 199–200,
    202–3, 219
    as myth 1–2
    need for empirical analysis 196–
    7, 218
    and new social contract 219–21
    phases of 82–4
    political economy of 77–99

and poverty/inequality 2–3, 13,
    14–19, 37–8, 79, 95, 97–100,
    141, 183
    radical agenda 186–90, 193
    reformist agenda 183–6, 192–3
    remedying defects of 173–95
    and space-time compression 110
    and state 81, 89–94
    and transformative resistance
    197–203
    understanding impacts of 23
    and vulnerability 3–4, 11, 72,
    92–3, 125–6, 141, 220
Gomes, Mary 159
Goodman, Douglas J. 114–15, 116
Gottdiener, Mark 43
Gramsci, Antonio 175, 176, 207
Great Depression 1929 84
Greece 163
Greenpeace 66
Gwynne, Robert N. 37, 68

Habermas, Jürgen 207
Hagan, Carl 45
Haider, Jorg 45
Hall, Stuart 104, 155
Hall-Matthews, David 83
Hamilton, Clive 59
Hampson, Fen Osler 165–6
Hardt, Michael 190
Harriss-White, Barbara 21, 213
Hay, Colin 80
Hay, John B. 165–6
Hayek, Friedrich 147
health 60–2, 63, 64
heart disease 61, 62
Hegel, G.W.F. 206
Held, David 2, 33, 78, 81, 82, 88,
    183–6, 192
Herman, Judith 161
Hertz, Noreena 44
Hillebrand, Ernst 37
Hillman, James 159
HIV/AIDS 9, 19, 51, 63, 68, 205
homo economicus 155, 158
Honduras 8–9
Hong Kong 63
Hough, Peter 6
Houghton Mifflin publishers 113
Human Development Report 1999 6

human person
  homo economicus 155, 158
  and natural world 24, 157–8,
    158–63, 194
  need for new myths 160–2
  as social being 144, 152, 169
  and spirituality 160–3
human rights, and protectionism
  189
Human Rights Watch 51
human security 20–2, 163–9
  definitions of 165–6
  and individualism 167
  and protection strategies 166–7
  as relational concept 167–8
  and state security 164, 166
Human Security Now 163, 164, 166–7
Hungary 44

identity 119–24
  immigrants and 104
  and individualism 121, 122
  national identity 120–1
  shifting identities 121–2
identity politics 101, 122–4, 125
  and masculinity 124
  and new terrorism 123
  and violence 123
Ignazi, Piero 44
immigrants, and cultural identity
  104
India 15, 16, 41, 62, 70
individual
  and freedom 147, 154
  and personal choice 153–4
  separateness 156–7, 158–63
  and society 50, 52, 134, 151–69,
    174, 191
individualism 121, 152, 158, 163,
  167, 220
individuation 156–7
Indonesia 37, 51
Indus Water Treaty 1960 70
Industrial Revolution 137, 144–5
infant mortality 61, 62
infectious diseases 61, 62
information revolution 84–9
  and inequality 86, 87
  innovations 85
  see also new technologies

informational economy, and
  changing social structures
  94–100
Inglehart, Ronald 201
INGOs (international NGOs) 204–5
insecurity 13, 20–2, 27
  see also human security
insurance industry 68
Intel 85
interdependence 5
internally displaced persons (IDPs)
  43
International Accounting Standards
  (IAS) 184
International Chamber of
  Commerce 212
International Institute for
  Democracy and Electoral
  Assistance (IDEA) 44
International Labour Office (ILO)
  37, 38, 66
International Monetary Fund (IMF)
  187, 215, 218
  and anti-globalisation movement
    1, 209
  and house prices 60
  and inequality 83, 95
  link with civil society 206
  and maintenance agenda 182
  and privatisation of health
    services 61–2
  vulnerability indicators 7–8
International Panel on Climate
  Change (IPCC) 71
International Political Economy
  (IPE) 23, 24–5, 32
International Year of Fresh Water 70
Internet
  access to 86
  and creation of imagined
    communities 111
  mediation of reality 109
  and sexual abuse 51
Iran 51
Iraq 43, 51, 71
Ireland 45, 59, 93, 163
Israel 51, 70
Italy 10, 45, 66

Japan 163, 199–200

Japanese Yakuza 39
Jessop, Bob 92
Jiaqing, Lu 37
Johannesburg conference 2002 216
Jordan 71, 163
Jordan, Bill 153, 154, 156, 202
Jubilee 2000 campaign 205

Kaldor, Mary 10, 101, 122, 123,
    203, 206–7, 219
Kanbur, Ravi 15, 17
Kanner, Allen 159
Kasabe language 107
Kay, Cristóbal 37, 68
Keay, Douglas 153
Kellner, Douglas 112
Keohane, Robert O. 5
Keynesian welfare state (KWS) 90
Kilby, Jack 85
Kim, Chigon 43
Kirchner, Néstor 214
Kiribati 7
Kjaersgaard, Pia 45
Kjeldgaard, Dannie 119
Korngold, Efrem 156, 157
Korten, David C. 177, 199, 201
Kosovo 123
Kuro, Jacek 202
Kyoto Protocol 216

labour, commodification of 174,
    191, 216
Lagos 43
Lagos, Ricardo 214
Laïdi, Zaki 101
land
    commodification of 174, 191,
        216
    degradation 69–71
languages 106–7
Laos 70
Latin America 36, 37, 40
    and education 62
    elections 44
    legitimacy of state 91
    and social protection 68
    women 38
Le Pen, Jean Marie 45
Lebanon 51
Leeson, Nick 34

Lesotho 7
Liberia 10, 43, 51, 123
Liberty Media 113
livelihood (human well-being) 31,
    142–8, 149, 150, 152–3, 220
    see also well-being
localisation 104, 105, 189, 197–203
    initiatives 199–200
Locke, John 206
Lufthansa 59
Lula da Silva, Luiz Inácio 188, 214

McCloskey, James 106
McDonagh, Sean 70
McDowell, Linda 124
McGrew, Anthony 2, 78
McSweeney, Bill 122, 164, 167
Macy, Joanne 157, 160, 162, 168
Madrid bombings 2004 44
Malaysia 36, 70
Mali 163
malnutrition 61
Malouf, David 107
Malta 17
Manila 43
Marcuse, Herbert 155
market fundamentalism 132
market mentality 131–6
    and economic determinism 133,
        134, 135–6, 191
    and human motivation 132–3,
        134–5, 144
market society 136–7, 139–42,
    191–2
    destructiveness of 140, 147–8
    and embedded liberalism 141,
        194
    and vulnerability 148–50
market system
    impact on society 129–50
    and individual freedom 147
    and public authority 129, 140,
        191, 192
    and reform 185
    and regulation 140, 191
    and social dislocation 145–6
    and supply-demand-price
        mechanism 132, 139
Marsh, David 80
Martin, Gus 45, 47

Martin-Boro, Ignacio 162
masculinity, crisis of 124
maternal mortality 62
Mauritania 7
media
    appropriation of messages 114
    and commercial interests 111
    deregulation of 111–12, 125
    mediation of reality 108–10
    monopolisation of 112–13
    and socialisation 110–11, 114
Mekong river 70
Melin, Harri 97
Mexico 7, 36, 51, 71, 123
Mexico City 43
Michelin 59
Michigan Militia 47
micro-resistances 198, 199–200,
    202–3, 219
microprocessors 85
migration 41–3
    migrant trafficking 39
Millennium Development Goals
    (MDGs) 40, 62, 168
Mishra, Ramesh 68
Mittelman, James H. 178, 181, 186,
    187, 189, 196, 198–200, 203
mobile phones 51
Le Monde 209
money laundering 38
Mongolia 7
Monsanto 205
Montreal Protocol on Substances
    that Deplete the Ozone Layer
    216
Moody's Investors Service 212
Mothers of East Los Angeles
    (MELASI) 199
Moulian, Tomás 117, 118
multiculturalism 187
Multilateral Agreement on
    Investment (MAI) 205, 209
multinational companies (MNCs)
    88
Munich Re Group 48
Murphy, Craig N. 210, 218
Myanmar 51, 70
myths, need for 160–2

Nairobi 43

Narayan, Deepa 18, 19
National Economic and Social
    Council (NESC), Ireland 93
National Front, France 45
natural disasters 8–9, 47–8, 49, 54
    and insurance 68
natural resources, erosion of 71, 157
Negri, Antonio 190
Nestlé 205
Netherlands 45, 59, 163
new technologies
    and communications 88
    and finance 87, 89
    impact on state 89–94
    and occupational categories
        97–100
    and production 87–8
    and trade 88
    see also information revolution
new wars 10
Newly Industrialised Countries
    (NICs) 36
News Corporation 113
Nike 205
Nile River 70
Nölke, Andreas 184
North American Free Trade
    Agreement (NAFTA) 205
Norway 45, 66, 163
Noyce, Robert 85
Nye, Joseph S. 5

obesity 61
OECD 182, 205, 209
Oklahoma bombing 1995 47
Olesen, Thomas 209, 211
Ostler, Nicholas 107
Oxfam 212
ozone-depleting substances (ODS)
    48–9, 216

Pakistan 70
Palestine 70
Panama Canal 70
Papua New Guinea 51, 107
Participatory Poverty Assessment
    (PPA) 18
Pauly, Louis W. 215
Pearson, Harry W. 129, 130
pensions 59

Perry, James 184
Peru 51, 71
pharmaceutical companies 205
Pim Fortuyn List (LPF) 45
Piot, Dr Peter 51
PlayStation 113
Polanyi, Karl 25, 26, 130–50, 158,
    168, 174, 210, 211
  commodification of land, labour
    and capital 174, 191, 215, 216
  human livelihood (well-being)
    142–8, 169, 193–4
  market mentality 131–6
  market society 136–42, 191
  and poverty 144–5, 147–8
political systems
  and electoral participation 44
  extreme right-wing parties 44–5
  membership of political parties
    65, 66
  and new terrorism 45–7
Ponniah, Thomas 187, 188–9
population growth 38, 39–40
Portland, Oregon, opposition to
    motorway 199
Portnoy, Jerry 36
Portugal 45
post traumatic stress disorder
    (PTSD) 161
Poverty Reduction Strategy Papers
    (PRSPs) 217
poverty/inequality 14–19, 37–8,
    40–1, 151, 154–6
  capability approach to 143, 147
  definitions of 16–17
  impact of globalisation 2–3, 13,
    14–19, 37–8, 79, 95, 97–100,
    141, 183
  and income 16, 17, 18, 25
  measurement of 14–16
  monetary approach to 143, 147
  participatory approach to 143–4,
    147
  Polanyi's view of 144–5, 147–8
  and population growth 40
  poverty eradication 154–5, 173,
    188
  poverty lines 16, 143
  social exclusion approach to 143,
    147

Progress Party, Norway 45
Pronk, Jan 77, 99
property 59–60
protectionism 84, 189
psychic numbing 160, 161
psychology/psychotherapy
  depth psychology 159
  ecopsychology 159
  existential psychology 168
  and individual 152–3, 156–7,
    159, 167
  transpersonal psychology 160
Putnam, Robert D. 65–6, 67
Pyöriä, Pasi 97

quantum mechanics 158, 176–8
Quayle, Dan 110

Radcliffe, Sarah A. 66
Rapley, John 90, 92, 94, 100, 121
Ravaillon, Martin 2
Reagan, Ronald 133, 153, 182
reciprocity 146
redistribution 146
refugees 42–3, 217
religion, and consumer choice 116
Report on the World Social Situation
    3, 4–5
resilience 55–6, 166
Rheingold, Howard 84
Rio De Janeiro conference 1992
    (Earth Summit) 216
risk 13, 19–20, 27, 31–53, 190
  concept of 31–2
  coping mechanisms 13, 54–73,
    190
    see also assets; resilience
  economic 25, 35–9, 89
  environmental 25, 47–9, 54
  financial 25, 33–5, 89
  manufactured 31
  personal 50–2, 94
  political 25, 43–7, 94
  social 25, 39–43, 94
risk society 19, 32
Rogers, Paul 10
Rolls Royce, pension scheme 59
Rosenau, James N. 212–13
Roszak, Ted 159
Rotstein, Abraham 146–7, 211

Ruggeri Laderchi, Caterina 142, 143–4
Ruggie, John Gerard 91, 94, 141
Russia 7, 51
Rwanda 10, 42, 123

Sainsbury 59
Salsano, Alfred 192
Salween River 70
sanitation 61
Sao Paulo 43
sarin nerve gas 46
SARS (Severe Acute Respiratory Syndrome) 63
Sassen, Saskia 197
satellites 85
savings 57
Scharpf, Fritz W. 68
Schirato, Tony 110–11, 114
Scholte, Jan Aart 10–11, 21, 33–4, 50, 67, 79–80, 88, 187, 192
Schumpeterian workfare state (SWS) 92
Seattle monorail system 199
Seed, John 160
Sen, Amartya 55, 60, 143, 147
Sennett, Richard 50
Serageldin, Ismail 70
Shell 205
Short, Clare 19
Sicilian Mafia 39
Sierra Leone 10, 51, 123
Singapore 17, 36, 63, 70
Sklair, Leslie 78, 95–6, 113, 118–19
Slovenia 163
Smith, Adam 138, 206
smoking 61
social capital 65–7, 68
social change 175–80, 194–5
  and historical structures 178–80
  and social forces 180, 183, 192
social contract 219–20
social dumping 217
social exclusion 143
social movements 66–7, 203
social protection 67–9
social reality, intransigence of 176–8
social sciences, and natural sciences 176–8

Social Vulnerability Index (SVI) 9, 72
socialism, collapse of 132, 133, 137
society 94–100
  and class 96–8
  denial of 153–8
  forms of integration 146
  and market system 129–50, 174, 191–2, 210
  social values 154
  and trauma 161–2
Solana, Javier 214
Solomon Islands 51
Somalia 10, 43, 51, 123
Sony 113
South Africa 163, 202
South Korea 36
Spain 10, 59, 66
species extinction 49, 71
Squire, Lyn 17
Sri Lanka 51
Standard & Poor Ratings Group 212
state(s)
  breakdown of 123
  impact of new technologies 89–94
  new state form 92–4
  and shift in power relations 92, 190
  types of contract 90
Steger, Manfred B. 108
Stevens, Anthony 151
Stiglitz, Joseph 15, 57, 58, 68, 72
stock market 57, 58, 59
Stockholm conference 1972 216
Strange, Susan 87
stress 10–11, 50
Sub-Saharan Africa 37, 39, 40, 41, 62, 70
Sudan 43, 51
Summit of the Americas, Quebec City 209
Sweden 59
Swimme, Brian 168
Switzerland 45, 163
Syria 70, 71
system theories 158

Taiwan 36

Tarrow, Sidney 206
TB 61
techno-hazards 32
television 67, 108, 109–10
terrorism 45–7, 123
Thailand 36, 70, 163
Thatcher, Margaret 133, 153–4, 156,
    158, 182
Thomas, Caroline 165, 217–18
Thomas, Jeremy 49
Thompson, John B. 114
Tobin Tax 189
Tocqueville, Alexis de 207
Tokyo underground attack 1995
    46
Tomlinson, John 120
Touraine, Alain 50, 52, 101, 111,
    121
toxic chemicals 71–2
trade unions
    and anti-globalisation movement
    187
    membership of 65, 66
transnational capitalist class (TCC)
    96
Tulloch, John 32
Turkey 51, 70
Turner, Stephen 155
Tuvalu 7
Twaddle, Andrew 62

Ubuh language 107
Uganda 51
UNAIDS 51
UNCTAD 7
UNDP (UN Development
    Programme)
    and consumerism 118, 119
    definition of globalisation 81
    and education and health 60–1
    and environment 8
    and family 65
    Human Development Index 17,
    143
    Human Development Reports 6,
    20, 21, 35–6, 40, 41, 151, 164
    and human security 20–1, 164
    and membership of political
    parties 66
    and organised crime 38

United Nations 83
    Department of Economic and
    Social Affairs 3, 4–6
    Economic Commission for Latin
    America and the Caribbean
    (ECLAC) 9, 55, 63, 72, 82,
    98–9, 191, 220
    Economic and Social Council 7
    Environmental Programme
    (UNEP) 8, 48, 49, 70, 71–2
    Global Compact 185, 220
    High Commission for Refugees
    (UNHCR) 42, 217
    Office for the Coordination of
    Human Affairs (OCHA) 48
    Office for Drug Control and
    Crime Prevention 12
    reform 185
United States
    asset ownership 57–8
    hegemony 179–80
    and identity politics 123
    illegal migrants 42
    illiteracy 45
    and postmaterialist values 201
    shopping malls 117
    and water 70
Universal Studios 113
urbanisation 41, 43, 61
Uruguay 214
USSR 123

values
    and consumerism 116–17
    postmaterialist 201
    social 154
    universal 189
Vargas Llosa, Mario 106
Vazquez, Tabaré 214
Venezuela 214
Vermont Family Forests 199
Viacom 113
Vietnam 37, 70
violence
    addressing 191–3
    against women 12, 42, 51
    and identity politics 123
    and stress 10–11
    and vulnerability 3, 4, 10–13, 169
Vivendi 113

Vlaams Blok 45
Voices of the Poor survey 13, 18–19, 55
Volcker, Paul A. 34
vulnerability
  economic 4, 7, 11
  environmental 4, 8–9, 11
  financial 4, 7–8, 11
  and globalisation 3–4, 6, 11, 13–23, 220
  and IPE 24–5
  remedies for 173–95, 197
  social 4, 5–6, 9, 11, 55
  social production of 54–5
  usefulness of concept 13–23, 163–4, 220
  uses of concept 4–13, 27
  and violence 3, 4, 10–13, 169
  see also assets; human security; insecurity; poverty/inequality; risk

Wade, Robert Hunter 14–15, 41
Wainwright, Hilary 208, 210
water, access to 69, 70
Waterman, Peter 207
Waters, Malcolm 77
Webb, Jen 110–11, 114
Weimann, Gabriel 109, 110
welfare state 68, 90, 91–2, 154
well-being
  and connection with biosphere 158–63
  and social belonging 69, 144, 145, 149, 153
  see also livelihood (human well-being)
Welwood, John 168
Western Aquifer System 70
westernisation 79, 104
Wheeler, John A. 177
Whitbread 59
Wilding, Paul 37
Wilkinson, Rorden 212, 213

Williams, Marc 204
Winter, Deborah Du Nann 160
Wolfensohn, James D. 19, 183
women
  employment 38
  and social risk 41, 42
  trafficking of 39, 42
  violence against 12, 42, 51
World Bank 1, 187, 209, 217, 218
  Assessing Vulnerability table 6, 72
  and history of globalisation 82
  and inequality 83, 95
  link with civil society 206
  and maintenance agenda 182
  and participatory approach 143–4
  and privatisation of health services 61–2
  reports on world poverty 14–16, 17, 40, 79
  and types of assets 13, 55, 56, 64
  use of vulnerability concept 6
World Development Indicators 6
World Development Report 2000–01 6, 15, 17, 18
World Economic Forum 1, 52, 188, 212, 214
World Health Organisation 42
World Social Forum 173, 187, 188, 209, 210, 212
World Trade Organisation 1, 187, 217
  and inequality 83, 95
  link with civil society 206
  and maintenance agenda 182
  Seattle summit 209
Worldwide Fund for Nature 212

Yeates, Nicola 217
Yugoslavia 10, 51, 123

Zapatista Army of National Liberation (EZLN) 123, 209–10
Zukav, Gary 178